P9-CAG-740

Contents

Piety, Politics, and Pluralism

Religion, the Courts, and the 2000 Election

Mary C. Segers, Editor

ROWMAN & LITTLEFIELD PUBLISHERS, INC.
Lanham • Boulder • New York • Oxford

ROWMAN & LITTLEFIELD PUBLISHERS, INC.

Published in the United States of America
by Rowman & Littlefield Publishers, Inc.
4720 Boston Way, Lanham, Maryland 20706
www.rowmanlittlefield.com

12 Hid's Copse Road
Cumnor Hill, Oxford OX2 9JJ, England

Copyright © 2002 by Rowman & Littlefield Publishers, Inc.

All rights reserved. No part of this publication may be reproduced, stored in a retrieval
system, or transmitted in any form or by any means, electronic, mechanical,
photocopying, recording, or otherwise, without the prior permission of the publisher.

British Library Cataloguing-in-Publication Information Available

Library of Congress Cataloging-in-Publication Data

Piety, politics, and pluralism : religion, the courts, and the 2000 election / edited by Mary
C. Segers.
    p. cm.
  Includes bibliographical references and index.
  ISBN 0-7425-1514-1 (alk. paper)—ISBN 0-7425-1515-X (pbk. : alk. paper)
    1. United States—Religion—20th century. 2. Freedom of religion—United States. 3.
  Smith, Alfred Leo—Trials, litigation, etc. 4. Religion and politics—United States. 5.
  Presidents—United States—Election—2000. I. Segers, Mary C.

BL2525 .P54 2002
323.44'2'0973—dc21

                                                                            2001048273

Printed in the United States of America

♾™ The paper used in this publication meets the minimum requirements of
American National Standard for Information Sciences—Permanence of Paper
for Printed Library Materials, ANSI/NISO Z39.48-1992.

Acknowledgments

This project had its origins in a major international conference, the fiftieth International Conference of Americanists, held in Warsaw in July 2000. Four panels at this meeting focused on religion and politics in the United States, with special attention to the role of religion in the 2000 presidential election and to the controversy over religious liberty provoked by the U.S. Supreme Court's decision in the *Employment Division, Oregon Department of Human Resources of Oregon v. Smith* case.

The presenters at these panels, who are contributors to this volume, included leading scholars in the field of religion and politics in the United States. I would like to acknowledge, first, these fellow authors who wrote and revised most of the chapters in this book. Together we spent three days in Warsaw discussing and analyzing the continuing American debate about the scope and limits of religious freedom, the influential role of religion in American politics, and the possible relevance of the American experience to Poland and other countries in postcommunist transition.

Thanks also to other scholars who participated in the original conference as panel chairs and discussants: Krzysztof Michalek, Cynthia Dominik, Bohdan Szklarski, Joanna Yastrebska-Szklarska, Andrzej Filipiak—all faculty at Warsaw University's American Studies Center—Halina Parafianowicz from the University of Bialystok and Warsaw University, and John Leo, Fulbright Distinguished Chair from Marie Curie Sklodowska University in Lublin. American scholars included Donald Scruggs, Eileen Sullivan, Joan Weiss, Jerome Travers, William Gould, Jo Renee Formicola, Timothy A. Byrnes, and Samuel Marotta. This book benefits from their valuable comments and suggestions.

Special thanks also to Andrzej Dembicz and to conference organizers at CESLA, the Latin American Studies Center of Warsaw University, and to

Krzysztof Michalek of the American Studies Center, who first suggested the idea for these panels at the fiftieth ICA meeting. Andrzej Dakowski, director of the Polish–United States Fulbright Commission, also met with us to discuss Fulbright lectureships in Poland.

Back here in the States, I am grateful to Steve Wrinn, editor at Rowman & Littlefield, and to Murray Karstadt, Warren Mayer, and Darrell Richardson of the Rutgers-Newark Computer Center, who helped at critical moments with file conversions.

Finally, a very special thank-you to my husband, Jerry Travers, who provided valuable editorial advice and a wealth of patience in the final stages of editing this volume.

The American experiment in religious liberty and church-state separation has been called the chief contribution of American political thought to the world community. Among liberal democracies, the United States is unusual in its high rates of religious affiliation and church attendance. Although Americans are constitutionally committed to church-state separation, they do not divorce religion from politics. This book examines two examples of the influence of religion in American public life: the role of religion in the 2000 presidential election, and the debate over the scope and limits of religious liberty.

1

Religion and Liberal Democracy: An American Perspective

Mary C. Segers

The role of religion in a liberal democracy is controversial, so controversial that it has been the subject of a national debate in the United States throughout most of its history. The debate currently centers on a wide range of issues: from school prayer, public funding of parochial schools, and the use of a Jewish yarmulke (skullcap) in the military—to church lobbying, public displays of Christian symbols during Christmas holidays, use by the clergy of the pulpit to issue voting instructions, and religious exemptions for the use of peyote or wine in worship services. Underlying these specific issues are deeper questions about the role of religion in a liberal democracy: Is liberal democracy, by definition, hostile to religion? Is religion dangerous and subversive, or does it play a constructive role in a secular liberal society?

This book addresses these questions by examining two areas at the intersection of religion and politics in the United States: the role of religion in American electoral politics, as illustrated in the 2000 presidential campaign, and the ongoing debate about religious liberty and the rights of religious minorities occasioned by the Supreme Court's 1990 decision in *Oregon v. Smith*.[1] In the 2000 presidential election, God-talk and religious activism played a prominent role in the campaign. Aside from the historic, unprecedented Florida recount that ended the election, the debate about the role of religion in public life was one of the more remarkable features of this presidential race. The *Smith* case triggered an intense debate not only about religious liberty but also about federalism, the separation of powers, congressional prerogatives, and the role of the Supreme Court in the American system of government.

In order to understand better these two controversies and to reflect critically on religion and public life, it is necessary to define liberal democracy. For better or for worse, the United States is a liberal democracy in a pluralistic society.

LIBERAL DEMOCRACY

"Liberal democracy" refers to a philosophy and a form of government that strongly emphasize individual rights and the values of freedom, equality, respect, and tolerance. Liberal democracies combine respect for individual liberty with the majoritarian practices of representative government. Such societies structure their political arrangements so as to dilute power and prevent tyranny, whether a tyranny of elites or the tyranny of the majority.

The American political system is a hybrid of two major traditions of political thought: democracy and liberalism. In the modern world, democracy is not simply majority rule or the rule of the many poor, as Aristotle defined it.[2] The type of democracy that is most important to the United States is constitutional, or liberal, democracy, which seeks maximum political participation and majority rule while stressing fundamental respect for individual and minority rights. Liberal democracy, as it has developed in the United States, emphasizes protective institutions such as representative government, periodic elections that hold representatives accountable, individual constitutional rights defended through an independent judiciary, and private ownership of property to guarantee political independence. The values essential to a liberal democratic society include personal freedom, tolerance, distributive justice, citizen participation in decision making, social discipline, and respect for the rule of law.

While democratic thought may be traced to the ancient Greeks, liberalism is a modern political tradition composed of many strands and varieties. It draws from the political thought of seventeenth-century English civil wars, the ideas of the eighteenth-century Enlightenment, nineteenth-century republican movements, and twentieth-century concerns with equal liberty. It is no accident that liberalism has been mischaracterized and that "the L word" has become, at times, a term of opprobrium. In the 1988 election, George H. W. Bush vilified his Democratic opponents as "liberals and card-carrying members of the ACLU." Distortions of such a rich, diverse tradition of political discourse can easily occur.[3]

As a tradition of political thought, liberalism emphasizes human rights, limited government, and pluralism in the service of human freedom. The liberal political theory of John Locke, for example, which influenced such statesmen as Jefferson and Madison, held that human beings had fundamental rights to life, liberty, and property—rights that existed prior to government and that limited governmental power.[4] Later liberals, such as John Stuart Mill, eschewed natural rights in favor of the principle of utility, but they still emphasized the civil rights of individuals and minorities as well as basic freedoms of religion, speech, press, and assembly as useful to both individual happiness and the public well-being.

Because liberals support human dignity and individual rights, they have always feared political tyranny and have therefore sought to limit governmental power. The Framers of the Constitution worked toward this goal. Within the context of American politics, as Bette Novit Evans reminds us (in chapter 9), the Constitution "creates a jurisdictional fragmentation almost unparalleled in institutional design." Federalism fragments power geographically, and the separation of powers reinforces this fragmentation at every level—national, state and local. The Framers believed that this fragmented structure of government was a better protection for individual rights than was any single document, even the Bill of Rights. This is a typically liberal approach to the problem of political tyranny: the use of structural and procedural innovations to limit government by diluting political power.

At the same time, dividing power and limiting government are not enough to achieve the liberal goal of maximizing the potential for moral autonomy and human freedom. Liberals therefore stress the need for a richly diverse, heterogeneous, pluralistic society, one that offers many opportunities for human flourishing. A good civil society, to a liberal, is one characterized by ethnic, cultural, and religious diversity. Such a multifaceted society creates opportunities for choice and the exercise of moral autonomy, and so enhances human freedom and virtue. Such a society is also, frankly, more interesting than a uniform, one-dimensional culture.

These liberal notions of individual rights, limited government, and social pluralism are reflected in how liberals view religion. The right to worship as conscience dictates is a fundamental liberty that needs to be protected by separating church and state. Historically, the union of altar and throne symbolized by religious establishment was, to European liberals, a formula for tyranny. Disestablishing state churches was, therefore, a necessary step toward protecting dissenters and preserving religious freedom. Religious commitment itself could be formulaic, even hypocritical, unless it was freely undertaken.[5]

Note that the liberal theory I have outlined here is a political philosophy of limited government, individual rights, and social pluralism. As Judith Shklar remarked in her essay "The Liberalism of Fear," what liberals most fear is the arbitrary, capricious cruelty of tyrannical government.[6] This is why they look to individual rights and the rule of law as necessary restraints on political power. This brings us to the matter of religion. The question is whether liberal democracy is, by definition, hostile to religion.

RELIGION AND LIBERAL DEMOCRACY

Questions about the compatibility of religion and democracy have been a continuing concern of Americans in almost every generation. For much of U.S. history, American thinkers and political leaders wondered whether religion could support the American experiment in democracy, and they worried about the divisive potential of religious belief. They attempted to control and manage the relationship between religion and politics by enshrining in the Constitution the religion clauses of the First Amendment: "Congress shall make no law respecting an establishment of religion, or prohibiting the free exercise thereof." But these First Amendment provisions are vague and raise as many questions as they solve.

The enduring debate about religion and liberal democracy centers on whether religion undermines or enhances democracy. Note that this is a very abstract formulation of the problem. Obviously, the answer to this question depends on the particular society and historical context in which the question is raised. In the American context, proponents of both views—religion is subversive, religion is beneficial—continue to debate the role of religion in a liberal democracy.

Religious minimalists and advocates of church-state separation contend that religion is a source of political dysfunction in a liberal polity.[7] They explain this idea of dysfunction in several ways. First, competition between churches in a diverse, pluralistic society can lead to sectarian strife. Second, religion threatens to undermine the process of public deliberation, because of the tendency of religious activists to be uncivil, intolerant, and disrespectful of nonbelievers' basic rights to freedom of speech, press, expression and assembly. Third, because of its appeal to divine authority, religion undermines or subverts the substantive prerogatives of democratic citizenship— namely, the autonomy and self-determination necessary for democratic self-governance. Fourth, while religion poses real dangers to the political process, politics itself threatens to undermine religion. By conflating religion with established culture, the political involvement of churches poses the danger of idolatry or the legitimization of contemporary political structures in religious terms.

Religious minimalists conclude that given these dangers and the risks posed by the intermingling of religion and politics in the United States, churches and governing agencies are wise to avoid unnecessary entanglement. Governments should neither endorse nor promote the expression of religious values in politics and public policy. For their part, churches should refrain from becoming heavily invested in political advocacy, lest they lose sight of their authentic spiritual mission. Or so the argument for separation runs.

The opposing view—that religion is not only compatible with liberal democracy but actually enhances democratic governance—also has many adherents.[8] They contend that religion supports democracy in the United States in three different ways. First, religion has the positive effect of broadening political representation—something all democrats should, in principle, applaud. Second, religion promotes democratic citizenship by training people in the political abilities and civic skills necessary for effective participation. Third, religion transmits moral values without which democracy could not thrive. In these ways, churches, mosques and synagogues act as powerful socializing agents and as effective barriers to political and social tyranny.

In this view, while religion can be inimical to democracy, religious values can also enhance and support such liberal democratic institutions and ideas as human rights, equality, political community, tolerance, and respect for the law. Moreover, many political thinkers, among them Machiavelli and Rousseau, have argued that religion can be useful in educating a virtuous citizenry, a body politic of civic-minded persons that is the basic prerequisite of a democratic republic. Religious values can be the source of public morality. Furthermore, in the history of the United States, religious traditions have often been fertile sources of constructive political action. Campaigns for human dignity—such as the antislavery, temperance, women's suffrage, civil rights, and 1960s antiwar movements—were all at least partly inspired and motivated by religious values and religious commitment. Thus, before we confine religion to the arena of private life, we need to be mindful of the many ways in which, historically, religion has contributed to American public life.

Proponents of accommodation contend that given these valuable functions of religion in a liberal democracy like the United States, government should not trivialize or privatize religion but instead should support the constructive social programs churches offer—from soup kitchens and homeless shelters to drug abuse programs and recreational programs for young children and teens. They suggest that perhaps it is time for Americans to move away from notions of strict church-state separation and toward government funding of "faith-based organizations" (as President Bush has suggested in his "charitable choice" initiative). These accommodationists propose that we Americans renegotiate the relationship between religion and public life.

There are no easy answers to the question of whether religion and liberal democracy are compatible. Perhaps it helps to see the American situation historically and concretely rather than in the abstract. Two observations help us understand the continuing debate about religion and politics in the United States. First, Americans do not think that church-state separation means the divorce of religion from politics. Keeping government agencies and religious institutions separate does not mean that citizens cannot bring religiously based moral convictions to bear in public policy debates. Second, it may be true that categories such as "separation" and "accommodation" are no longer useful in describing the role of religion in public life. They may apply, narrowly, to Supreme Court jurisprudence in interpreting the First Amendment religion clauses, but they do not capture the fluid and dynamic role religion plays in political discourse and community action. As American society grows more diverse, the challenge is to preserve the liberal value of religious freedom by both keeping the government out of the way and protecting the free expression of believers.

RELIGIOUS PLURALISM IN AMERICAN SOCIETY

A major factor impinging on the relationship between religion and American democracy is the fact that religion itself is changing. As a result of changes in immigration patterns in the last half-century, American religion is becoming much more diverse.

As an immigrant nation, the United States has been open to new groups bringing different religious traditions to the country. Changes in immigration laws in the 1960s have shifted migration sources and patterns away from Europe and toward Asia and Africa. As a result, groups such as Muslims, Buddhists, and Hindus have been increasing in numbers. Muslims, for example, now number 5.5 million and operate about a thousand Islamic religious centers in the United States. There are approximately 1.9 million Buddhists (with immigrants outnumbering converts three to one). Hindus number 1.3 million. If we add to the many Christian denominations the approximately's 350,000 members of the Native American Church, almost a million Jehovah's Witnesses, some 5.6 million Mormons, about 133,000 members of the Bahai faith, and nearly six million Jews, we can get some sense of the vast variety in American religion today.[9]

These may seem like small numbers in such a large nation; after all, Americans number approximately 281 million, according to the 2000 census.[10] At sixty-two million, for example, Catholics remain the largest single denomination in the country, representing 22.7 percent of the population.[11] But the fact is that today there are more Muslims than Episcopalians in the United States. Representing both major traditions of Islam, Sunni and Shi'ite, these Muslims come from such countries as Pakistan, Iran, Bangladesh, Nigeria, Egypt, the Philippines, Indonesia, and the states of the Middle East. In short, there is remarkable ethnic diversity within the Islamic community here in the United States—which, of course, adds to the cultural, ethnic, and religious pluralism of the country as a whole.[12]

The point in citing these statistics, of course, is to illustrate the remarkable diversity of American society—the ethnic, religious, and cultural pluralism of this liberal democracy. Kenneth Prewitt, director of the Census Bureau, puts it this way: "The 21st century will be the century in which we redefine ourselves as the first country in world history which is literally made up of every part of the world."[13]

Such diversity provides the context for the intense debate about the freedom of religious minorities triggered by the Supreme Court's 1990 decision in *Oregon v. Smith*. As one commentator noted, "If we want to be a democracy that supports the rights of minority groups, including religious minorities, we can't have a government that stands behind and supports one world view."[14] A government policy of equal treatment of religion is necessary—and in a liberal democracy, the principle of church-state separation is a necessary corollary to the idea of religious liberty.

The decline of Protestant hegemony and the growing diversity of American society pose new challenges. As our authors show, tolerance and respect for the religious and cultural diversity of Islam, Confucianism, Buddhism, and Hinduism may require that Americans rethink issues of school prayer, public holiday displays, issues of dress in the military, and a host of other issues. But a liberal democracy in a pluralistic society welcomes such rich cultural diversity. Although America may be 85 percent Christian, the religious liberty of the 15 percent who are non-Christian must be preserved. The 1990 *Smith* case and protection of religious minorities remain central issues for American society.

PART ONE: THE ROLE OF RELIGION IN THE 2000 ELECTION

One reason Americans continue to argue about religion and politics is the role that religion plays in our elections. In choosing our governors, we inevitably ask certain questions. For example: What is the connection, if any, between religion, morality, and public policy? Can a legislator constitutionally bring his or her religious beliefs to bear in formulating public policy? Should political candidates discuss their religious and ethical convictions so that voters may judge their fitness for high office? To what extent should voters rely upon their own religious beliefs in evaluating candidates for public office?

These issues may be compressed into one basic question: Is religion relevant in a presidential election? Or should campaign rhetoric and public debate be sanitized of all forms of God-talk, all references to the Almighty?

This question was raised very dramatically in the 2000 presidential election. The Clinton/Lewinsky scandals and the deeper matter of presidential character were issues in the campaign. American voters were therefore treated to the discomfiting, embarrassing spectacle of all nine Republican presidential candidates and one of the two Democratic candidates professing their faith openly for all to see and hear. The only candidate who refused to discuss his religious beliefs was former Senator Bill Bradley (D-N.J.), who said simply, "I've decided that personal faith is private, and I will not discuss it with the public."[15]

Religion was influential in the campaign in other ways as well. In the primaries, the Christian Right played a major role in delivering the Republican nomination to George W. Bush, governor of Texas. Republican Party leaders considered the Catholic vote to be so crucial in key "swing" or "battleground" states that they set up a special task force within the Republican National Committee to target Catholic voters. For his part, to distance himself from the scandals associated with the Clinton presidency, Vice President Al Gore chose as his running mate Senator Joseph Lieberman (D-Conn.), an Orthodox Jew and a political moderate best known for his 1998 Senate speech denouncing Clinton's immoral conduct in the Lewinsky affair. Gore's selection of Lieberman was historic, since the Connecticut senator was the first Jew ever to be nominated by a major political party for president or vice president. Like John F. Kennedy in 1960 and Geraldine Ferraro in 1984, Lieberman's candidacy represented a major step forward in ending prejudice in American life—be it anti-Catholicism, anti-Semitism, or antipathy to women in high office.

The chapters in Part One of this book examine the singular role of religion in the 2000 presidential election. Mark Rozell describes the primary contests between candidates John McCain and George W. Bush in South Carolina and Virginia, and he explains how conservative evangelicals delivered the Republican nomination to Bush. Mary Segers examines the controversy over anti-Catholicism provoked by Bush's appearance at Bob Jones University in South Carolina and discusses its impact on GOP campaign strategy and on Catholic voting patterns in the general election. Molly Andolina and Clyde Wilcox suggest that key moral, social, and religious issues supplanted, to some extent, traditional economic concerns in the 2000 election, and they analyze four such issues: abortion, gay rights, the death penalty, and a set of broader church-state considerations. Describing the campaign's approach as "stealth politics," the authors argue that these social issues mattered even though they did not get a lot of attention from Bush and Gore. Mary Segers examines the Lieberman nomination as well as the remarkable debate his comments on religion and politics triggered during the 2000 campaign.

To be sure, the controversy over religion and politics was not the only remarkable feature of the 2000 election. The Florida voting fiasco clearly overshadowed all other aspects of this election. By contrast with the postelection recount in Florida and its culmination in a highly controversial Supreme Court decision, the pre–Election Day campaign looked tame indeed. But we should not let the historic endgame of the 2000 race distract us from important aspects of the campaign, such as the debate about the role of religion in public life. In fact, we need to pay attention to this question, because this debate continues to reverberate in the new presidential administration of George W. Bush.

In the first month of his presidency, Bush made major appointments and undertook major policy initiatives bearing on questions of religion and politics. He proposed educational reforms, including school vouchers, that raised the question of the constitutionality of public funding of church-related schools. He imposed restrictions on funding of international family planning agencies that provide abortion counseling. In his second week in office, he established by executive order a new Office of Faith-Based Action to provide government assistance to churches and other religious groups that run soup kitchens, drug abuse programs, job training programs, and other social services. He named former Senator John Ashcroft of Missouri

and Governor Tommy Thompson of Wisconsin—both pro-life candidates—
to the sensitive cabinet posts of attorney general and secretary of health and
human resources. These first actions of the new president were paybacks
to the Religious Right constituency of the Republican Party. They were also
invitations to file lawsuits challenging these policies as violations of the religion clauses of the First Amendment. There is every indication that the debate about religion and politics, church and state, will intensify during the
Bush presidency.

At the same time, no discussion of the 2000 election can ignore the historic
thirty-six-day postelection recount that kept the nation in suspense about the
identity of the next president. There will be many books written about this
extraordinary election. The Florida follies raised so many issues—the machinery of voting, states' rights versus federal rights, and the constitutional
separation of powers, to name but a few—that it will take political scientists
and historians years to sort it all out. At the same time, some attempt must be
made here to give a brief overview of the postelection endgame so that read-
ers can understand the chapters on the 2000 election in this volume.

Accordingly, Part One of this book begins with a chronology of the Florida
recount, together with a short summary of the highlights of this fascinating
postelection drama. Elizabeth A. Hull then analyzes *Bush v. Gore,* the December 12, 2000, decision of the U.S. Supreme Court that stopped the recount and made George W. Bush president-elect. The Court's decision has
been criticized as an "act of judicial usurpation" by an "imperial judiciary"
that anointed George Bush as president. Hull analyzes the Supreme Court's
reasoning in this case and discusses the continuing controversy among constitutional lawyers, scholars, and citizens over the significance of the decision.

PART TWO: RELIGIOUS LIBERTY IN A PLURALISTIC SOCIETY

Bette Novit Evans remarks that the *Smith* case "is at the heart of the most
tangled Free Exercise controversy of the generation. . . . No constitutional
controversy . . . illustrates as sharply the immensely complex relation among
institutions of government as does the series of events that began with this
case." Moreover, many scholars are concerned that the *Smith* opinion has
had devastating implications for the rights of religious minorities.

Part Two of this book focuses on this debate about limits to religious freedom and protection of the rights of religious minorities—a discussion that
occupied the attention of scholars, legislators, and jurists throughout the
1990s. In the *Smith* decision, the Court ruled that a religiously neutral Oregon law, which did not directly burden the free exercise rights of two Native
Americans, was constitutional. At issue was the denial of unemployment

benefits to two men who had lost their jobs over their use of peyote in religious rituals of their Native American Church. In effect, the Court refused to
uphold the free exercise rights of these two Native Americans.

In deciding this case, the Court reversed thirty-year-old precedents holding that First Amendment rights to religious freedom are fundamental guarantees that warrant strict scrutiny of any state statute limiting a citizen's free
exercise rights. This Supreme Court decision stunned many religionists in the
United States, to such an extent that in 1993 Congress passed, by an overwhelming vote, the Religious Freedom Restoration Act (RFRA) to protect the
religious freedom of minorities. Not to be outdone, the Supreme Court in
1997 overturned RFRA, in *City of Boerne v. Flores*.[16]

The chapters in Part Two examine this controversy. George Garvey provides an overview of the debate and suggests a possible resolution. Bette
Novit Evans analyzes the structural and constitutional factors that sustain religious freedom in the United States, while Ted Jelen discusses the cultural
and political factors that account for the persistence of church-state conflict
in the nation. Finally, Clyde Wilcox, Rachel Goldberg, and Ted Jelen examine the impact of increasing diversity on church-state attitudes of residents in
the Washington, D.C., metropolitan area. They report that exposure to citizens of different religious faiths may foster greater tolerance for religious
practices and more support for free exercise by minority religious groups.
Together, these four chapters provide a sustained analysis of this controversy
and suggest what is unique about the American experiment in religious liberty, as well as what might be transferable to other contexts.

Each of these essays takes a position on the relationship between pluralism and religious freedom. Describing the current state of free exercise law
as "unsettled and unsettling," George Garvey examines the major struggle
over separation of powers and lawmaking authority that occurred between
Congress and the Supreme Court in the aftermath of the *Smith* decision. In
Smith, the Supreme Court opted for a standard that promotes neutrality of
state laws at the price of protection of the rights of religious minorities (such
as Native Americans). Congress tried to restore the old strict-scrutiny doctrine in the 1993 Religious Freedom Restoration Act, but its revised standard
was too extreme in practice and was therefore overturned. Garvey proposes,
as a more realistic principle, an intermediate standard of review that both
values highly the rights of citizens to practice their faiths freely and simultaneously recognizes that majoritarian policies cannot be held hostage to every
personal claim to religious exemption from the law.

In general, Garvey regards the tensions between the establishment and free
exercise clauses as inherent and healthy in a complex society that is both intensely religious and highly diverse. He emphasizes that the ethnic and cultural pluralism resulting from immigration necessitates tolerance and religious
freedom. Tolerance may be a reluctant duty, but it is a duty nonetheless.

The empirical study by Clyde Wilcox, Rachel Goldberg, and Ted Jelen addresses the issue of religious pluralism in more concrete fashion. Noting that Americans tend to be "abstract separationists but concrete accommodationists," they compare a 1993 survey of residents of the Washington, D.C., area with a similar survey conducted in 2000. Since the Washington metropolitan area is one of great and growing religious diversity, these two surveys seven years apart might provide a glimpse into how traditionally mainstream believers in the United States react to the advent of new faith groups in their communities.

The authors report that their data provide some support for the notion that "increased exposure to citizens with different religious faiths may foster greater tolerance for religious practices, and a concomitant decrease in support for public displays of majority religious symbols." At the same time, they are cautious in extrapolating from their study. As they note, the area surrounding the District of Columbia is not typical of the rest of the United States. In coastal cities, such as New York, Washington, or San Francisco, exposure to neighbors from outside the Judeo-Christian tradition is rather common. However, in rural areas and in parts of the South or Middle West, social interaction with people whose religious beliefs differ fundamentally from one's own is much less common. So the opportunities for developing tolerance presented by religious pluralism do not obtain for all regions of the United States.

Bette Novit Evans takes the argument one step farther. She contends that religious liberty has succeeded in the United States because it is consistent with both the pluralism of its major political institutions and the diversity of American society and culture. On balance, then, pluralism is not only necessary but positively beneficial, because while it implies conflict, it also promotes liberty.

For Evans, the genius of the Framers in fashioning American constitutional arrangements lay in arranging multiple points of access to the nation's political institutions, providing citizens with many opportunities to remedy unfairness—through the courts, legislatures, executive clemency, or administrative discretion. Thus the Supreme Court's departure, in *Smith,* from a strict-scrutiny interpretation of the free exercise clause is not the end of the matter. There are always other opportunities to seek religious exemptions from otherwise neutral laws. As Evans recognizes, however, this does put the burden of protecting religious freedom on minorities themselves.

In contrast with Evans's more positive view, Ted Jelen focuses on the potential, inherent in a pluralistic society, for sectarian strife and church-state conflict. He is somewhat dismayed by the fact that conflict over the proper relationship between church and state remains a permanent feature of politics in the United States. Disputes over religious freedom are never-ending in the American context. Jelen regards this persistence of church-state conflict as negative, because it contains an implicit, if not explicit, bias toward accommodation.

> The problem with the unsettled nature of the debate in U.S. politics is that such dynamic tension has a definite accommodationist bias. That is, those Americans who assert rights with respect to the Establishment Clause are forced by the permanent nature of the church-state debate to defend those rights over and over again. Such persons or groups are typically disadvantaged politically, and perhaps legally as well. The fact that religious rights are continually renegotiated in American politics often means that the politically weaker side (typically separationists) is forced to contest issues that religiously defined minorities would like to see settled.

Ultimately, Jelen sees this as an issue of equal freedom: the burden of proof falls regularly on those citizens (Native Americans, for example) whose beliefs lie outside the prevailing range of acceptability. By contrast, the fact that the American political system provides multiple access points for those who would accommodate the public expression of religious belief suggests that citizens holding mainstream beliefs are advantaged in the continuing church-state debate. "Absent some sort of resolution of these issues, the religious rights of some citizens will remain 'more equal' than those of others."

These contrasting views of the relation between pluralism and religious freedom in the United States indicate the importance of the Court's decision in *Oregon v. Smith*. If the American political system contains an implicit bias toward accommodating religious majorities, one might look to the courts to protect the freedom of religious minorities. If, on the other hand, the fragmented nature of the American political system offers many access points to advocates of religious freedom, the judicial system and juridical notions of strict scrutiny are not the only ways to protect minorities. Legislative action and administrative discretion might be adequate, as they were in the case of Capt. S. Simcha Goldman, an air force officer and an Orthodox Jew.[17] At the same time, greater exposure to religious diversity (as for example, in the Washington metropolitan area) might conceivably change the attitudes of Americans, making them more tolerant of the religious customs of the ancient traditions of Hinduism, Islam, and Buddhism now becoming more visible in the United States. Yet the findings of our authors (Wilcox et al.) suggest a cautiously realistic approach here.

These essays illuminate this fundamental debate about the freedom of religious minorities in the United States. Controversies over the First Amendment's religion clauses show no signs of abating. Paradoxically, these debates reinforce the nation's commitment to religious freedom. As E. J. Dionne notes, "Precisely because every generation of Americans has been willing to argue about it, we have managed not only to preserve but also to expand religious liberty."[18]

CONCLUSION

What can these controversies about *Smith* and about the role of religion in the 2000 presidential election tell us about religion and politics in the United States? The essays in Part Two remind us that preserving the freedom of religious minorities remains a fundamental challenge in an increasingly pluralistic society. They tell us that religious freedom is a never-ending struggle—that the role of religion in public life must be renegotiated all the time; that Americans must work continually to reconcile the imperatives of belief and tolerance, discipleship and citizenship, faith and democracy, religious commitment and political obligation.

The impact of the 2000 election on religion and politics in the United States is less clear. Although candidates were willing to discuss their religious beliefs at length, they were silent about the policy implications of those beliefs. Many candidates used God-talk to prove their bona fides on the character issue, while refusing to address substantive policy considerations on matters of deep importance to voters. Such a "stealth" campaign is a real disservice to voters, who must decide on the basis of hard information rather than cloudy mystification.

Of course, this strategy of obfuscation tells us much about coalition building in American elections and also a great deal about American religion—how superficial it can be, and yet how powerful religious rhetoric can be in attracting support. If religious rhetoric seems effective in appealing to voters, it will continue to be used in American elections despite risks of superficiality, hypocrisy, and demagoguery. If this is the case, perhaps Lieberman's intelligent, forthright discussion of religion and politics was a substantial contribution to our political discourse.

On the other hand, a case could be made that religious rhetoric is best left outside a presidential campaign. It cheapens religion and misguides voters, who are, after all, engaged in a process of democratic deliberation about officials and policies for all Americans, believers and nonbelievers. A. J. Reichley describes well the restraint and discretion necessary in a judicious approach to religion and politics in American democracy:

> The religious problem for democracy . . . is how to maintain a social environment favorable to the free exercise of religion, while avoiding the hazards, for both religion and secular society, of mingling institutional religion too closely with governmental authority. These hazards—principally, violation of individual conscience, manipulation of religion by the state, and incitement of group antagonisms—can largely be overcome through reasonable and consistent application of the First Amendment. . . . Beyond that, politicians honoring religious freedom should forego using religion as a campaign device. And the churches, to preserve their autonomy and their integrity, should usually hold themselves some distance above the rough-and-tumble of ordinary politics, whether in election campaigns or on Capitol Hill.[19]

NOTES

1. *Employment Division v. Smith,* 494 U.S. 872 (1990). There is a vast literature on this historic case. See the bibliographic essay in Carolyn N. Long, *Religious Freedom and Indian Rights: The Case of Oregon v. Smith* (Lawrence: University Press of Kansas, 2000), 293–300. Long also provides a useful chronology of the case.

2. Ernest Barker, ed., *The Politics of Aristotle* (New York: Oxford University Press, 1962), book 3, chaps. 6–13, 179–88.

3. By liberalism here I do not mean "neoliberalism," a term used recently to describe an economic doctrine of free markets, free trade, privatization, and deregulation. Along with "globalization," neoliberalism commonly refers to the increasing interdependence—financial, environmental, economic, technological—of peoples in the world community.

4. John Locke, "The Second Treatise of Civil Government," in *Two Treatises of Government,* ed. Peter Laslett (New York: Cambridge University Press, 1960).

5. An eloquent statement of this view is James Madison's *A Memorial and Remonstrance on the Religious Rights of Man,* in John E. Semonche, *Religion and Constitutional Government in the United States* (Carrboro, N.C.: Signal, 1986), 96–102.

6. Judith Shklar, "The Liberalism of Fear," in *Liberalism and the Moral Life,* ed. Nancy L. Rosenblum (Cambridge: Harvard University Press, 1989), 21–38.

7. Religious minimalists and separationists include, for example, Leonard Levy, *The Establishment Clause: Religion and the First Amendment* (Chapel Hill: University of North Carolina Press, 1994); Leo Pfeffer, *Church, State, and Freedom* (Boston: Beacon, 1967); and Ted G. Jelen, "In Defense of Religious Minimalism," in *A Wall of Separation? Debating the Public Role of Religion,* ed. Mary C. Segers and Ted G. Jelen (Lanham, Md.: Rowman & Littlefield, 1998), 3–51.

8. They include Stephen L. Carter, *The Culture of Disbelief: How American Law and Politics Trivialize Religious Devotion* (New York: Basic, 1993); William Lee Miller, *The First Liberty: Religion and the American Republic* (New York: Knopf, 1986); A. James Reichley, *Religion in American Public Life* (Washington, D.C.: Brookings Institution, 1985); E. J. Dionne Jr. and John J. DiIulio Jr., *What's God Got to Do with the American Experiment?* (Washington, D.C.: Brookings Institution, 2000); Mary C. Segers, "In Defense of Religious Freedom," in *A Wall of Separation?* ed. Segers and Jelen, 53–114.

9. Sources include *World Almanac 2000* (which uses the *1999 Yearbook of American and Canadian Churches* of the National Council of Churches of Christ in the USA); *The American Jewish Yearbook 1999* of the American Jewish Committee; U.S. Census Bureau, *Statistical Abstract of the United States* (Washington, D.C.: U.S. Census Bureau, 1999). For statistics on the Native American Church, see Long, *Religious Freedom and Indian Rights,* 15–16. See also Richard N. Ostling, "America's Ever-Changing Religious Landscape," in *What's God Got to Do with the American Experiment?* ed. Dionne and DiIulio, 17–24.

10. Data from the 2000 census are now being made available, with the appropriate media coverage. See, for example, Susan Sachs, "What's in a Name? Redefining Minority," *New York Times,* 11 March 2001, sec. IV, 1. Also Tony Pugh, "Multiracial U.S.: Census Reflects an Increasingly Diverse America," *Newark (N.J.) Star-Ledger,* 13 March 2001, 3.

11. For statistical information on the number of Roman Catholics in the United States, see chapter 5 below, on "Catholics and the 2000 Presidential Election."

12. In the case of Muslims, there are signs that Americans are beginning to recognize their presence in public life. In 1997, a crescent-and-star sculpture joined the Christmas tree and the menorah in the park in front of the White House. During the Clinton administration, the White House began holding dinners for Muslim Americans to celebrate the end of the Ramadan fast. Dean E. Murphy, "For Muslim Americans, Influence in Politics Still Hard to Come By," *New York Times,* 27 October 2000, A1.

13. Lizette Alvarez, "Census Director Marvels at the New Portrait of America," *New York Times,* 1 January 2001, A10.

14. Derek Davis, quoted by E. J. Dionne, "The Third Stage: New Frontiers of Religious Liberty," in *What's God Got to Do with the American Experiment?* ed. Dionne and DiIulio, 119.

15. Richard L. Berke, "Religion Center Stage in Presidential Race," *New York Times,* 15 December 1999, A20.

16. *City of Boerne v. Flores,* 521 U.S. 507 (1997).

17. *Goldman v. Weinberger,* 475 U.S. 503 (1986). At issue here was a conflict between the duty of Captain Simcha Goldman, an air force officer and an Orthodox Jew, to wear a yarmulke or skullcap in fulfillment of his religious obligation to keep his head covered at all times, and an air force regulation that prohibited wearing "headgear" indoors. At first, Captain Goldman had been unofficially accommodated by commanders, but eventually he was challenged for wearing his yarmulke indoors. (See the description of this case in chapter 9, by Bette Novit Evans, below). On appeal, the Supreme Court decided to uphold the military regulations in deference to the armed services' judgment about the need to uphold military discipline. That is, the Court did not judge Goldman's free exercise rights important enough to exempt him from the military regulations. But the case did not end there. Congress then passed a law allowing Jews to wear yarmulkes in the military, but it did so without challenging the authority of the federal government to decide such matters.

18. Dionne, "The Third Stage," in *What's God Got to Do with the American Experiment?* ed. Dionne and DiIulio, 120.

19. A. James Reichley, "Democracy and Religion," *PS: Political Science and Politics* 19, no. 3 (Fall 1986): 805.

One

The Role of Religion in the 2000 Presidential Election

2

The Extraordinary Election of 2000

Mary C. Segers

"Selected, Not Elected!"
"Legal, but Illegitimate!"
"Re-elect Gore in 2004!"
"No Recount, No Democracy!"

These poster slogans, carried by protesters at President George W. Bush's inauguration on January 20, 2001, expressed the views of many American voters about the 2000 presidential election. These citizens argued that not only had Bush lost the popular vote nationwide but that he had lost the state of Florida and therefore the Electoral College vote as well.

Some protesters carried signs saying "Jail to the Thief," a variation of "Hail to the Chief," the ruffles and flourishes played by military bands whenever the president appears. They felt that the Bush campaign had stolen the election in Florida, with the help of the U.S. Supreme Court. The Supreme Court's controversial decision in *Bush v. Gore*, handed down at 10 P.M. on December 12, put a permanent stop to the Florida vote recount and effectively gave the election to Bush. This is how Election 2000 ended. In the United States of America, which professes to be a liberal democracy, President Bush lost the popular vote by a whopping margin and barely eked out a razor-thin victory in the Electoral College (271 to 266). An unelected Supreme Court anointed him president. Thanks to the Court, he was "selected, not elected."[1]

Republicans, on the other hand, claimed that Bush won the state of Florida "fair and square," according to Florida election law. After an official recount mandated by state law, Florida's twenty-five electoral voters were certified to George W. Bush by Florida's secretary of state, Katherine

Harris, on November 26, 2000. In their view, the Supreme Court's ruling in *Bush v. Gore* confirmed the official count showing that Bush won the state of Florida by 537 votes.

Americans are still trying to sort out these two views of the 2000 presidential election. It will be a long time before we know what really happened in Florida's 5,885 election precincts.

We do know that the race in Florida ended in a statistical tie. A few hundred votes, out of six million cast in Florida and a hundred million cast nationwide, separated George Bush and Al Gore. Neither Bush (the proclaimed victor) nor Gore (the putative loser) could claim a decisive mandate for the White House.

As the whole world now knows, the real drama in the 2000 election occurred after Election Day, not before. Prior to Election Day, both candidates ran completely scripted campaigns, relying heavily on focus groups and political advertising to target key voters. Both candidates moved to the center of the political spectrum in a search for independent, "swing" voters in key battleground states. The real excitement began during the evening of Election Day, when television networks twice called a victor in Florida's race, only to retract each call. On Wednesday morning, November 8, the day after Election Day, voters awoke to learn that there had been no winner and that Florida law officially required a recount in a race too close to call.

In the extraordinary five-week period that followed, the state of Florida and the nation witnessed machine recounts, manual recounts in selected counties, a variety of lower court decisions at federal and state levels, two major rulings of the Florida Supreme Court, and two decisions of the U.S. Supreme Court. The brief chronology appended to this chapter describes the major events of this remarkable political finale.

While other states (New Mexico, Wisconsin, Oregon, and Iowa) were also too close to call, Florida attracted the most attention, because of the closeness of its vote and the large number of its electoral votes (twenty-five). Two things soon became clear: Florida would decide the presidential election, and Florida's election procedures were woefully inadequate.

WHAT WENT WRONG IN FLORIDA?

First in the "parade of horribles" in Florida, media coverage on election night was a disaster. The television networks twice declared a victor in Florida's contest and twice retracted. They also erred by projecting the outcome in Florida before the polls closed in the western part of the state, which is in a different time zone. Viewers spent a bewildering election night, with network anchors declaring and then undeclaring winners.

The networks' difficulties stemmed in part from flawed data supplied by the Voter News Service, a consortium run jointly by the networks and the Associated Press to help them in their projections. But the competition to be first in calling the election also pressured TV executives to rush to judgment and project winners before independent confirmation was obtained. Later, CBS, NBC, and ABC all did internal reviews of their election-night failures. While they have not said they will avoid projecting winners in future elections, they have agreed not to call an election in any state when the polls remain open.[2]

But network reforms of future election coverage cannot compensate for the negative impact of flawed reporting in the 2000 election. An external review commissioned by CNN excoriated TV election-night coverage as a "news disaster that damaged democracy and journalism." The CNN report blamed the networks for creating a political climate of "rancor and bitterness." In particular, the report said that the unanimous network declarations of a Bush victory on election night "created a premature impression" that Bush had defeated Gore in the crucial race for Florida's twenty-five electoral votes. "That characterization carried through the postelection challenge. Gore was perceived as the challenger and labeled a 'sore loser' for trying to steal the election." In other words, "reckless" TV coverage put the burden of proof on Gore in contesting what the media had led the public to believe was a final determination about Florida's twenty-five electoral votes.[3]

Conflict of interest presented a second problem in Florida. Once it became clear that Florida had to recount its vote, both Governor Jeb Bush and his attorney general, Robert Butterworth, recused themselves from any involvement in the process. For obvious reasons—Jeb Bush is George Bush's brother—the governor had to bow out. Butterworth, who had served as Gore's campaign manager in Florida, explained that he could not, in the interests of impartiality, participate in the election challenge.

Conspicuously absent from the joint press conference at which Bush and Butterworth announced their decisions was Florida's secretary of state, Katherine Harris. She had been George Bush's campaign co-manager in Florida during the 2000 campaign. She had also campaigned for Bush in New Hampshire during the February primary earlier in the year.

In such an unusual challenge as the Florida contest, public officials must respect the appearance as well as the substance of justice. If the public is to have confidence in the neutrality, nonpartisanship, fairness, and impartiality of recounts of contested votes, officials must appear to be fair and impartial. Harris did not withdraw; instead, she made key decisions about absentee ballots and deadline extensions that favored Bush. Concern for public confidence and for the appearance as well as the substance of justice dictates that Harris, like Governor Bush and Attorney General Butterworth, should have recused herself. Because of her prior partisan activities, she had a conflict of interest.[4]

Third, Florida's voting procedures were woefully inadequate. Reports emanating from precincts on Election Day described chaos: voters struggled with long lines, confusing ballots, outdated voter lists, and faulty machinery. The most egregious example of voting irregularities was the infamous "butterfly ballot" used in Palm Beach County, a largely Democratic county in southeast Florida populated by Jewish voters living in retirement villages and also by African American and Hispanic communities.

This ballot differed in its layout from ballots elsewhere in the state. Instead of placing candidates' names on the left and a punch hole to the right of each, as specified by Florida statutes, the butterfly ballot placed some names on the left and some on the right, and all punch holes in the middle. It was difficult to line up a name with the correct punch hole. Moreover, contrary to Florida statutes, the butterfly ballot did not list candidates' names in proper order—the two major-party candidates followed by eight minor-party candidates. Instead, Bush's name was first, with Pat Buchanan below him and Gore listed third.

This confusing ballot resulted in the disqualification of nineteen thousand ballots because citizens voted for two or more candidates (technically, such "overvotes" result when voters mistakenly punch one hole, then try to correct the mistake by punching another, "correct" hole). Moreover, Buchanan's vote in this heavily Democratic county increased dramatically from his vote share in the 1996 election (Buchanan got 5 percent of the vote in 1996 and 20 percent in 2000). Buchanan himself stated on public television that he simply had not expected to win so many votes (3,400) in Palm Beach County and suggested that something was amiss.

In Palm Beach County, miscast votes (overvotes and undervotes—the latter occurring when punch styluses do not fully penetrate the cards and leave "dimples" or "hanging chads") totaled thirty thousand in the 2000 election compared with fourteen thousand in 1996. The rate of overvoting was 4.4 percent in Palm Beach, compared with one-half of 1 percent in other large Florida counties; it was as high as 15 percent in some predominantly African American precincts and about 10 percent in some Palm Beach precincts with large numbers of Jewish retirees. There was so much confusion over this butterfly ballot that significantly large numbers of voters made mistakes and then overvoted; their ballots were automatically disqualified. Unlike undervotes, which can be studied to discern voter intent, overvotes are simply indecipherable and illegal.[5]

The butterfly ballot had been designed by Theresa Le Pore, a Democrat and the election supervisor in Palm Beach, in a good-faith effort to comply with a 1998 change in Florida statutes stipulating that all minor party presidential candidates had to be listed on the ballot. Whereas Florida voters chose among four presidential hopefuls in 1996, they chose among ten such candidates in Election 2000. Le Pore was concerned that the large numbers of seniors in Palm Beach County would have trouble reading the ballot; she designed a large-print "butterfly ballot" that managed to list all ten presidential candidates on one card. It was ironic, in light of Le Pore's good intentions, that the card created more confusion than clarity. In Duval County in the Jacksonville area, officials spread the names of the ten presidential candidates across two pages but left the existing instructions to "vote every page." This ballot design also confused voters and probably cost Al Gore votes.[6]

Additional Obstacles to Voting

Other difficulties facing voters included an inaccurate master voting list and obstacles to the restoration of the voting rights of ex-felons who had served their sentences. In testimony before a Florida gubernatorial task force later commissioned to recommend improvements in the state's voting system, Pat Hollam, a Republican and the elections supervisor of Okaloosa County, in the Panhandle, criticized the state for its poorly funded, error-prone central voter file. Because the state legislature did not have enough people working on the voter file, she said, the list is updated only quarterly, which means that much of its information was obsolete, Florida being a state with high rates of immigration and emigration. According to Hollam, "The whole process of the central voter file is fraught with error. Our records change by the minute. . . . The pain we have caused people has been grievous."[7]

Hollam noted that the clemency process of restoring voting rights takes up to a year, is expensive, and is not well known to most former felons. In addition, some qualified voters were wrongly listed as felons on the master list and denied the right to vote. Linda Howell, elections supervisor from Madison County, in central Florida, later testified before the U.S. Civil Rights Commission that she got a letter from the state saying—in error—that she was a convicted felon. A black pastor from Tallahassee, Willie D. Whiting Jr., testified that when he tried to vote with his family, he was told his name had been purged from the rolls because he was a convicted felon. He insisted that he had never spent a night in jail anywhere, but only after threatening to retain a lawyer was he permitted to vote. The confusion was so great that in some counties convicted felons were improperly allowed to vote, while others mistakenly labeled as felons were prevented.[8]

Minority voters in particular lodged many complaints about voting irregularities in the election. African Americans testified before the U.S. Civil Rights Commission that antiquated voting machinery was concentrated in poor and minority communities; that police checkpoints on roads leading to certain polling places were intended to intimidate voters; and that some citizens were wrongly told they had been purged from the voter rolls. Latino advocates noted that on Election Day many Latinos were turned away at the polls, were ignored when they requested language assistance, were required to present additional photo identification, and were subjected to other forms of harassment—all of which resulted in thousands of uncast votes.[9]

Systemic Problems

Florida's election difficulties resulted from the use of different voting machinery in different counties, lack of uniform vote-counting standards, poor direction from the secretary of state's office, lack of support from the director of elections, and the refusal of the state legislature to spend the time and money necessary to update the central voter list or improve voter education. Ion Sancho, election supervisor in Leon County, near Tallahassee, testified before the U.S. Civil Rights Commission that Florida is "a state that spends $35 million to tell people how to play Lotto" but not nearly enough to tell them how to vote.[10]

In Election 2000, voters used four different types of voting systems, depending on the counties they lived in. One county (Union) used the old-fashioned paper ballot, and one county (Martin) used a lever voting machine. In forty more of the state's sixty-seven counties, voters used optical scanners. The punch-ballot system was used in the remaining twenty-five counties, including heavily populated counties in southeastern Florida— Palm Beach, Broward, Miami-Dade—where Gore asked for recounts, as well as Duval in the northeast and Pinellas in the Tampa–St. Petersburg area. Counties using punch-card machines had nearly three times as many ballots discarded as counties that used optical scanners.

Statewide, a total of 185,000 ballots were discarded, rejected as either undervotes (failing for whatever reason to mark a ballot or punch out a chad) or overvotes (selecting more than one candidate, for whatever reason). Voting machinery and ballot design played large roles in rejections. Palm Beach, of butterfly-ballot fame, and Duval County, where presidential candidates' names were spread across two pages, accounted for 31 percent of the uncounted ballots but only 12 percent of the total votes cast.

Statistics show that the Votomatic punch-card voting system (described above) did not serve voters well. Of the fifty-one precincts in which more than 20 percent of ballots were rejected, forty-five used punch cards—88 percent. Of the 336 precincts in which more than 10 percent were tossed out, 277 used punch cards—78 percent. Most discarded ballots came from punch-card counties in urban Democratic strongholds, such as Broward and Palm Beach Counties. Moreover, in nearly all of Florida's majority-black precincts, presidential ballots were invalidated at higher rates than in mostly white neighborhoods. The lopsided loss of black votes occurred throughout Florida, not just in widely publicized instances in Palm Beach and Duval Counties. A *Miami Herald* analysis confirmed that, statewide, voters in Democratic precincts had a far greater chance of having their ballots rejected. Only one in every forty ballots was rejected in precincts Bush won, while one of every twenty-seven ballots was discarded in precincts Gore won.[11]

Leon County election supervisor Ion Sancho summarized the Florida fiasco in these terms: "There was failure in voter technology, failure in training the voters in technology, and a failure in administration." Mary Frances Berry, chair of the U.S. Civil Rights Commission, noted that state officials knew that voter turnout, especially among minorities, would be higher in 2000 than in previous elections but did nothing to ensure that all precincts had enough resources to handle that increase. Nevertheless, when Governor Bush and Secretary of State Harris appeared before the Civil Rights Commission, they both denied responsibility for the Florida voting disaster, saying it was the responsibility of the county election supervisors. Harris described her administrative style as one of delegation; daily operations and implementation of the state election code, she stated, were the responsibility of the elections director, Clay Roberts. Local control of elections, according to Harris, fell to county elections supervisors.

At the same hearing, however, several county elections supervisors testified that Harris's office had not given help they had requested to educate voters or to pay for sample-ballot mailings (a problem in some cash-strapped counties). Three current supervisors and a former one said they had stopped making requests, because they knew they would be turned down. The Division of Elections in the secretary of state's office did little to help the counties. It set up a voter-fraud hot line and spent a small amount of money on public service announcements, but according to Clay Roberts, the bulk of voter education duties were left to the counties.[12]

Conditions in Florida were so inferior that former President Jimmy Carter, who has monitored dozens of elections in troubled spots around the world, said he would not assist a foreign nation that had election procedures as flawed as Florida's. He listed three conditions that the Carter Center requires before monitoring an election in a foreign country. First, the country must have a bipartisan election commission to oversee elections and help to resolve disputes. Second, it must have uniform voting procedures and machinery throughout the country. Third, the country must have standards for counting the vote, not a standardless situation as in Florida.

Florida met none of the three conditions. "I was really taken aback and embarrassed by what happened in Florida," Carter said. "I could not believe that in Florida the error rate was expected to be four or five percent, which is an enormous amount of votes, many of which, of course, were not counted." According to Carter, such a built-in expectation of error in Florida's voting practices should have been a warning flag and a harbinger of disaster in a close election.[13]

THE POSTELECTION CAMPAIGN IN FLORIDA

In the midst of the immediate postelection confusion, Democratic and Republican campaign personnel rushed to Florida to observe the mandated ballot review. Wading into essentially uncharted waters, campaign managers for both Bush and Gore sought to shape public opinion in their respective candidate's favor and to put the "correct spin" on the developing recount. The Bush spokesman, former Secretary of State James Baker, suggested that to prolong the election was to invite a constitutional crisis. With George Bush ahead, initially by 1,784 votes, Baker was content to comply with the machine recount required by Florida law; however, once that was completed, he held, the winner should be certified.

But the Gore campaign, aware of the voting irregularities in the heavily populated, Democratic-leaning (traditionally Democratic) counties of south Florida, called for a manual recount to cope with the large number of undervotes. As the media and the public became more aware of the serious flaws in the state's voting procedures, sentiment grew in favor of a fair and accurate recount of ballots.

Both sides waged a battle for public opinion. It is worth reviewing the arguments put forth by the Bush camp; they were examples of masterful spin doctoring. These are some of the themes repeatedly sounded by the Bush communications people, chief of whom was James Baker.

(1) Baker suggested that the issue was finality rather than fairness. After all, Bush had been declared the winner by the networks, and it was just a matter of time before the machine recount would be completed and he would be declared president-elect. It would be best to keep the Florida postelection period as brief as possible; if it dragged on too long, there would be instability in Florida, in the nation, on Wall Street, and in the world. So all sides should accept the conclusions of the machine recount mandated by Florida law. But the Gore campaign pointed out that while the situation was unusual, there was no crisis. While they kept one eye on the news, Americans were going about their daily business calmly and quietly; they were not taking to the streets or manning the barricades.

(2) Baker and other Republican spokespersons suggested that Gore was a whiner and a spoilsport for not accepting the results of the initial tally. Gore-Lieberman posters were changed to "Sore-Loserman." The Republicans argued that the burden was on Gore to show why it was necessary to strive for a complete and accurate count of the Florida vote. But Gore was simply executing his lawful rights as a candidate seeking a recount in a very tight election. Florida law mandated a machine recount in very close elections and permitted manual recounts if requested by a candidate. Both sides could request manual recounts. Gore did; Bush did not.

(3) In their haste to finalize a Bush victory, Baker and other Republican advocates originally said the courts should stay out of this challenge. They

were particularly critical after the Florida Supreme Court called for a thorough manual recount of contested ballots and extended the deadline for certification of the vote by Secretary of State Harris from November 17 to November 26. Despite arguments by Gore lawyers that Florida election law was vague and needed judicial interpretation, the Bush managers described the Florida Supreme Court's decision as an act of judicial usurpation, not a legitimate exercise of judicial review.

(4) Baker and other GOP spokespersons often raised issues of partisanship and partisan bias about officials involved in the process. They charged that the Florida Supreme Court was biased because six of the seven justices had been appointed by Democratic governors. They responded to criticism of the butterfly ballot in Palm Beach County by saying the ballot had been designed by a Democrat and that therefore the Gore Democratic campaign should not criticize it—as though the independent matter of good or bad ballot design was a merely partisan issue.

(5) Concerned that Gore might pull ahead in the manual recounts, the Republicans threatened to have the GOP-controlled Florida state legislature certify its own slate of presidential electors. This threatened to reveal what some have called "the dirty little secret" of the American political system—that there is no right to popular election of presidential electors. Under Article II of the Constitution, state legislatures—not the people—are empowered to decide the allocation of their respective states' electoral votes. This move raised the distinct possibility that Florida might present two slates of presidential electors to the U.S. Congress, one certified by the legislature and the other certified as the result of a recount of Florida's popular vote. This prospect did indeed raise the specter of chaos and political instability.

(6) Ultimately, the Bush handlers fought tooth and nail against every recount—machine, manual, undervotes—until they finally appealed to the U.S. Supreme Court, which stopped the last Florida recount and declared that time had run out.

Why did the Bush campaign resist so strenuously a full and complete vote count? After eight years out of the White House, they were determined to win and feared a recount would give victory to Gore. But beyond this obvious motive, what about the democratic principle that every vote must be counted? The contrast between the Bush campaign's sense of urgency and the American public's commonsense insistence upon a full and fair recount was striking. The Bush people wanted it over fast, while the public said: get it done, and get it right.

The Gore people also wanted desperately to win the election. Armed with a sizable lead in the popular vote and with knowledge of significant voting irregularities in heavily populated southeast Florida, they called for a manual recount of the ballots in four counties: Palm Beach, Miami-Dade, Broward, and Volusia. By insisting that maximum efforts be made to count every vote, the Gore campaign took the high road and appeared to stand for the democratic principles of one man, one vote, and government with the consent of a majority of the governed. But by initially calling for a manual recount in four Democratic-leaning counties rather than in all of Florida's sixty-seven counties, the Gore people left themselves vulnerable to a Republican accusation of partisanship.

In the end, there may not have been much hope for Gore's contesting of the Florida count. He was perhaps unfairly burdened by the network's premature projection of Bush as president-elect, so that even his rightful, legal challenge of the election made him look like a sore loser. Both Gore and Lieberman ultimately took the high road of insisting that in a country claiming to be the world's leading democracy, people's votes must be counted as fully, fairly, and accurately as possible. While this stance was appealing, a case could be made for the other side, and that case was reflected in the U.S. Supreme Court's decision in *Bush v. Gore.* Since this controversial decision was crucial in ending the Florida postelection contest, a thorough analysis by Elizabeth Hull of the Court's decision is included here (see chapter 3).

LONG-TERM CONSEQUENCES OF THE 2000 ELECTION

Long-term consequences of the Florida recount are both positive and negative. They include a sobering awareness of the imperfections of our electoral system, widespread acknowledgment of the need for electoral reform, possible loss of public confidence in the American political system, and a legacy of bitterness and intense partisanship.

Knowledge of Imperfections in Voting

A bevy of bipartisan commissions and independent panels have investigated the Florida vote in an effort to understand what went wrong and to make recommendations for reform of the system. Governor Bush appointed a bipartisan task force, the Select Task Force on Election Procedures, Standards and Technology, comprising ten Republicans, ten Democrats, and one independent, to conduct hearings and recommend changes to him and to the Florida legislature. The U.S. Civil Rights Commission conducted hearings and used its subpoena powers to compel testimony from high state officials (including Bush and Harris). A task force of the National Association of Secretaries of State adopted a set of guidelines for future elections. As of this writing, the *Miami Herald* has conducted a statewide review of sixty thousand undervotes in Florida's sixty-seven counties. Other news organizations—the *New York Times,* the *Wall Street Journal,* the *Palm Beach Post,* the *St. Petersburg Times,* the *Washington Post,* CNN, the Associated Press, and the *Orlando Sentinel*—are conducting jointly an independent review of the same ballots (see appendix, page 37). Finally, a National Commission on Election Standards and Reform, an independent commission sponsored by the National Association of Counties and the Association of County Recorders, Election Officials and Clerks, is conducting its own investigation and plans to make recommendations to Congress and the president.[14]

This effort should be undertaken for the nation's historical and electoral record. Americans need to gain a fuller understanding of what happened in this strange election. This knowledge is necessary in order to devise reforms that will prevent a recurrence of what was clearly an electoral disaster.

At the same time, we will probably never know with any real certainty which candidate actually won the Florida presidential race. Of the 175,000 disqualified Florida ballots, only sixty thousand were undervotes (for which it is possible, in theory, to decipher voter intent). The remaining 115,000 were overvotes—cases where voters punched two choices for president—and they present a formidable problem: they are illegal, and it is virtually impossible in such cases to discern voter intent.

A recent report from the *Miami Herald* suggested that Gore would not have gained enough votes in Miami-Dade County to win the presidential race. Based on their recount of 10,644 undervotes—ballots bearing no machine-readable vote for president—the *Herald* found 1,555 ballots that might be interpreted as a vote for Gore. An additional 1,506 ballots bore some kind of mark that could be interpreted as a vote for Bush. There were 106 markings for other candidates. Based on this tally, the *Herald* concluded that Gore picked up only forty-nine additional votes in Miami-Dade, not enough to enable him to overtake Bush.

However, no markings for president were found on 4,892 punch-card ballots, and another 2,058 ballots bore markings in spaces that had been assigned to no candidate. In another words, careful inspection by the *Miami Herald* (and the public accounting firm retained by the *Herald* to conduct the review) could not decipher voter intent in 70 percent of the 10,644 undervotes in this one county alone.[15]

Almost simultaneously, the *Palm Beach Post* reported that Al Gore would have gained 784 votes in Palm Beach County if officials there had counted every ballot that had a hanging chad, pinhole, or dimple. The newspaper suggested that, had the *Post*'s standard been used and its tally applied without any changes in counting procedures in Florida's other sixty-six counties as well, the revised tally would have been enough for Gore to erase Bush's 537-vote margin of victory in the state. The newspaper examined the 9,150 ballots that county officials said had no vote for president (undervotes) and found that 5,736 had marks for either Bush or Gore. There were 462,350 ballots cast in the county, which Gore carried by an almost two-to-one margin.[16]

Based on these two examples, I think it is safe to say that review of the ballots will be inconclusive and that we will probably never know who won Florida. What we do know, however, is that electoral reform in Florida is an urgent necessity.

The Need for Electoral Reform

Reforms proposed by the Florida gubernatorial task force are extensive, but the question is whether the state legislature and the governor will implement them. The bipartisan task force recommended that all counties switch to on-site optical-scan voting machines by the 2002 election in order to avoid the problems of the antiquated punch-card system. The optical-scan system is more accurate and allows voters to correct ballots if they have marked them incorrectly; in 2000, it was used in thirty Florida counties, with a very low rate of error. The task force also suggested that the state should establish thorough voter education programs, hire and train higher numbers of qualified poll workers, and make the position of county election supervisor a nonpartisan job (currently, supervisors are elected officials nominated by the two major parties). It is noteworthy that county election supervisors themselves have repeatedly proposed this last reform to the legislature— without success.

The recommendations of most of the other panels reiterate the needs for voting equipment, training, and education. They suggest that the federal government should help states and local governments pay for upgrades in voter equipment. They also stress the need to maintain up-to-date lists of registered voters and to ensure the integrity of absentee ballots.

The Florida task force's recommendations were sent to the state legislature in March 2001. Election reform was the last item mentioned in Governor Bush's address to the lawmakers. There is some worry that lawmakers will be unwilling to spend the twenty million dollars necessary to lease optical-scan equipment for the counties, let alone the forty million to enable counties to purchase it. Some are concerned that the governor and the Republicans in the Florida legislature will not make electoral reform a top-priority issue this year. Mary Frances Berry, chair of the U.S. Civil Rights Commission, which held hearings on minority voting in the 2000 election, indicated that the commission will subpoena the governor, the secretary of state, and legislative leaders at the end of the session to ascertain what reforms have been approved.[17]

Money, of course, is not the only obstacle to electoral reform. Neither of the major political parties wants to adopt any reform that will tip the balance of power to the other side. In the struggle for partisan advantage in elections, each party has preferences. A truism that has guided strategies for years is that higher voter turnout usually favors Democrats, lower turnout generally favors Republicans. Democrats therefore favor measures that make it easier for everyone to vote (such as "motor voter" registration laws). Republicans, on the other hand, worry that there is too much "deadwood" on the voting rolls, leading too easily to fraud. They therefore want to control access to the ballot box as much as possible—by, for example, purging voter lists of people who have not voted in some time period, have moved, are felons, or are otherwise ineligible.[18]

In this debate, the Democrats have the better part of the argument. That is, so long as the United States professes to be a liberal democracy, the ideals of government with the consent of the governed and one man, one vote should be guiding principles. The voting booth may be the last vestige of political equality in an otherwise oligarchic society—a sad fact that underscores the need for care in the conduct of our elections. As African Americans insisted during the Florida recount, the principle that every vote must be counted is absolutely fundamental. While every step must be taken to avoid fraud, electoral reform is imperative.

Loss of Public Confidence in the Electoral System

Five weeks of Florida follies were a giant civics lesson for the American public, as citizens struggled to understand the Electoral College, separation of powers, federalism, judicial review, and the intricacies of voting. Suddenly all these abstractions became dramatically real as the nation watched the Florida Supreme Court struggle with the issues, and as it heard oral arguments before the U.S. Supreme Court in *Bush v. Gore.* Americans were riveted to their television sets, watching daily for signs of resolution in the contest. One journalist described this civic lesson as an "immersion course on Article II of the U.S. Constitution, forced upon us by Florida's Great Chad Hunt."[19]

But the Supreme Court abruptly ended this civics lesson with its decision to stop the Florida recount and, in effect, declare George Bush president-elect. The Court's intervention stunned many voters. For weeks afterward, the Court was deluged with mail criticizing its decision. Some voters were so angry that they mailed their voter registration cards to the justices, implying that voting was a waste of time.[20]

So this extended civics lesson was a two-edged sword. This was illustrated dramatically for me in a course I was then teaching on religion and politics in the United States. During the five-week Florida challenge, we would spend a few minutes at the beginning of each class discussing new developments in the recount (for political scientists this was a great teaching moment!). At the beginning of the Florida recount, I asked my students what we might learn from all this postelection confusion, and they replied, "The importance of voting, that every single vote counts." When I asked the same question at the end of the process, they replied, "Voting? Why bother?"

This was not exactly the desired civics lesson. A loss of public confidence in the electoral system may be a long-term consequence of the 2000 election. To dissipate such citizen anger and despair, major electoral reforms are absolutely essential.

A Legacy of Bitterness and Rancor

Finally, a long-term negative effect of the 2000 presidential election may be a legacy of intense partisanship and rancor. As the Florida recount stretched into days and then weeks, the rhetoric became increasingly bitter. The lack of civility was quite disturbing. The effect of it was to delegitimize the notion of a "loyal opposition." A long-range democratic process is at stake here. In democracies, there is such a thing as a valid, legitimate, loyal opposition. A loyal opposition keeps those in power accountable and is a needed balance in a stable polity. But the idea and the practice require that politicians in both parties respect one another. Respect for political opponents was one of the singular casualties of the Florida debacle.

POSTSCRIPT ON ELECTORAL REFORM IN FLORIDA

On May 10, 2001, Governor Jeb Bush of Florida signed into law a sweeping election-reform bill that had been approved 120 to zero by the Florida House of Representatives and thirty-eight to two by the Senate. The new law requires that by September 2002, all of Florida's counties must abandon punch cards and lever machines and instead use precinct-based optical scanners using ballots that are uniform statewide. Counties will receive twenty-four million dollars over the next two years to replace outdated equipment. In addition, counties will divide six million dollars for better education of voters and poll workers, and another two million to create a central voter database.

The law requires that ballots in extremely close elections be recounted by hand—the very practice that Florida election officials and the Bush campaign had opposed so vehemently in the 2000 election. Moreover, the law requires manual review of *both* overvotes and undervotes in close elections (defined as an election where the margin of victory is one quarter of 1 percent or less). The secretary of state's office would establish rules for the manual review, including how ambiguous ballots would be counted. Such a statewide standard for recounts would eliminate confusion over counting questionable ballots, which was a major point of contention in the 2000 postelection imbroglio.

The new law addresses another problem that arose in the last election—the disenfranchising of citizens in heavily black precincts who were erroneously eliminated from the voter rolls because they had been mistakenly purged along with ex-convicts. The law creates provisional ballots, which will enable people whose registration is in question to vote pending verification by canvassers after the election.

The Florida election reform also makes absentee ballots easier to get and cast, and it lengthens to eleven days, from the current seven, the time for certifying general election results. Finally, the new law requires electronic tabulation of ballots in each precinct, offering voters a chance to redo spoiled ballots before leaving the polling place.

The new election law does not reflect all the reforms proposed by the Florida gubernatorial task force. For example, the legislature did not make the county elections supervisor races nonpartisan, like those for judges and school board members. Nor did the legislature change the law barring felons from voting. A provision that would have been a step toward automatically restoring the voting rights of felons was dropped in negotiations between the Senate, which favored it, and the House, which opposed it. Moreover, the law does not guarantee uniformity in voting machinery. While the law funds optical scanners for most counties, it allows wealthier counties to purchase more expensive touch-screen technology. This loophole means that the state's voting machinery will not be uniform statewide, a measure the U.S. Supreme Court recommended in *Bush v. Gore.*

Nevertheless, passage of this voting reform package is remarkable—especially in view of the fact that six months ago, Florida's Republican-controlled legislature was hell-bent on ignoring manual recounts and certifying the election of George Bush to the presidency. Apparently, legislators were moved by pressure from Florida constituents who demanded change now to avoid ever again becoming a national embarrassment. Legislators also became aware of the flaws in the electoral system once they began to examine the system carefully, as if through a microscope.

While Florida has taken the lead among the states in electoral reform, other states have also updated their election procedures. Georgia enacted legislation to place touch-screen-voting systems in all precincts, while the Maryland legislature passed a bill requiring the state and counties to split the costs of a new system. Since Election 2000, more than 1,500 bills relating to electoral change have been introduced in the fifty states. More than 130 have been signed into law, and more than a thousand are pending in thirty-five states.

At the federal level, however, Congress seems to be dragging its feet on providing funding for electoral reform. The Senate's Government Affairs Committee began hearings only on electoral reform in May 2001. Senator Joseph Lieberman opened these hearings by saying that he did not want to revisit the 2000 election or discuss the Florida recount. Instead, Lieberman described the subject of the hearings as "a much larger problem that we stumbled upon on Election Day 2000 concerning the voting process nationally. The fact is, countless Americans were disenfranchised last year."[21] Lieberman estimated the number at 2.5 million voters nationwide. Given the magnitude of this problem, the nation's commitment to democracy, and the civics lessons Americans learned in Florida, it is imperative that the federal government in Washington follow the example set by Florida in enacting and funding major electoral reforms.[22]

APPENDIX: CHRONOLOGY OF THE FLORIDA RECOUNT

November 7—Election Day. At 7:50 P.M., CBS and other major television networks project Gore as the winner of Florida's twenty-five electoral votes. The networks retract this projection at approximately 10 P.M.

November 8—In the early morning hours, the networks declare Bush the winner of Florida, only to retract that projection two hours later. The closeness of the Florida vote triggers an automatic machine recount in the state's sixty-seven counties. Bush's lead is 1,784 votes.

November 9—Gore campaign requests a hand recount in four of Florida's more populous counties: Miami-Dade; Broward, which includes Fort Lauderdale; Volusia, which includes Daytona Beach; and Palm Beach. Secretary of State Harris says it is up to county election boards to decide whether to conduct these, but that if they took place, they would have to be completed by the state deadline of November 14. Democrats also request in court that a new presidential balloting be held in Palm Beach County, claiming the butterfly ballot was illegal and caused massive confusion among voters in the county.

November 11—Automatic machine recount concluded. Bush lead reduced to 961.

November 12—Palm Beach County officials vote to conduct a full hand recount of presidential votes. Volusia County begins its own hand count. Bush's legal team goes to federal court seeking to block manual recounts.

November 13—Secretary of State Harris says she will not extend a deadline of 5 P.M. EST on November 14 for receiving all state election results except for absentee ballots coming from overseas. Gore's lawyers promise a legal challenge. A federal judge turns down Bush's attempt to stop manual recounts.

November 14—Date for initial vote certification. Bush lead reduced to 327 votes, according to unofficial Associated Press estimates. Harris delays certification of the state's votes until 2 P.M. EST on November 15 so that three heavily Democratic counties can explain why they should conduct hand recounts of their ballots.

November 15—Harris says she will not accept further hand recounts and asks the Florida Supreme Court to order the halt of manual recounts. Broward County decides to begin a hand recount.

November 17—The Florida Supreme Court blocks Harris from any vote certification until it can rule on the Democrats' motion to allow hand recounts to be tallied. The midnight deadline passes for counties to receive overseas absentee ballots. The Eleventh Circuit Court of Appeals denies on constitutional grounds a Republican request to stop manual recounts.

November 18—Addition of overseas absentee ballots increases Bush's lead to 930.

November 20—Florida Supreme Court hears oral arguments on whether Harris should consider hand-recounted ballots before she certifies results of the presidential election. A Florida lower-court judge says he lacks authority under the U.S. Constitution to order a new presidential election in Palm Beach County.

November 21—Florida Supreme Court orders hand counts to continue and gives counties five days to complete them.

November 22—Bush running mate Dick Cheney suffers a heart attack. He undergoes surgery to open a constricted artery at a Washington hospital and is released two days later.

November 23—Miami-Dade County officials stop the hand recount, saying they will not have enough time to complete it before the deadline given by the Florida Supreme Court. Democrats blame the canvassing board's decision on a raucous Republican demonstration, accusing the GOP of intimidating the board into quitting—a charge that Republicans deny.

November 24—The U.S. Supreme Court agrees to hear Bush's appeal of the Florida Supreme Court's ruling allowing hand recounts to proceed.

November 26—Harris certifies the results of the Florida vote after the state supreme court's deadline expires, giving Bush a 537-vote lead over Gore. Harris does not include results from Palm Beach County, which completed its manual recount about two hours after the deadline.

November 27—Gore's lawyers move to contest the Florida result in a circuit court in Tallahassee. Gore tells the nation the result Harris certified wrongly excluded thousands of votes that were never tallied.

November 28—Judge N. Sanders Sauls, the circuit court judge hearing Gore's election contest, refuses Gore's request for a speedy resolution and sets a December 2 hearing on the case.

December 1—The U.S. Supreme Court hears oral arguments over whether the Florida Supreme Court overstepped its authority in ordering Harris to include the manual recounts in certified state results. Meanwhile, the Florida Supreme Court upholds Judge Sauls's ruling putting off a hand recount in Gore's contest.

December 2—Judge Sauls opens two days of proceedings on Gore's challenge to the Florida results. The vice president asks for a count of about fourteen thousand "undervotes" from Palm Beach and Miami-Dade Counties.

December 4—Judge Sauls rules against Gore's request for a manual recount of the disputed south Florida votes. Gore appeals Sauls's ruling to the Florida Supreme Court. Meanwhile, the U.S. Supreme Court asks the Florida Supreme Court to explain its reasoning in extending the hand recounts, returning the case to Tallahassee and putting off any action in Bush's appeal objecting to the recounts.

December 7—In oral arguments before the Florida Supreme Court, Gore's lawyers argue that Sauls was wrong to uphold the certification of Florida's election results.

December 8—Divided four to three, the Florida Supreme Court orders a manual recount of all undervotes in Florida counties where such a recount has not yet occurred. The Florida court also adds to the state total 215 votes for Gore from Palm Beach County and 168 votes from Miami-Dade County, all of which had been rejected earlier by Secretary of State Harris but that the high court said were legal votes. This reduces the Bush lead to 193 votes. Bush appeals the decision to the U.S. Supreme Court and seeks injunctive relief to stop the hand counts. Meanwhile, the Florida legislature meets to begin the process of choosing electors on its own. Also, circuit court judges in Tallahassee rule against Democratic challenges to absentee ballots in Martin and Seminole Counties; they decide not to throw out nearly twenty-five thousand absentee ballots where GOP workers were improperly allowed to fix Republican ballot-request forms that had been rejected (had those ballots been eliminated, Gore would have won Florida). The judges in both cases condemned the altering of absentee ballot requests but said that it was simply not a grave enough offense to disenfranchise voters.

December 9—In the midst of the Florida hand count, the U.S. Supreme Court, in a five-to-four ruling, issues a stay to stop the count and sets a hearing for December 11 to decide the case.

December 11—The Supreme Court hears oral arguments in *Bush v. Gore.* Florida's Republican-controlled state legislature meets in committee to appoint its own slate of presidential electors for Bush.

December 12—The U.S. Supreme Court ends the recount. The Court overturns the Florida Supreme Court and rules, by a vote of five to four, that there should be no further counting of Florida's disputed presidential votes. In an unsigned decision that drew four dissents, the justices reverse the Florida high court's recount decision, saying it had due-process and equal-protection flaws. At the same time, the Florida Supreme Court rejects the appeals of two lawsuits filed by Gore supporters concerning altering of absentee ballot requests.

December 13—Gore concedes the presidential election and calls for unity. President-elect Bush calls for bridging partisan divisions and promises to be president for "one nation."

December 18—Electors for each state meet in state capitals and cast electoral votes. Florida casts twenty-five electoral votes for George W. Bush. One District of Columbia elector pledged to Gore refused to vote and left her ballot blank in protest against the denial of statehood to the District.

January 6—As president of the Senate, Vice President Al Gore chairs a joint session of Congress that certifies the Electoral College vote, showing that George W. Bush defeated him by 271 to 266 votes. Members of the Congressional Black Caucus protest the Florida electoral vote in vain.

November 12, 2001—One year after the disputed 2000 presidential election, a consortium of news organizations publishes the results of a comprehensive ballot review of 175,000 uncounted Florida votes. The media consortium, which included the *New York Times,* the *Wall Street Journal,* CNN, the *Washington Post,* the Tribune Company, the *Palm Beach Post,* the *St. Petersburg Times,* and the Associated Press, hired the National Opinion Research Center at the University of Chicago to examine both overvotes and undervotes. The results of this extensive review reveal that Bush would have won the presidential election even if the U.S. Supreme Court had allowed the statewide manual recount of undervotes that the Florida Supreme Court had ordered to go forward. Similarly, Bush would have retained a narrow lead if Gore's request to recount ballots in just four counties had been completed. However, the consortium, looking at a broader group of rejected ballots than those covered in the court decisions, found that Gore would have won if the courts had ordered a full statewide recount of all the rejected ballots—overvotes as well as undervotes. Gore would have eked out a victory if he had pursued in court a course like the one he publicly advocated when he called on the state to "count all the votes."

The review also found statistical support for the complaints of many voters, the elderly in Palm Beach County and minorities in Duval County, who said in interviews after the election that confusing ballot designs may have led them to spoil their ballots by voting for more than one candidate. And the review determined that predominantly black precincts had more than three times as many rejected votes as white precincts, even after accounting for differences in income, education, and voting technology.

This most thorough examination of Florida's uncounted ballots provides ammunition for both sides in what remains the most disputed and mystifying presidential election in modern times. It also provides indisputable evidence of the need for federal and state electoral reform.[23]

Table 2.1. Final National Vote Count

	Popular Vote	Electoral Vote	States
Gore	50,996,116 (49%)	266	21
Bush	50,456,169 (48%)	271	30

Gore lead in popular vote: 539,947 (0.516 percent)

Table 2.2.   Final Vote Count in Florida

Gore	2,912,253 (49%)
Bush	2,912,790 (49%)
Nader	97,500

Bush lead in Florida: 537 votes (0.009 percent)[1]

[1]*New York Times,* 30 December 2000, A17.

NOTES

1. Susan Ferrechio, "Anger over Election Fuels Raucous Protests in D.C.," *Miami Herald,* 21 January 2001. About twenty thousand people assembled in Washington to protest Bush's election. As one demonstrator from Florida put it, "This was not a fair election, and it breaks my heart." See www.herald.com/content/archive/news/elect2000/decision/107744.htm.

2. Felicity Barringer, "CBS Plans Changes in Election Night Reporting," *New York Times,* 5 January 2001, A10.

3. Daniel J. Wakin, "Report Calls Networks' Election Night Coverage a Disaster," *New York Times,* 3 February 2001, A10.

4. Harris, a former Republican state senator from Sarasota, was elected secretary of state in 1998. Claiming that she followed the law strictly, Harris insisted that she did not tip the result in Bush's favor. Appearing on CBS's Diane Sawyer interview show, she acknowledged that she had her preferences but insisted that she had "had to act with integrity in the system because I have to live with myself for the rest of my life, regardless of who the president is." See Terry Jackson, "Prime Time for Election Official," *Miami Herald,* 12 January 2001, www.herald.com/content/archive/news/elect2000/decision/052411.htm.

5. Firsthand account of Palm Beach voting problems provided by Ben Austin, whose mother was a Palm Beach precinct clerk on Election Day. Electronic message from Ben Austin to scholars on the "law and courts list," lawcourts-l@usc.edu, 10 November 2000.

6. John Dorschner, "Any of Many Twists May Shape Outcome: Factors Range from Rowdy Republicans to Ballot Design," *Miami Herald,* 5 December 2000, www.herald.com/content/archive/news/elect2000/decision/005229.htm. The *Miami Herald* Website provided thorough coverage of the campaign, the election, and the post-election difficulties in Florida. It has been actively engaged in the media recount of the Florida undervote.

7. Steve Bousquet, "Panel Gets Input on Fixing Florida's Election Flaws," *Miami Herald,* 24 January 2001. See the paper's Website at www.herald.com/content/archive/news/elect2000/decision/071148.htm.

8. See Andrea Robinson, "Harris Rejects Voting Blame," *Miami Herald,* 13 January 2001. See www.herald.com/content/archive/news/elect2000/decision/082187.htm. See also Dana Canedy, "Rights Panel Begins Inquiry into Florida's Voting System," *New York Times,* 12 January 2001, A20.

9. Sarah E. Rios, "Let All Voters Vote," *New York Times,* 7 March 2001, A18. See also Canedy, "Rights Panel Begins Inquiry into Florida's Voting System," A20.

10. Andrea Robinson, "Harris Rejects Voting Blame," *Miami Herald,* 13 January 2001. See www.herald.com/content/archive/news/elect2000/decision/082187.htm.

11. Anabelle de Gale, Lila Arzua, Curtis Morgan, "If the Vote Were Flawless . . . ," *Miami Herald,* 2 December 2000, www.herald.com/content/archive/news/elect 2000/decision/104268.htm. See also Andres Viglucci, Geoff Dougherty, and William Yardley, "Blacks' Votes Were Discarded at Higher Rates, Analysis Shows," *Miami Herald,* 28 December 2000, 1A and 18A.

12. Andrea Robinson, "Harris Rejects Voting Blame," *Miami Herald,* 13 January 2001. See www.herald.com/content/archive/news/elect2000/decision/082187.htm; Andrea Robinson, "Governor Refuses Blame for Florida Election Problems," *Miami Herald,* 12 January 2001, www.herald.com/content/archive/news/elect2000/ decision/026553.htm; Steve Bousquet, "Panel Gets Input on Fixing Florida's Election Flaws," *Miami Herald,* 24 January 2001, www.herald.com/content/archive/news/ elect2000/decision/071148.htm; and Katharine Q. Seelye, "Rights Panel Chief Warns Florida on Elections," *New York Times,* 9 March 2001, A12.

13. President Jimmy Carter made these remarks on the *Lehrer News Hour,* PBS, Wednesday, 10 January 2001. He also appeared on National Public Radio's *Morning Edition* with Bob Edwards on 9 January 2001. This interview was written by Mark Silva, in "Carter: Florida Voting Too Flawed," *Miami Herald,* 10 January 2001. See www.herald.com/content/archive/news/elect2000/decision/058861.htm.

14. Dana Canedy, "Florida Panel to Recommend Statewide System for Voters," *New York Times,* 23 February 2001, A12; Dana Canedy, "Familiar Cast but Less Talk of Florida Voting Reform as Jeb Bush Unveils Plan," *New York Times,* 7 March 2001, A12; Katharine Q. Seelye, "Panel Suggests Election Changes That Let States Keep Control," *New York Times,* 5 February 2001, A16; "Election Panel Calls for More Money for Equipment and Training," *New York Times,* 11 January 2001, A21; Canedy, "Rights Panel Begins Inquiry into Florida's Voting System," A20. The *Miami Herald* reviewed the Florida recount in a series of articles beginning on 1 December 2000 and continuing to this writing. See www.miami.com/herald/ special/news/flacount/

15. Amy Driscoll, "Dade Undervotes Support Bush Win," *Miami Herald,* 26 February 2001. See www.miami.com/herald/special/news/flacount/docs/review.htm. See also "Miami Count Suggests Gore Still Falls Short," *New York Times,* 27 February 2001, A21. See also "Newspaper Vote Count Points to Bush Win," *Newark (N.J.) Star-Ledger,* 26 February 2001, 2.

16. "Review of Florida Ballots Shows Gore Advantage," *Newark (N.J.) Star-Ledger,* 11 March 2001, 8. See also "Paper Says More Votes Were Meant for Gore," *New York Times,* 11 March 2001, 30. The *Miami Herald* conducted an extensive review of the undervotes in all Florida counties; the results of this study appeared in Martin Merzer, *The Miami Herald Report: Democracy Held Hostage* (New York: St. Martin's, 2001). The book appeared in May 2001. Simultaneously, the *Miami Herald* published the results of its review of the overvotes in all Florida counties. See Martin Merzer, "Overvotes Leaned to Gore," *Miami Herald,* 11 May 2001, available at www. miami.com/herald/content/news/local/dade/digdocs/072902.htm. St. Martin's Press maintains a Website where expanded information from the survey of overvotes is available free of charge—www.overvote.net. Finally, for information on what happened to absentee ballots in the Florida election, see David Damron and Roger Roy,

"Mangled Ballots Resurrected," *Orlando Sentinel,* 7 May 2001, available at www. orlandosentinel.com/news/nationworld/orl-vote050701.story.

17. Katharine Q. Seelye, "Rights Panel Chief Warns Florida on Elections," *New York Times,* 9 March 2001, A12. At the national level, some twenty reform proposals have been introduced in Congress. Senators Charles Schumer (D-N.Y.) and Sam Brownback (R-Kans.) have cosponsored a bill calling for a commission to study all aspects of ballot reform—from new voting technologies to ways of protecting the integrity of voter registration lists—and providing $2.5 billion in matching grants over five years to help states carry out its recommendations.

18. Katharine Q. Seelye, "From Selma to Florida: Election Reform, Meet Politics," *New York Times,* 4 March 2001, sec. IV, 1.

19. Clyde Haberman, untitled column on germ limits and the New York City Council, *New York Times,* 24 February 2001, B1.

20. Joan Biskupic, "Election Still Splits Court," *USA Today,* 22 January 2001, 1A.

21. Katharine Q. Seelye, "Old Disagreements Emerge in Election Reform Hearings," *New York Times,* 4 May 2001, A22.

22. See Dana Canedy, "Florida Leaders Sign Agreement for Overhaul of Election System," *New York Times,* 4 May 2001, A1; Dana Canedy, "A Ban on Punch Cards and a Lull in Division," *New York Times,* 5 May 2001, A8. See also Phil Long, "Gov. Bush Visits to 'Celebrate' Voting Reforms," *Miami Herald,* 10 May 2001, available at www.miami.com/herald/content/news/local/florida/digdocs/076427.htm.

23. Ford Fessenden and John M. Broder, "Study of Disputed Florida Ballots Finds Justices Did Not Cast the Deciding Vote," *New York Times,* 12 November 2001, AI; see also Richard L. Berke, "Who Won Florida? The Answer Emerges, But Surely Not the Final Word," *New York Times,* 12 November 2001, A16; Ford Fessenden, "Ballots Cast by Blacks and Older Voters Were Tossed in Far Greater Numbers," *New York Times,* 12 November 2001, A17; and the editorial, "The Time for Ballot Reform," *New York Times,* 12 November 2001, A18.

3

Bush v. Gore: Judicial Activism, Conservative Style

Elizabeth A. Hull

The much-dreaded cataclysm, prophesied to occur on the first day of the New Millennium, did not actually strike until the following November, taking the form of a presidential election from hell. This was the election in which the American public went to bed November 7 thinking the Republican candidate, George W. Bush, had won the election but woke up to discover his Democratic rival, Vice President Albert Gore, might triumph after all. In this extraordinary, neck-and-neck contest the popular vote in Florida was too close to call, but whoever ultimately won that vote would also capture the state's twenty-five all-important electoral votes—and with them the presidency. Yet determining the state's victor, seemingly a straightforward enterprise, took a full thirty-six days.

According to Florida's first, incomplete tally, out of the six million ballots cast statewide Bush led by a mere 1,784 votes. This microscopic margin, three one-hundredths of 1 percent of the votes cast, triggered the automatic machine recount that state law mandates whenever the difference between candidates is less than one-half of 1 percent. As the recount began, however, so did revelations that complicated and compromised what is ordinarily a routine process. Thousands of ballots cast in poor, largely minority, neighborhoods had never been recorded, because of antiquated voting machines. Several thousand other poor people had been denied the franchise, because their names had erroneously been crossed off registration rosters. A confusing "butterfly ballot" had prompted thousands of voters in West Palm Beach County, including many Jews, to pull the lever mistakenly for Patrick Buchanan, a candidate whom many believed was anti-Semitic. In many ballots, "pregnant" or "dimpled" chads, products of punch-card machines, were the only indication of the voters' intentions. Absentee ballots had been lost, or not counted, or counted twice.

During the next five weeks the nation and much of the world watched Teams Bush and Gore feint and thrust, shift tactics and rhetoric with remarkable agility depending upon their day-to-day fortunes, and fight, alternately with bare knuckles and velvet gloves, the all-important public relations war. In a contest heavy on partisanship and light on principle, Gore stalwarts rooted as the vice president's lawyers fought for hand recounts in counties where they suspected "irregularities" had distorted the original vote count. Those backing the Texas governor, on the other hand, applauded his legal team's valiant efforts to prevent Democratic partisans from "stealing" the election.

The 2000 presidential election was a wildly improbable, virtually unique spectacle. It was the longest and costliest in this country's history, and certainly the only one in which postelection events outshone the campaign itself in terms of sheer drama. George W. Bush ultimately won, but with the closest electoral margin since 1876, when Rutherford B. Hayes beat Samuel Tilden by a single electoral vote. Bush became the first president since Benjamin Harrison defeated Grover Cleveland in 1888 to capture the Electoral College without winning the popular vote.

Finally, Bush became the only president in this country's history who triumphed not because of politics, although partisanship was relentless, brazen, and unprincipled; and not because either the Florida legislature or the U.S. Congress intervened to break the deadlock, although both were prepared and constitutionally empowered to do so; but because the U.S. Supreme Court placed the crown on his head. The Court made critical decisions on the vote recount, it plunged into the "political thicket" it had long avoided, and it cobbled together new rules of jurisprudence that flew in the face of its own past rulings. In so doing it seriously threatened its institutional standing.

CHRONOLOGY

During the thirty-six-day standoff, attorneys for Bush and Gore bombarded all levels of state and federal courts with challenges—to the recounts, ballot designs, alleged absentee ballot improprieties, and certification deadlines. The Gore camp desperately wanted hand recounts in counties where such recounts would presumably benefit the vice president, while the secretary of state of Florida, Katherine Harris—a Republican who also headed Bush's presidential campaign in Florida—refused to extend the deadline for delivery of recount results beyond the November 14 deadline established by the state legislature. In a unanimous ruling on November 21, however, the

Florida Supreme Court held that the state had to accept hand-recounted votes until November 26.[1] Lawyers for Bush immediately appealed this ruling to the U.S. Supreme Court, claiming that the state's highest tribunal was attempting to "usurp" the authority of Florida's election officials and violate the federal constitution by rejecting the secretary of state's November 14 certification of the statewide tally.[2]

On Monday, December 4, in an unsigned opinion the Supreme Court remanded the case to the Florida Supreme Court for clarification of an issue: In ordering the recounts to continue, had it relied for its authority on the state constitution or merely interpreted conflicting Florida election statutes?[3] The answer was critical, because the U.S. Constitution authorizes state legislatures to pass laws governing elections and therefore the judiciary can only interpret these laws, not seek independent "guidance" from the state constitution.

The Florida high court implicitly answered this question four days later when it ordered inclusion of recounts completed after November 14 and commanded all counties that had not already undertaken manual recounts to begin immediately examining the "undervotes"—that is, ballots that had not been counted because they did not register a vote for president. Within minutes of the ruling, the Bush team was on television excoriating the state judiciary for its "lawlessness" and "shameless partisanship."[4] For the second time in less than two weeks the governor's attorneys also appealed to the Supreme Court, this time seeking a stay on the ground that the Florida Supreme Court's ruling "imperils Governor Bush's proper receipt of Florida's 25 electoral votes" by raising "a reasonable possibility that the votes will be called into doubt—or purport to be withdrawn—at a time when the December 12 deadline for naming Florida's electors would make any later judicial relief futile."[5] In their opposing brief, Gore's lawyers said the assertion that "a candidate for public office can be irreparably harmed by the process of discerning and tabulating the will of the voters" was "surprising" and "remarkable."[6]

Counting of the Florida undervotes had no sooner begun on December 9 than it was abruptly halted by the U.S. Supreme Court, which in a five-to-four ruling granted Bush's request for a stay and scheduled a hearing for the following Monday.[7] Now it was members of the Gore team, whose spirits over the last two days had first soared and then tumbled, who were on television lambasting the high court for "short-circuiting the democratic process."[8]

THE "POLITICAL THICKET"

Legal authorities were amazed, and many clearly appalled, that the Supreme Court had agreed to hear the case, given its politically explosive subject matter. With one major exception (when it intervened to allow challenges to the country's starkly malapportioned congressional districts), the modern Court has resolutely heeded former Supreme Court Justice Felix Frankfurter's admonition to stay clear of electoral politics, or what he called the "political thicket," where its constitutional authority is minimal and its institutional competence slim. By accepting *Bush v. Gore,* however, the Court leapt into the "thicket," head first and eyes open.

The snares of the political thicket became evident once five justices voted to halt the statewide recount; it could not continue, they decreed, until the Court determined whether the Florida Supreme Court had violated the U.S. Constitution.[9] With an (apparent) December 12 deadline for certifying electors looming, Gore feared that by issuing the stay the majority had essentially installed his opponent in the White House.[10]

The Supreme Court issues a stay, according to its own rules, only if at least five members agree to do so and the party seeking the stay has a "likelihood of success" and would suffer "irreparable injury" if the Court refused to intervene on an emergency basis. The Court's five conservatives—Chief Justice William Rehnquist, and Justices Sandra Day O'Connor, William Kennedy, Antonin Scalia, and Clarence Thomas—voted for the stay. Justice John Paul Stevens filed a two-page dissenting opinion, which Justices Ruth Bader Ginsburg, Steven Breyer, and David Souter joined. "To stop the counting of legal votes," Stevens charged, "the majority today departs from three venerable rules of judicial restraint that have guided the Court throughout its history: respect for state court rulings on questions of state law; the cautious exercise of its jurisdiction on matters that largely concern other branches of government"; and refusal "to exercise jurisdiction over federal questions that were not fairly presented to the court whose judgment is being reviewed."[11]

While "counting every legally cast vote cannot constitute irreparable harm," Stevens continued, there was a danger that the stay itself would cause irreparable harm not only to Al Gore but "more importantly, the public at large," because given the deadlines, it was equivalent to deciding the case in favor of Bush.[12] "Preventing the recount from being completed will inevitably cast a cloud on the legitimacy of the election," Stevens said. "As a more fundamental matter," he concluded, "the Florida court's ruling reflects the basic principle, inherent in our Constitution and our democracy, "that every legal vote should be counted."[13]

Although the majority did not issue an opinion in support of its order, Justice Scalia felt obliged to include a statement in response to the Stevens dissent. "One of the principal issues in the appeal we have accepted," he said, "is precisely whether the votes that have been ordered to be counted are, under a reasonable interpretation of Florida law, legally cast votes." "Count first, and rule upon legality afterwards, is not a recipe for producing election results that have the public acceptance democratic stability requires."[14]

What the majority apparently feared—at least as Scalia interpreted its views—was that a completed recount might result in an electoral victory for Gore. If that were to happen, then even if Bush were eventually to win on the legal merits, his victory would be marred. This reasoning prompted many observers to conclude that the Rehnquist bloc was intent upon protecting Bush from any embarrassment a full recount might present.[15]

Terrance Sandalow, the former dean of the University of Michigan Law School and a noted judicial conservative, found that the "balance of harms so unmistakably were on the side of Gore" that granting the stay was "incomprehensible."[16] The stay, he said, was "an unmistakably partisan decision without any foundation in law."[17] Charles Fried, a former solicitor general in George H. W. Bush's administration, countered that it was the Florida Supreme Court's decision to order statewide recounts that was "lawless," that the stay merely prevented it "from garnering the fruits of [its] lawless behavior."[18]

Millions of viewers sat tethered to their television sets as one improbable event after another unfolded—culminating in the Supreme Court's release, late in the evening of December 12, of its unsigned per curiam opinion. Viewers watched as network correspondents shot forth like cannon balls from the Supreme Court's side entrance clutching freshly minted opinions. These correspondents, many still out of breath, began reading their copies, fumbling and visibly confused as they attempted to decipher what the majority had decreed.

The ruling itself was buried within the sixty-five-page document. There were, altogether, six different opinions. In addition to the unsigned majority opinion, there were dissents signed by Justices Brewer and Souter—who also appeared to have joined the majority opinion—and individual ones by Justices Ginsburg and Stevens. Who had won? Who had lost? (The elder George Bush called his son and asked, "What does this mean?")[19]

George Bush had "won," it seemed—although in an opinion as obfuscating and slapped together as *Bush v. Gore,* even that crucial fact became apparent only upon a focused rereading. One thing was obvious from even a casual perusal, however: The opinion had emerged from a severely fractured, acrimonious Court. As correspondents for the *Washington Post* observed, a public "used to seeing the mulled, sanded, and lacquered work of a leisurely court now caught a glimpse of the human passions that run behind the marble."[20]

The majority opinion was labeled "per curiam," meaning "for the court"— a strange designation, since per curiams are used almost exclusively for decisions that are unanimous and uncontroversial.[21] Although the opinion was unsigned, students of the Court believe it was written by one of its two "swing" justices—either O'Connor or more probably, given its style, Kennedy.

The enormity of its undertaking was clear to the majority: "None are more conscious of the vital limits on judicial authority than are the members of this Court," it said, referring to "our unsought responsibility to resolve the federal and constitutional issues the judicial system has been forced to confront."[22] It then proceeded to overturn the Florida Supreme Court and hold, by a one-vote margin, that there was no time for any further counting of the state's disputed presidential votes.

The majority rested its decision on the Fourteenth Amendment's equal protection clause: "The recount mechanisms implemented in response to the decisions of the Florida Supreme Court do not satisfy the minimal requirement for nonarbitrary treatment of voters necessary to secure the fundamental right to vote."[23] The majority implicitly chastised Florida's high court for not establishing uniform standards for determining which ballots should and should not be counted, beyond instructing enumerators to be guided by the vague "intent of the voters" language used in the relevant state statute. As a result, said the majority, the standards being used varied, "not only from one county to another, but also from one recount team to another."[24] (This criticism seems disingenuous, since only eight days earlier the Supreme Court had advised the Florida tribunal that if it made any postelection changes in the law—say, by imposing recount standards—it would be usurping the state legislators' constitutional prerogatives.)

Rehnquist, Scalia, and Thomas protested that the decision did not go far enough. They cited what they saw as more fundamental objections to the recount and asserted that by ordering it the Florida Supreme Court had violated state law. Among the four dissenters, Justices Breyer and Souter agreed with the majority that the varying standards in different Florida counties for counting the punch-card ballots raised both due process and equal protection problems. They believed, however—in sharp contrast to the majority—that the case should be remanded to the Florida court "with instructions to establish uniform standards for evaluating the several types of ballots that have prompted differing treatments" before December 18, when the electors were scheduled to meet.[25] Souter said that such a recount would be a "tall order" but that "there is no justification for denying the state the opportunity to try to count all the disputed ballots now."[26] "Unlike the majority," he added, "I see no warrant for this Court to assume that Florida could not possibly comply with this requirement before the date set for the meeting of electors, December 18."[27]

The majority insisted, however, that the recount could not continue until December 18, the date established in the Constitution. Rather, it said, the process must be completed by December 12, the federal deadline for immunizing a state's electors from challenge in the House of Representatives—a deadline that would occur a scant two hours after the Court released its opinion. Moreover, the majority asserted, the state's supreme court had itself indicated its desire to adhere to the December 12 deadline.[28] This assertion, upon which the entire majority opinion was founded, is simply wrong.

The deadline controversy is a long-term consequence of the 1876 presidential election between Rutherford B. Hayes and Samuel Tilden. Although Hayes was eventually declared the winner, disputed electoral votes called into question the legitimacy of his victory. To prevent such a contretemps from recurring Congress subsequently passed the so-called Safe Harbor Act. This act provides that no electoral slate certified by a state at least six days before the Electoral College is scheduled to convene (December 12 in the year 2000) would face a congressional challenge. States have often certified their slates after this date, however, and indeed, in the aftermath of the 2000 presidential election many continued to do so.[29]

The Florida Supreme Court had noted in passing that the state legislature intended to secure the benefits of the December 12 "safe harbor" provision, but not once had it suggested that this strictly optional deadline *should* be observed if a recount were ordered. (As Thomas Oliphant observed, "The Supreme Court decided which provision of what law the Florida court hadn't cited, in order to proceed with their order that reversed the judgment allowing the recount to proceed.")[30]

The Rehnquist pentarchy nevertheless proceeded as if December 12 were a mandatory deadline and asserted that extending certification beyond that date would violate the Florida election code. This code, however, also mandates that ballots be counted as accurately and fully as possible. According to the high court's own, time-honored principles, conflicts in state law should be resolved by the states themselves rather than by the federal judiciary. "I might join the Chief Justice were it my commission to interpret Florida law," Justice Ginsburg stressed in her dissenting opinion. "The extraordinary setting of this case has obscured the ordinary principle that dictates its proper resolution: federal courts defer to state courts' interpretations of their states' own law. This principle reflects the core of federalism, on which all agree."[31]

The "time problem" the state was now facing, Justice Breyer said, was "in significant part, a problem of the Court's own making."[32] The recount had been moving ahead in an "orderly fashion" when "this Court improvidently entered a stay."[33] He discussed at length the political maneuvering undertaken by Supreme Court Justice Joseph Bradley during the deadlocked election of 1876 to secure the presidency for Hayes. "This history may help to explain why I think it not only legally wrong, but also most unfortunate, for the Court simply to have terminated the Florida recount," Breyer said.[34] There was no need for the Court to have involved itself in the election dispute this time. "Above all," he added, "in this highly politicized matter, the appearance of a split decision runs the risk of undermining the public's confidence in the Court itself."[35] "As a result," he concluded, "we will never know whether the recount could have been completed." (Justice Ginsburg agreed: "The Court's conclusion that a constitutionally adequate recount is impractical is a prophecy the Court's own judgment will not allow to be tested. Such an untested prophecy should not decide the presidency of the United States.")[36]

The dissenters protested in vain. The game was over. On December 13, at 9 P.M., Al Gore conceded. At 10 P.M. George W. Bush declared victory, and five weeks later he was formally sworn in by Justice William Rehnquist. Given the circumstances, the ceremonial investiture seemed especially fitting.

EQUAL PROTECTION JURISPRUDENCE

The majority in *Bush v. Gore* concluded that because neither the Florida courts nor the state legislature had devised a uniform standard for recounting ballots, the recount process violated the equal protection clause of the Fourteenth Amendment. The equal protection clause, part of a Civil War–era amendment enacted in 1868, prevents "any state from denying to any person within its jurisdiction the equal protection of the laws"; it was intended to prevent official discrimination against newly liberated blacks. Over the years it has been expanded to shield other, similarly vulnerable classes from invidious treatment at the hands of state officials.

When the Supreme Court grounded its opinion in the equal protection clause, it caught by surprise virtually the entire legal community. While it has invalidated malapportionment schemes on equal protection grounds, until *Bush v. Gore* the Court had never suggested that states or their subdivisions might be violating this constitutional provision by using different means of tabulating ballots. When the Court agreed to hear Bush's first challenge on November 22, it did not do so on equal protection grounds, and indeed it remanded the case to the Florida Supreme Court without so much as a bow to this clause. (If the Florida court had been apprised that the recount raised equal protection issues, of course, it would have had sufficient time to address them.)

Conservative legal scholars were at least as discomfited as their liberal colleagues by the Court's quixotic behavior. Professor Cass Sunstein described the equal protection holding as "a bolt out of the blue."[37] "There is no precedent for it, and there's no support in history for this type of ruling. It's a real embarrassment, the worst moment for the Court, at least since *Roe v. Wade*," he said.[38] Virginia law professor A. E. Dick Howard echoed Sunstein's sentiments: "This is a remarkable use of the equal protection clause. It is not consistent with anything they have done in the past 25 years."[39]

Legal authorities were stunned also because the implications are staggering if election processes are subject to equal protection challenges. The majority condemned the Florida recount because "standards for accepting or rejecting contested ballots might vary not only from county to county but indeed within a single county."[40] Yet thirty-three states, including George

Bush's own Texas, use the same standard as Florida—that is, ballot counters are to be guided by the "clear intent of the voter."[41] Surely, then, all these states and their manifold subdivisions are equally vulnerable to challenge. In this country, moreover, not only different standards but every other conceivable variation in its decentralized voting system is potentially susceptible to suit: the way instructions are worded, or ballots designed, counted, recounted, or certified. At a minimum, *Bush v. Gore* will spawn scores of federal lawsuits after every close election.

The majority says, "Not to worry." It says its consideration "is limited to the present case," because "the problem of equal protection in election processes generally presents many complexities."[42] Such assurances ring false. If the Court subsequently denies relief to other plaintiffs who challenge voting schemes that are arguably as vulnerable as Florida's, it will confirm the widespread suspicion that the legal principles articulated in *Bush v. Gore* were invoked only to guarantee a particular outcome.

In reality, the Court turned the equal protection clause on its head—employing it not to expand the rights of minorities, as those who ratified the Fourteenth Amendment intended, but rather—in a perverse sleight of hand—to constrict these rights. By claiming that the absence of uniform standards compelled a halt to the recount, the majority obscured the very real and pervasive inequalities that had marred the Florida election process. "The majority's concern for equal treatment now applies to the dimpled and pregnant chad," said one observer, but not to the "parade of horrors" that disproportionately affects the black electorate.[43] Indeed, in focusing on recount methodology the majority ignored altogether the real outrage—that citizens reliant upon the decrepit voting machinery typically used in poor neighborhoods are much less likely to have their votes counted than are their better-heeled neighbors who use state-of-the-art optical scanners.[44]

Still, something good might come out of the Florida imbroglio: The Supreme Court, in spite of itself, might have provided the impetus for genuine electoral reform. By holding that the equal protection clause is violated when voters are treated in unfair or disparate ways, it may encourage states to replace faulty voting machines, biased supervisors, and other impediments that disenfranchise poor people no less than poll taxes and literacy tests did in the past. If this happens, said Michael Glennon, a law professor at the University of California–Davis, then "Vice President Gore's forces may have lost a big battle, but actually have won the war."[45]

WHITHER CONSERVATIVE PRINCIPLES?

After the majority in *Bush v. Gore* overturned the recount ordered by the Florida Supreme Court, Democratic Senator Bob Kerry of Nebraska marveled that "it would be one thing if this were the Warren Court. This is the Rehnquist Court. The Court that has established in case after case the principle of state sovereignty."[46] Indeed, the Rehnquist Court has endorsed wide-ranging new theories of state immunity against federal law, jettisoning in the process nearly seventy years of precedent. It has declared, for instance, that Congress is powerless under either the commerce clause or the Fourteenth Amendment to address violence against women, impose liability on state governments that discriminate on the basis of age or disability, or even hold states accountable for violating copyright law.[47]

Chief Justice Rehnquist recently published a book, *The Supreme Court,* in which he made this statement: "Save as restricted by the United States Constitution, the states are themselves sovereign entities within their own systems of laws and courts, and the supreme court of a state is concededly the final authority in construing the meaning of its own constitution and laws."[48] These words were penned by the same jurist who, in overturning the Florida Supreme Court's recount order, said: "To attach definitive weight to the pronouncement of a state court, when the very question at issue is whether the court has actually departed from the statutory meaning, would be to abdicate our responsibility."[49]

There is indeed irony, as Senator Kerry pointed out, in the fact that the Supreme Court's five most committed federalists found themselves overturning a decision by a state's highest judicial tribunal and then imposing upon the state its own interpretation of that state's election law (and justifying its action with logic, Justice Breyer pointed out, that "would seem to invalidate any state provision for a manual recount of individual counties in a statewide election").[50]

According to John DiIulio, a conservative academic who now heads the Bush administration's "faith-based" programs, the majority in *Bush v. Gore* ignored two principles enshrined in the conservative pantheon— not just the importance of state autonomy, but also the need for judicial restraint. The logic by which the majority "gave" Bush the presidency is "disingenuous," he said, and would come back "to haunt conservatives and confuse the principled conservative case for less judicial activism."[51]

Yet "judicial activism," says newspaper columnist John Farmer, "lies in the ideology of the beholder."[52] For fifty years conservatives have been "belly-aching" about liberal judges who "legislate from the Bench," who cavalierly overturn state laws and discover individual rights that are nowhere mentioned in the Constitution. Yet in *Bush v.* Gore the Rehnquist majority elevated judicial activism to heights never contemplated by its liberal brethren: It decided a presidential election. "Now," Farmer concludes, "that's real judicial activism."[53]

THE SUPREME COURT: WHERE THE "BUCK STOPS"

In 1974, during the height of the Watergate turmoil, the Supreme Court commanded President Richard Nixon to turn over incriminating secret recordings, thereby precipitating his resignation. The Court's intervention was defensible on many grounds, but it served to truncate the impeachment process that was then under way, and it short-circuited the mechanisms established in the Constitution for resolving profound national crises. With or without its involvement, however, the substantive result would have been the same: Nixon would be forced from office.

Many thoughtful people draw a parallel to the election of 2000, supporting the Court's action in *Bush v. Gore* on the ground that it imposed order on a chaotic state of affairs. Richard Posner, a judge on the Seventh Circuit Court of Appeals and an influential conservative spokesman, concedes that the majority's ruling may have been neither constitutionally "conclusive" nor based on principles that predate the election. But, he says, its interference headed off a major threat to the country's well-being.[54]

Should the Court assume the role of what columnist Benjamin Wittes calls "self-appointed saviors"? What, Judge Posner responds, is the Supreme Court there for if not to head off national crises?[55]

Yet the "national crises" he fears—an election decided either by the Florida legislature or by the U.S. Congress—would simply have been the process envisioned by the Constitution. What if the recount *had* gone forward in Florida? Maybe George Bush would have won, thereby acquiring a legitimacy that his ascension at the hands of the judiciary denied him. Maybe the dispute would have ended up in Congress. The public might not have liked whatever decision lawmakers reached, but in contrast to federal judges, who enjoy lifetime tenure, at least legislators can be held accountable when they run for reelection.

It is an unfortunate commentary on American democracy that both the citizenry and its elected officials look almost reflexively to the Court to handle every Big Issue that comes along—as if Congress, the presidency, or state legislators are incapable or at least unwilling to grapple with contentious or divisive issues.[56] However, democratic institutions quickly become flaccid and irresponsible when it is the judiciary that ends up resolving each era's vital controversies. (Besides, the Court does not have a great long-term track record: consider *Dred Scott,* or the Japanese internment case. Some might add *Roe v. Wade.*)

CONCLUSION: A "SELF-INFLICTED WOUND"

The majority in *Bush v. Gore* appears to have capitulated totally to raw partisanship. How else are we to explain its willingness to leap recklessly into the political fray, to disregard states' rights, and flout every tenet of judicial restraint? The Court, moreover, failed in its obligation to explain its actions in terms the public could understand—perhaps not agree with, but accept as intellectually honest. Failure by the Court to provide an adequate accounting is always regrettable. Its failure is unconscionable when it renders an opinion that not only decides a presidential election but also, because of future nominations to the Court, may well influence its own composition for decades to come. It has invited the suspicion that it acted as it did for one reason only: it wanted George W. Bush to be the president.

New York Times columnist Linda Greenhouse compared the majority's stance in *Bush v. Gore* to the one it had assumed eight years ago in *Planned Parenthood v. Casey*. The *Casey* case presented the Court with an opportunity to overrule *Roe v. Wade*, the enormously controversial opinion in which the Court declared that a woman has a constitutional right to an abortion. In *Casey,* Justices O'Connor, Kennedy, and Souter wrote a joint opinion explaining their decision to adhere to precedent even though they might have dissented had they been on the bench when *Roe* was decided.

The court's only "real power" lies, they said, "in its legitimacy, a product of substance and perception that shows itself in the people's acceptance of the judiciary as fit to determine what the nation's law means and to declare what it demands."[57] Sometimes it was not sufficient, they continued, for a decision to have a plausible basis in the law. Rather, "the court must take care to speak and act in ways that allow people to accept its decisions on the terms the court claims for them, as grounded truly in principle, not as compromises with social and political pressures having, as such, no bearing on the principled choices that the court is obliged to make."[58]

Overturning *Roe v. Wade* would cause "profound and unnecessary damage to the court's legitimacy," the three justices said, emphasizing that "the court's concern with legitimacy is not for the sake of the court but for the sake of the nation to which it is responsible."[59] (Ironically, Chief Justice Rehnquist spoke for the majority in a case last year that presented the Court with an opportunity to overrule *Miranda v. Arizona,* a 1966 opinion that Rehnquist and his conservative colleagues have long considered "wrongly decided." He explained that he ultimately voted to uphold *Miranda,* however, out of respect for the principle of "stare decisis": "*Miranda,*" he said, "has become embedded in routine police practice to the point where the warnings have become part of our national culture.")[60]

Although Justices O'Connor and Kennedy have apparently abandoned the convictions they had articulated in *Casey,* the dissenters in *Bush v. Gore* again gave them voice. The latter made clear, in their individual and joint opinions, that the Court should never have embroiled itself in this case. "Our doing so," Justice Stevens lamented, "can only lend credence to the most cynical appraisal of the work of judges throughout the land. It is confidence in the men and women who administer the judicial system that is the true backbone of the rule of law.[61] Time will one day heal the wound to that confidence that will be inflicted by today's decision. One thing, however, is certain: Although we may never know with complete certainty the identity of the winner of this year's presidential election, the identity of the loser is perfectly clear. It is the nation's confidence in the judge as an impartial guardian of the rule of law."[62]

Justice Breyer agreed with his fellow dissenter: What the court did today, "it should have left undone." He said: "By embroiling ourselves in this political maelstrom, we undermine public confidence that has been built slowly over many years," and without much confidence "we cannot protect basic liberty or, indeed, the rule of law itself." By hearing this case, the Supreme Court risked "a self-inflicted wound—a wound that may harm not just the court, but the nation."[63]

NOTES

1. Todd S. Purdum and David Firestone, "Florida Court Unanimously Affirms Gore's Case," *New York Times*, 22 November 2000, in *36 Days: The Complete Chronicle of the 2000 Presidential Election Crisis*, ed. *New York Times* correspondents (New York: Henry Holt, 2000), 125–27.

2. Frank Bruni, "Bush Camp Angrily Vows to Fight Ruling," *New York Times*, 22 November 2000, in *36 Days*, 277–78.

3. *Palm Beach Canvassing Board v. Harris*, 2000 VVL 1725434, 13 (Fla. 2000).

4. Richard L. Berke, "Angry Republicans Vow Bitter Fight," *New York Times*, 9 December 2000, in *36 Days*, 268–69.

5. Linda Greenhouse, "Bitterly Divided High Court Suddenly Steps In," *New York Times*, 10 December 2000, in *36 Days*, 276–78.

6. Text of the Supreme Court's decision, quoted in *36 Days*, 279.

7. Greenhouse, "Bitterly Divided High Court Suddenly Steps In."

8. Richard L. Berke, "Stunned Democrats Attack the Court's Decision," *New York Times*, 10 December 2000, in *36 Days*, 281–82.

9. "U.S. Supreme Court Halts the Recount," *New York Times*, 10 December 2000, in *36 Days*, 275.

10. Berke, "Stunned Democrats."

11. Supreme Court's decision granting stay, quoted in *36 Days*, 279–81.

12. Supreme Court's decision, 280–81.

13. Supreme Court's decision, 280–81.

14. Supreme Court's decision, 280.

15. Berke, "Stunned Democrats."

16. Berke, "Stunned Democrats."

17. Berke, "Stunned Democrats."

18. Berke, "Stunned Democrats."

19. *Washington Post* political staff, eds., *Deadlock: The Inside Story of America's Closest Election* (New York: Public Affairs, 2001), 227.

20. *Deadlock, 227.*

21. For discussion see Linda Greenhouse, "Court's Action Brings Confusion, Not Clarity," *New York Times,* 14 December 2000, in *36 Days,* 314–16.

22. *Bush v. Gore,* 121 S.Ct. 525, 532 (2000).

23. 121 S.Ct., 531.

24. 121 S.Ct., 530.

25. 121 S.Ct., 524.

26. 121 S.Ct., 546.

27. 121 S.Ct., 547.

28. 121 S.Ct., 537.

29. Richard D. Friedman, "*'Bush' v. 'Gore'*: What Was the Supreme Court Thinking?" *Commonweal,* 12 January 2001, 10–11.

30. "A Dishonest Rehnquist Five," *Boston Globe,* 17 December 2000, 8(C).

31. 121 S.Ct., 549.

32. 121 S.Ct., 553.

33. 121 S.Ct., 553.

34. 121 S.Ct., 556–57.

35. 121 S.Ct., 550.

36. 121 S.Ct., 550.

37. Quoted in Sidney Zion, editorial, *New York Post,* 19 December 2000.

38. Zion, *New York Post,* 19 December 2000.

39. Zion, *New York Post,* 19 December 2000.

40. 121 S.Ct., 530.

41. Jeffrey Rosen, "The Supreme Court Commits Suicide, Disgrace," *The New Republic,* 4 February 2001.

42. 121 S. Ct., 531.

43. Margaret A. Burnham, "A Cynical Supreme Court," *Boston Globe,* 14 December 2000, 23(A).

44. "U.S. Probing Bias Claims in Florida Vote," *Newark Star-Ledger,* 4 December 2000, 10; Jeff Diamant, "Jackson, Invoking King, Says Black Voters Still Shorted," *Newark Star-Ledger,* 14 December 2000, 32; Ford Fessenden, "No-Vote Rates Higher in Punch-Card Counts," *New York Times,* 1 December 2000, 29(A).

45. Quoted in Susan Milligan, "In Long Run, Ruling May Aid Voters' Rights," *Boston Globe,* 14 December 2000, 1(A).

46. Berke, "Stunned Democrats."

47. For discussion see Rosen, "Supreme Court Commits Suicide."

48. Bob Braun, review of William Rehnquist, *The Supreme Court* (New York: Knopf, 2000), *Newark Star-Ledger,* 25 February 2001, 4.

49. Braun, book review, 4.

50. 121 S.Ct., 551.

51. "Supreme Court Action Run Amok," *Washington Post,* 5 December 2000.

52. "An 'Activist' High Court Conservatives Can Love," *Newark Star-Ledger,* 18 December 2000.

53. An 'Activist' High Court."

54. Quoted in Benjamin Wittes, "Maybe the Court Got It Right," *Boston Globe,* 21 February 2001, 23(A).

55. Wittes, "Maybe the Court Got It Right."

56. For discussion see Friedman, *"Bush v. Gore."*

57. "The Court's Credibility at Risk," *New York Times,* 11 December 2001, in *36 Days,* 289–90.

58. The Court's Credibility at Risk."

59. "The Court's Credibility at Risk."

60. *Dickerson v. United States,* 120 S.Ct. 2326 (2000).

61. 121 S.Ct., 542.

62. 121 S.Ct., 542.

63. 121 S.Ct., 557.

4

The Christian Right in the 2000 GOP Presidential Campaign

Mark J. Rozell

As is so often the case, the early conventional wisdom regarding the Christian Right's role in the Republican presidential contest in 2000 ultimately did not mirror reality. Indeed, the conventional wisdom was not even close to describing the movement's ultimate role in the contest. Prior to the nomination battle between Texas Governor George W. Bush and Arizona Senator John McCain, observers were nearly uniform in their assessments that the Christian Right was a minimal player in the GOP's presidential candidate selection process. At most, many suggested, the movement would influence the vice presidential nomination and some platform positions at the national party convention.

Although ultimately wrong, these analyses were by no means foolish, even in hindsight. There were sound reasons for observers to believe that the Christian Right was not going to be a major player in the party nomination process. Consider:

First, the Christian Right lacked a standard-bearer candidate. Throughout 1999 Missouri Senator John Ashcroft—a Christian social conservative with a strong electoral record of appealing to different constituencies—appeared to be in the running for the nomination, and he was clearly the favored candidate of the movement. When he announced his intention not to seek the presidency, there was no obvious candidate to unify the Christian Right and help the movement flex its muscle in the primaries. Numerous candidates competed for the Christian Right's support, but none unified the movement.

Second, the nation's leading Christian Right organization, the Christian Coalition, was in serious trouble. Its fund-raising and membership were in substantial decline. The organization was beset by infighting and by resignations of staff and of state and local chapter chairs; some of its state and local-based chapters had either disappeared or continued to exist merely on paper. *Fortune* magazine had dropped the organization from its list of the top twenty-five Washington lobby groups. The conservative *National Review* had featured an article about the Coalition entitled "Slouching toward Irrelevance." Some scholars suggest that the organization's decline reflected the waning influence of the Christian Right movement more generally.[1]

Third, without a single standard-bearer, numerous GOP candidates all tried to appeal to the Christian Right, thus potentially splintering the movement. Each one of them had a credible claim to the movement's support. For example:

Former Vice President Dan Quayle had become something of a hero to grassroots social conservatives when he lambasted the values of Hollywood and of popular culture more generally, and when he had openly professed his religious faith as inspiration for his policy views. Gary Bauer, the former Reagan administration liaison to the social conservatives and the director of the Family Research Council, had perhaps the most impeccable credentials as a true Christian rightist. Multimillionaire Steve Forbes had spent his time since his failed 1996 presidential nomination campaign successfully building bridges with social conservative leaders, many of whom worked for his 2000 campaign.

Former Cabinet Secretary and FTC Commissioner Elizabeth Dole, a born-again southern Baptist and pro-life advocate, also pitched her appeals to the social conservatives while claiming she could broaden the GOP electoral base. Senator Orrin Hatch (Utah), a devout Mormon, also had impeccable credentials as a conservative pro-life advocate, and he had the credibility of leadership in elective office. Senator Bob Smith of New Hampshire was an unapologetic pro-life advocate with a consistently conservative voting record in Congress.

Senator John McCain (Arizona) had a long record of pro-life votes and other social conservative positions during eighteen years in Congress. Former ambassador and talk-show host Alan Keyes, a devout Roman Catholic and the only African American in the race, was a most stirring orator who focused on his uncompromising social conservative views. Before he left the GOP, Patrick Buchanan, conservative commentator and former White House aide, had also sought the party presidential nomination focusing on the social issues agenda.

Finally, Governor George W. Bush of Texas emphasized socially conservative views couched in the liberal rhetoric of compassion and tolerance. Many leading Christian Rightists, particularly the Christian Coalition's founder and leader Rev. Pat Robertson and its former executive director Ralph Reed, signed on early to back Bush as the most electable candidate in the field. Yet their early support of Bush was not matched by evident grassroots Christian Right enthusiasm for his candidacy. Many openly decried his use of liberal language, his support from party officials, and his frequent self-description as a "compassionate conservative" as evidence that Bush was, like his father, an establishment figure more than a true movement conservative.

Therefore, in its early stages the race appeared to be between the moderate-establishment wing of the Republican Party, supporting Bush, and the movement conservative wing, which lacked a single standard-bearer. That Robertson and Reed backed Bush was of no moment to many in the Christian Right. To many activists and some other leaders in the movement, these two figures represented the pragmatist wing of the movement; it was evident to them that Robertson and Reed were more interested in gaining access to power than promoting a cause. With other prominent Christian Rightists variously backing any one of the numerous GOP candidates, it was impossible for the movement to be united.

In the face of Bush's major party endorsements, family network, and historically unmatched campaign fund-raising, GOP candidates dropped from the campaign early, and at a remarkably fast pace. Quayle, Elizabeth Dole, and Hatch dropped out the earliest; Buchanan left the GOP to seek the Reform Party nomination. Many social conservatives complained openly of "the big fix" by the establishment wing of the GOP to ensure Bush's nomination without a serious challenge. Forbes and Bauer stayed in the campaign through several early primaries but then also dropped out. Keyes remained in the race even though he was never a factor; it appeared that he cared more about making a statement than making a quiet and graceful exit as the other social conservative candidates had done. Buchanan remained in the race as a Reform Party candidate, but he could draw hardly any attention to his candidacy during the GOP primary contests.

The Republican nomination race quickly became a bitter contest between Bush and McCain, with the Christian Right taking central stage in the drama and ultimately delivering victory to Bush. After all of the predictions of the movement's political irrelevancy in 2000, Christian Right activists became the kingmakers in the GOP contest.[2] The remainder of this essay explores the impact of the movement on the GOP nomination process and explains the factors that suggest the continued influence of the Christian Right in U.S. politics, despite many predictions to the contrary. The essay begins with a description and analysis of the GOP contests in the crucial primary states. It concludes with an analysis of the lessons of the Bush-McCain race for the future of the Christian Right in U.S. electoral politics.

THE REPUBLICAN PRIMARY CAMPAIGN

As so often happens, the New Hampshire primary, the nation's first, narrowed the Republican candidate field effectively to two candidates: Bush and McCain. Bauer dropped out after receiving just 1 percent of the vote.[3] Forbes pulled a disappointing 13 percent; he stayed in the campaign, but only temporarily. Keyes received 6 percent of the vote, but he was not leaving the race no matter how poorly he fared. McCain stunned the GOP establishment with a resounding 49 percent to 30 percent victory over Bush.[4]

Although McCain won New Hampshire easily, the exit polling data showed a GOP fissure that would become problematic for his campaign later on: Whereas McCain did exceptionally well in the primary among independents, Democrats, and some Republicans, Bush showed his greatest strength among Christian social conservatives.[5] Unfortunately for Bush, the social conservative voting base in the New England states is quite small. But the exit polls provided some encouraging news for Bush as the campaign moved toward the crucial South Carolina primary.

Among the 53 percent of the Republican identifiers who voted in the GOP primary in New Hampshire, 41 percent chose Bush and 38 percent McCain. The Arizona senator nonetheless overwhelmingly won among independents (62 percent to 19 percent), who constituted 41 percent of the vote, and Democrats (78 percent to 13 percent), a mere 4 percent. Self-identified liberals and moderates also overwhelmingly backed McCain, whereas he and Bush split the conservative vote almost evenly. Those who identified themselves as "very conservative" went for Bush 33 percent to 21 percent (with 24 percent going to Keyes and 20 percent to Forbes). McCain had therefore demonstrated broad-based appeal, whereas Bush showed strongly among the most conservative wing of his party.

Bush won the Christian Right vote. Among self-identified "Religious Right" voters, he prevailed 36 percent to 26 percent over McCain (19 percent for Keyes and 14 percent for Forbes). Yet these voters were only 16 percent of the GOP primary electorate, suggesting that Bush had strong vote-getting potential in the more culturally conservative primary states outside of the Northeast. Bush also won among those voters who said that they attended church more than once per week (10 percent of the voters) and those who opposed abortion in all circumstances (12 percent of the voters)—a position not compatible with the governor's own views. Similarly, McCain did very well among pro-choice voters, even though his own views on abortion were strongly at odds with abortion rights advocates.

Somewhat surprising, perhaps, was the fact that McCain had become the candidate of the more moderate wing of the GOP and Bush the candidate of the Christian Right. Both candidates were strongly pro-life, and it was almost impossible to detect any differences at all between the candidates in their views on abortion and other social issues. Bush's gubernatorial record and McCain's eighteen-year voting record in Congress clearly gave them equally valid claims to support from the Christian Right. Yet the New Hampshire results made it clear that Bush had become the favored candidate of the social conservatives and that McCain had much work to do to appeal to that constituency.

A key explanation for this division was the fact that McCain had staked much of his presidential quest on his commitment to campaign finance reform. His campaign positions, as well as his earlier efforts as a senator on behalf of reforming campaign finance laws, were anathema to such interest groups as the National Right to Life Committee and the Christian Coalition. Both of those organizations, among many others, rely very heavily on the use of independent expenditures in elections; McCain's favored reforms, if enacted, would force such groups to refocus their efforts. Consequently, both of these organizations geared up to oppose McCain's presidential quest, with Christian Coalition director Rev. Pat Robertson leveling the inaccurate charge that the Arizona senator was actually hostile to the pro-life policy agenda. Robertson's attacks at times seemed personal; he even suggested that McCain lacked the temperament and emotional stability to be president. The director of Focus on the Family, Rev. James Dobson, even more bluntly criticized McCain's personal fitness as a moral leader because of the senator's admitted adultery during his first marriage, and then divorce.

The leaders of the nation's three most prominent socially conservative organizations were thus united in their opposition to McCain. They put forth a major effort to stop his candidacy in South Carolina, backed by extensive independent spending efforts. In the period leading up to the primary, Robertson in particular made numerous appearances on television news and commentary shows denouncing McCain and asserting that social conservatives would sit out the general election if the Arizona senator were nominated by the GOP.

The Christian Right, for its part, unleashed an all-out assault on McCain's campaign in South Carolina. The movement based its attack on his credibility as an advocate of the social conservative cause on four factors: (1) McCain's suggestion that the GOP should soften the language of the party's anti-abortion platform plank to make the party more inclusive; (2) the senator's vote to allow fetal-tissue research for combating Parkinson's disease; (3) his suggestion in a newspaper interview, later retracted, that he would not support a repeal of the *Roe v. Wade* decision; and (4) McCain's statement that if his daughter became pregnant he would leave the abortion decision up to her.[6]

To any nonpartisan observer, altogether these factors hardly could justify the severity of the attacks on McCain, especially given his consistently pro-life voting record in Congress for eighteen years. The National Right to Life Committee, in fact, had consistently given McCain nearly 100 percent ratings for his votes in Congress. McCain frequently affirmed his pro-life stand in the campaign. Declared one of his position papers, "John McCain is pro-life. He recognizes that 'all human beings are endowed by their creator with certain inalienable rights.' Life is one of those rights."[7] The National Right to Life Committee nonetheless led the attack on McCain, with mass mailings (one with a picture of a baby on the front and the words, "This little guy wants you to vote for George Bush"), radio ads, and telephone calls to voters throughout the state.[8]

The Christian Coalition, in contrast, was remarkably quiet in the South Carolina campaign—a reflection of the organization's weakened state rather than any decline in the influence of the socially conservative voters in the GOP. Pat Robertson, however, was a highly visible spokesperson during the primary, throwing most of his efforts against McCain. While the National Right to Life Committee did the grassroots campaigning, Robertson commanded much attention on the national airwaves. The consistent message was that McCain was unacceptable to the Christian Right. The attacks on McCain were relentless and often very personal in nature.

The role of religion in the campaign took center stage when McCain attacked Bush's decision to speak at the controversial Bob Jones University—a fundamentalist institution that prohibited interracial dating and characterized Catholicism as "a satanic counterfeit." The university's founder had made disparaging comments about the pope and had referred to the Catholic Church as a "satanic cult."

Bush was initially stunned by the attack, because GOP candidates for years had made seemingly obligatory visits to that university, and McCain himself had been considering an offer to speak there. None of the earlier GOP presidential candidates had come under criticism for speaking at the university. Yet McCain took the unprecedented step in the GOP of making a visit to that university a campaign issue, blasting Bush for failing to criticize the institution's overtly bigoted policies and statements. McCain focused much of his attack on Bush's failure to say anything about the university's anti-Catholicism.

The campaign took on a highly personal nature between the leading GOP candidates. Bush reacted angrily to suggestions that he had somehow endorsed anti-Catholic sentiment by addressing the university. Yet the criticism clearly hurt his standing with Catholic voters, and Bush ultimately expressed regret for his appearance at the university. In a letter to former Cardinal John O'Connor of New York, Bush referred to his own visit at the university and failure to address its anti-Catholic views as "a missed opportunity causing needless offense, which I deeply regret." Bush admitted that "on reflection, I should have been more clear in disassociating myself from the anti-Catholic sentiments and racial prejudice."[9]

McCain could not concede the Christian Right vote to Bush in South Carolina and hope to have any chance at all of winning the state. When Bauer dropped out before the South Carolina primary, the McCain camp heavily lobbied for the Christian Right leader's endorsement. Bauer agreed to endorse McCain and his campaign. McCain scheduled an appearance at Furman University in Greenville; the campaign trumpeted that the candidate's speech there would be followed by a major endorsement. First to introduce McCain was Rep. Lindsay Graham (R-S.C.), who made an extraordinary statement that seemingly suggested that McCain had been ordained by God to run for president and heal the country.

> God has placed John McCain here for a reason, in the right spot at the right time. We have in our midst a man who can heal the wounds of the nation. Really, he shouldn't be alive. . . . [a reference to McCain's being shot down in the Vietnam War] John McCain was supposed to die, but he didn't. You're here [turning toward McCain] because God wants you to be here. And God has given us in South Carolina the opportunity to raise you to the needs of the nation.[10]

Bauer later made his endorsement, an action that would cause him to be disavowed by many Christian Right leaders. But for the time being, the McCain campaign thought it had achieved a major coup in breaking into Bush's support from the Christian Right.

Bush handily won South Carolina, 53 percent to 42 percent (and 5 percent for Keyes). The Christian Right carried the state for Bush. Among the 61 percent who said in exit polls that they were *not* members of the Religious Right, McCain won 52 percent to 46 percent. Among the 34 percent self-described Religious Right voters, Bush won overwhelmingly 68 percent to 24 percent. Bush once again prevailed heavily among the voters who said that abortion never should be legal (67 percent to 19 percent, with 13 percent for Keyes). McCain handily prevailed among the 39 percent of the South Carolina Republican voters who said they were pro-choice. Forty-three percent of the primary voters chose either "moral values" or abortion as the most important issue in their voting decision. Bush won those voters heavily. McCain prevailed among those 25 percent who said that either campaign finance or social security was the most important issue.[11]

Two major factors boosted Bush's showing in South Carolina over his disappointing performance in New Hampshire. First, after the stunning McCain victory in the first primary, the Christian Right had made a unified and heavy push for Bush's candidacy. Bush's margin over McCain among Religious Right voters went from a mere 10 percent in New Hampshire to 44 percent in South Carolina. Second, the percentage of socially conservative voters in the South Carolina primary was substantially higher than in New Hampshire. Most analysts suggested that a loss in South Carolina would have ended Bush's candidacy. If true, the Christian Right vote surely could claim to have saved his presidential bid.

With each candidate claiming one major state primary victory, the campaign focus now shifted to the crucial Michigan contest. With Michigan having a heavy Catholic population, the McCain campaign counted on anger at

Bush's appearance at Bob Jones University to aid the senator's candidacy. Once again, Christian Right and pro-life groups became heavily involved in the race. The powerful Michigan Right to Life Committee sent pro-Bush, anti-McCain mailings to four hundred thousand Michigan voters and followed up with phone calls to those same voters. The mailing featured a picture of a smiling baby with the words "George W. Bush, a Pro-Life Vote." Inside the mailer were statements favorable toward Bush's views on social issues and critical of McCain's alleged views. The mailing also made an issue of the fact that McCain had fared well in New Hampshire among pro-choice voters.[12]

Pat Robertson of the Christian Coalition taped an anti-McCain phone message for socially conservative Michigan voters. Robertson crossed the line of propriety in the message, lambasting McCain's New Hampshire campaign manager, former GOP Senator Warren Rudman, as "a vicious bigot" who had once made disparaging comments about the Christian Right. Rudman indeed had a history of clashing with the social conservative wing of his party, particularly when he criticized religious-based political organizations for their opposition to a potential presidential candidacy by Gen. Colin Powell. Robertson later backed away somewhat from his charge of bigotry: "I may have gone on that phrase a little far."[13] Nonetheless, the taped calls became the core of a national news story about the tactics of the Christian Right, and even the Bush campaign privately urged Robertson to tone down his rhetoric.

McCain's campaign fought back by targeting Catholic voters for support. The candidate himself initially denied any knowledge of efforts by an independent group to conduct mass phone calls to Catholic voters to alert them to Bush's appearance at Bob Jones University. Eventually McCain admitted that he had known, and he too came under criticism for playing the "religion card" too heavily in the campaign—and for not being honest in his initial response.

McCain easily won the Michigan primary 51 percent to 43 percent (Keyes with 5 percent). Generally, the same voter pattern held: McCain won independent and Democrat votes in the open primary, Bush won the Republican identifiers. Among the two-thirds of voters who were *not* members of the Religious Right, 60 percent went to McCain, 36 percent to Bush. Bush again overwhelmed McCain among self-identified Religious Right voters (but they were only 27 percent of the Michigan GOP primary voters), 66 percent to 25 percent (8 percent for Keyes). Perhaps significantly, Bush's numbers declined somewhat among pro-life voters, suggesting that although he lost nothing in Religious Right appeal, he indeed lost some Catholic pro-life voters. Among pro-life voters, Bush won only 54 percent, although again his numbers were strongest among those who said that abortion "never" should be legal (62 percent for Bush, 27 percent for McCain).[14]

McCain's strong showing in Michigan led to a round of analyses suggesting that he was clearly the strongest candidate for the GOP in the general election. In a record primary turnout for the GOP in Michigan, 29 percent of the voters said that they were casting their first GOP primary vote ever. Those voters went heavily to McCain. A substantial turnout among labor unionists, independent voters, and Democrats all favored McCain heavily. As in all of the earlier primary states, Bush carried the most conservative voters, particularly the Christian Right.

Although these facts bolstered the case for McCain's electability in November, they also underscored a large problem in his nomination candidacy: He could not win the nomination by appealing to largely non-GOP voters. Most of the upcoming key primaries were "closed"—that is, open only to formally registered Republicans. The next major contest was in Virginia—the state that is the home to the Christian Coalition, the former Moral Majority, and widely considered among the most fertile territory for Christian Right candidates in the GOP.[15]

Although an "open" primary state, the Virginia GOP instituted a requirement that all voters in the Republican primary must sign a "loyalty oath" as a condition for voting. The oath was a nonbinding statement in which the voter, in signing, affirmed that he or she would be loyal to the party and vote for its nominee in November, regardless of who won. Not all voters understood the purpose of the oath, and many believed that it was somehow legally binding. The effect was to lower substantially participation among non-Republican identifying voters, most of whom backed McCain. That was the goal of the state GOP leaders, all of whom backed Bush.

Early polls after the Michigan primary victory showed McCain running behind Bush but still competitive. For months Bush had been spending heavily in the state on mass mailings and television ads. McCain initially appeared not to be contesting the state. Indeed, without a substantial turnout of non-GOP voters, he stood little chance. But once the polls showed McCain had moved within a single-digit margin of Bush, the senator took a remarkable gamble that some likened to a political "Hail Mary" pass.

The day before the February 29 primary, McCain went to Virginia Beach, Virginia, the hometown of Rev. Pat Robertson, to make a speech laced with stinging criticism of the founder of the Christian Coalition founder and Rev. Jerry Falwell, founder of the former Moral Majority. McCain was very careful in the speech to draw a clear distinction between Christian social conservatives and their values on the one hand, and the political tactics of two Christian Right leaders on the other. At the urging of his supporter Gary Bauer, McCain also drew a distinction between a number of widely admired Christian Right leaders on the one hand and, again, Robertson and Falwell on the other. Yet these distinctions were largely lost on the media and the electorate—especially supporters of the Christian Right, who widely interpreted McCain's remarks as an attack on involvement in politics by people of faith.[16]

The McCain speech precipitated an emotionally charged national debate over the role of the Christian Right in the GOP. Because his statement was so widely misinterpreted, it is worth quoting key sections at some length here:

> Let me be clear, evangelical leaders are changing America for the better. Chuck Colson, head of Prison Fellowships, is saving men from a lifetime behind bars by bringing them the good news of redemption. James Dobson, who does not support me, has devoted his life to rebuilding America's families. Others are leading the fight against pornography, cultural decline, and for life. I stand with them.
>
> I am a pro-life, pro-family, fiscal conservative, and advocate of a strong defense. And yet, Pat Robertson, Jerry Falwell and a few Washington leaders of the pro-life movement call me an unacceptable presidential candidate. They distort my pro-life positions and smear the reputations of my supporters. Why?
>
> Because I don't pander to them, because I don't ascribe to their failed philosophy that money is our message. . . .
>
> The union bosses who have subordinated the interests of working families to their own ambitions, to their desire to preserve their own political power at all costs are mirror images of Pat Robertson. Just as we embrace working people, we embrace the fine members of the religious conservative community. But that does not mean that we will pander to their self-appointed leaders. . . .
>
> My friends, I am a Reagan Republican who will defeat Al Gore. Unfortunately, Governor Bush is a Pat Robertson Republican who will lose to Al Gore.
>
> I recognize and celebrate that our country is founded upon Judeo-Christian values. And I have pledged my life to defend America and all her values, the values that have made us the noblest experiment in history.
>
> But political intolerance by any political party is neither a Judeo-Christian nor an American value. The political tactics of division and slander are not our values.
>
> They are corrupting influences on religion and politics and those who practice them in the name of religion or in the name of the Republican Party or in the name of America shame our faith, our party, and our country.
>
> Neither party should be defined by pandering to the outer reaches of American politics and the agents of intolerance whether they be Louis Farrakhan or Al Sharpton on the Left, or Pat Robertson or Jerry Falwell on the Right. . . .
>
> We are the party of Ronald Reagan, not Pat Robertson. We are the party of Theodore Roosevelt, not the party of special interests. We are the party of Abraham Lincoln, not Bob Jones.[17]

McCain affirmed his own religious faith several times in the speech. But ultimately it was his most severe rebukes of Robertson and Falwell that made headlines nationally and were the focus of the extensive commentary about the speech. Immediately after the speech, political scientist John C. Green told the *Washington Post* that McCain's effort to draw a distinction between admirable Christian Right leaders (Dobson and Colson) and offensive ones (Robertson and Falwell) would be lost on most politically motivated religious activists. Furthermore, he correctly predicted that "instead of turning out and voting 66 percent against McCain, they [Christian Right activists] may vote 88 percent" against the senator in future GOP primaries.[18]

Indeed, McCain lost Virginia 53 percent to 44 percent, and once again the Christian Right had delivered the victory to Bush.[19] The Christian Right turned out and voted 86 percent against McCain. Among the one in five voters who were self-described members of the Religious Right, 80 percent supported Bush, 14 percent McCain, and the rest (about 5 percent) backed Keyes. McCain prevailed 52 percent to 45 percent over Bush among the nearly four in five voters who said that they were not members of the Religious Right. McCain overwhelmingly won the pro-choice vote, and Bush overwhelmingly won the pro-life vote. McCain handily won the votes of Democrats and independents. Bush defeated McCain among Republican identifiers 69 percent to 29 percent.[20]

McCain's strategists clearly saw an opening in the senator's attack on the two unpopular Christian Right leaders. Although the strategy hurt McCain substantially in Virginia, the GOP contest soon turned to more progressive states with smaller Christian Right voting blocs, among them New York and California. Many analysts indeed suggested that it was McCain's intention all along to accept defeat in Virginia but to take the high, principled ground by denouncing the Christian Right leaders in their home state.

There would be no electoral payoff for McCain in the subsequent primary states. Indeed, his attacks ultimately sank his candidacy. After the Virginia loss, McCain gave an interview to reporters on his campaign bus. Asked about his strong language against Robertson and Falwell, McCain rhetorically replied: "You're supposed to tolerate evil in your party in the name of party unity?"[21] It was the worst moment of McCain's campaign. He later backtracked from the comment, but the damage to his candidacy already had been done. Commentators lambasted McCain for crossing the line of allowable criticism by calling his Christian Right opponents "evil." Bauer stopped defending McCain and issued a statement asking the senator to apologize for his "unwarranted, ill-advised and divisive attacks on certain religious leaders."[22]

The "Super Tuesday" primaries took place one week after the Virginia primary. Among the crucial states were New York, California, Maryland, Georgia, Mississippi, and Ohio. Pro-life groups stepped up their attacks on the senator's campaign. The National Right to Life Committee alone spent over two hundred thousand dollars on anti-McCain phone calls in the Super Tuesday primary states. Phone calls told voters that McCain was not a genuine pro-life advocate and that Bush had the stronger record on the social issues. "For the children's sake, please vote for George Bush," said the phone message.[23]

The Right to Life Committee's spending to defeat McCain was extraordinary. In all, the organization spent over five hundred thousand dollars against McCain in the primaries, more than one-half its total spending on all races in the 1998 election cycle. Their spending about equaled the organization's total budget reported at the beginning of 2000.[24]

McCain's standing among key religious constituencies began a precipitous decline in the wake of his "evil" comment. The senator had staked much of his effort on New York State, hoping to capitalize on the large Catholic vote and possible continued anger at Bush's appearance at Bob Jones University. But a Zogby poll prior to the New York primary showed a once-substantial McCain lead among Catholics fast disappearing. Many leading politically conservative Catholics rallied to Bush's defense. Deal Hudson, the editor and publisher of *Crisis*, called McCain a "demagogue" for portraying Bush as insensitive to Catholics. "He is creating a division among traditional allies, including religiously active Catholics and evangelical Christians," Deal said of McCain.[25]

Super Tuesday ended McCain's candidacy. Although the senator won several New England states with low Christian Right populations, he lost all the important large contests. His attacks on Robertson and Falwell had backfired. One-third of the voters in New York and Ohio said that McCain's comments had influenced their voting decisions, and those voters opposed the senator by a four-to-one margin. McCain's negative rankings in the Super Tuesday exit polls were the highest of any in his campaign.[26]

The Christian Right delivered the key votes to Bush in most of the states. For example, in Ohio McCain won the three in four voters who said that they were *not* members of the Religious Right (52 percent to 44 percent). Among the one in four who were members, Bush won strongly (74 percent to 19 percent).[27] In New York, only 15 percent of the voters were self-described members of the Religious Right, and they backed Bush over McCain 62 percent to 28 percent. The rest of the GOP vote was split evenly between Bush and McCain (47 percent each). McCain again took the pro-choice vote, and Bush overwhelmingly won the pro-life vote. The New York electorate was 50 percent Catholic, and those voters favored Bush over McCain 52 percent to 43 percent, lending credibility to the argument that there had been a backlash against McCain's efforts to link Bush with anti-Catholic bigotry. Bush, of course, easily carried the Protestant vote, and McCain won only one religious bloc, the Jewish vote (a mere 6 percent of the GOP primary voters in New York).[28]

McCain "suspended" his candidacy after Super Tuesday and several weeks later gave a tepid endorsement to Bush. McCain disavowed any future interest in running for the presidency. He also told Bush that he would not accept selection as a vice presidential candidate under any circumstances. Indeed, the animosity between the two candidates was real, and it was hard to imagine the two running on the same ticket. Just in case, Robertson and other Christian Right leaders piled on, continuing to push their argument that having McCain on the national ticket in any capacity would result in socially conservative voters sitting on their hands on Election Day. Robertson told the press in late April, "To think that that man is one heartbeat away from the presidency would scare me to death!"[29] Ironically, at about the same time, the Christian Coalition issued its annual scorecard of legislative votes, which gave McCain a 91 percent positive score. That followed his 100 percent score from the organization the previous year—the most recent score that was readily available during the GOP primaries.[30]

THE GOP CONTEST IN RETROSPECT: CHRISTIAN RIGHT KINGMAKERS

McCain had a long record as a conservative voter in Congress, including on social issues. Yet he was anathema to the conservative movement in 2000, especially the Christian Right. Social conservative opposition cost him the nomination. Tables 4.1 and 4.2 make the case quite clearly that the Christian Right delivered Bush's nomination.

An *ABC News* poll in late February underscored McCain's challenge running for the GOP nomination. Seven in ten Americans believed that McCain was either a liberal or a moderate, or could not place him ideologically. Only 28 percent could correctly identify him as a conservative. Six in ten were unaware that he opposed abortion rights.[31]

Christian Right groups effectively distorted his record. But McCain also contributed to the Christian Right's unease with his support for moderating GOP platform language, his own campaign rhetoric, which often alienated the most conservative voters in his party, and especially for his attacks on movement leaders.

What should scholars make of the role of the Christian Right in delivering the GOP nomination to Bush? The answer is not a simple one. Scholars have written recently of the Christian Right's growing pragmatism, led by such

Table 4.1. Religious Right Voters

State	N.H.	S.C.	Mich.	Va.	N.Y.
Percent Religious Right	16	34	27	19	15
Bush-McCain	**36**–26	**68**–24	**66**–25	**80**–14	**62**–28

Table 4.2. Non-Religious Right Voters

State	N.H.	S.C.	Mich.	Va.	N.Y.
Percent Non-RR	80	61	67	77	80
Bush-McCain	28–**54**	46–**52**	36–**60**	45–**52**	47–**47**

figures as Reed and Robertson.[32] The early decision to back Bush seems the ultimate act of pragmatism. Bush was the candidate of the establishment wing of the GOP and was widely hailed as having the best chance for uniting the party and winning the general election. There were plenty of more genuinely social conservative candidates from which to choose, but Robertson, Reed, and others early on jumped on the Bush bandwagon, hoping to become players in the next GOP administration. To be sure, the Christian Right was not united early in supporting Bush. But many of the other movement leaders gravitated to candidates such as Forbes, who also may have appeared as pragmatic choices.

The case for Christian Right pragmatism is less easily made with regard to the Bush-McCain race. All of the polls suggested that McCain had a much stronger chance than Bush to defeat Democratic Vice President Al Gore in the general election. One possible explanation is that once the Christian Right leaders so strongly backed Bush, they had to protect their own credibility and stay loyal to their candidate. Nobody anticipated the strength of McCain's challenge for the nomination. Yet not only did the Christian Right leaders stand behind Bush, but they launched an extraordinary offensive against McCain. The severity of the response to McCain's candidacy would be understandable from the Christian Right perspective were he a moderate, pro-choice Republican. But his voting record in Congress and issue positions made him an almost ideal candidate for the Christian Right.

It is plausible that some Christian Right opposition to McCain was more personal than political in nature. Dobson was candid about his view that past adultery, divorce, and a tolerant attitude toward gays made McCain unacceptable, no matter how "right" the senator was on the issues. Bush clearly was more comfortable than McCain in the role of articulating "family values" issues and defending the Christian Right against its critics. Throughout his congressional career, despite a conservative voting record, McCain had never shown much interest in the intersection of religion and politics. By contrast, Bush spoke very openly of his faith, of his redemption from an undisciplined youth and early adulthood, and he made much of his own belief in the value of faith-based institutions in solving social problems. Furthermore, Bush projected a warm and likeable personality, whereas McCain at times appeared self-righteous. Bush was eager to show that he listened to the views of different groups. McCain wore his stubborn independence and refusal to pander to group leaders as a badge of honor.

Nonetheless, it is difficult to come to any conclusion other than that, more than any other reason for opposing McCain, Christian Right leaders perceived his emphasis on campaign finance reform as an assault on the political activities of their various interest-group organizations.[33] Opposition to McCain therefore had much to do with Christian Right leaders' protecting their own power and little or nothing to do with McCain's views on the social agenda. Yet in their attacks on McCain, the Christian Right leaders worked to mobilize their supporters by wrongly characterizing the senator as hostile to the pro-life agenda while saying very little about opposition to his campaign finance reforms.

The greatest risk in backing Bush so strongly was that the Christian Right might have borne the brunt of criticism for once again consigning the GOP to defeat when victory had been at hand. The heavy push by Christian Right groups for the Clinton impeachment in 1998 clearly hurt the GOP's electoral fortunes in the midterm elections.[34] Bush's Electoral College victory spared the Christian Right from further criticism for harming the party's fortunes.

Bush's victory, however narrow, could be a major gain for Christian Right politics. Having delivered the nomination to Bush, the Christian Right has a strong claim to a "place at the table" in a Bush administration. Given GOP control of the House of Representatives, however slight and tenuous, with a Bush administration, there is real potential for policy gains for the Christian Right. Indeed, at this writing during the earliest days of the Bush presidency, there is much evidence of Christian Right influence on Bush appointments and policies. Among actions that have pleased the Christian Right are: the nomination of former Senator John Ashcroft (R-Mo.) as attorney general; the executive order prohibiting federal funding for international agencies that provide abortions and abortion counseling; the creation of a "faith-based" initiatives office in the White House; and the president's support for an education vouchers program.

It remains to be seen whether Bush continues to support Christian Right–favored policies throughout his term. At least one of Bush's efforts to please the Christian conservative community has somewhat backfired. Christian Right leaders have strongly criticized elements of the faith-based initiative, especially the proposal that the federal government take the lead in funding certain church-based programs. Bush appointed a Democrat and university professor, John DiIulio, to head the White House office of faith-based initiatives. DiIulio incensed Christian Right critics of the faith-based initiative by declaring that they did not care about the plight of inner-city poor minorities.[35] Because of this controversy, during the early months of Bush's term there were serious tensions between some Christian Right leaders and the White House.

Moreover, Sen. James Jeffords's (R-Vt.) departure from the Republican Party, which gave Democrats control of the Senate for the first time since 1994, may influence the Bush administration to move toward the center of the political spectrum and away from Christian Right policies. Finally, soon after the September 11, 2001, terrorist attacks on the United States, Falwell and Robertson made controversial statements suggesting that a general moral decline in the country had played a role in the success of the attacks, which killed thousands of innocent people. The Bush White

House denounced these comments, further distancing the president from the Christian Right leaders. Bush's focus on fighting terrorism also took the spotlight off other agenda items, including social issues.

In the end, the GOP nomination contest in 2000 shows that despite many predictions to the contrary, the Christian Right remains an active and powerful force in U.S. politics. When the movement is united behind a candidate, as it was for Bush once the race became a two-man contest, the Christian Right can be the true kingmaker in the Republican Party. There is no convincing evidence at this point that the Christian Right is a dwindling force in the United States.

NOTES

1. See, for example, the analysis in Liz Szabo, "Christian Coalition Losing Clout," *The (Norfolk, Va.) Virginian Pilot*, 19 February 2000, www.pilotonline.com/news/nw0219sou.html; and Hanna Rosin, "Christian Right's Fervor Has Fizzled," *Washington Post*, 16 February 2000, A1, 16.

2. See Mark J. Rozell, ". . . Or, Influential as Ever?" *Washington Post*, 1 March 2000, A17.

3. It is surprising that Bauer staked his candidacy early on in a state with a very small Christian Right population rather than save his resources for upcoming primary states with more voters hospitable to a social movement candidate.

4. On the World Wide Web: cnn.com/ELECTION/2000/primaries/NH/results.html.

5. Exit polling data from cnn.com/ELECTION/2000/primaries/NH/poll.rep.html.

6. McCain had made it clear that his support for softened platform language did not lessen his own commitment to the pro-life agenda. Rather, he thought a softened platform position would signal that the GOP was a broad-based party. The issue of his support for fetal tissue research is more complicated. He had long opposed it until his close friend, former Arizona Senator Morris Udall, who was suffering from Parkinson's disease, urged McCain to rethink the issue. As for his statement about the *Roe* decision, McCain said that he had simply misspoken. McCain stood by his statement about letting his own daughter decide for herself the abortion issue. When asked the same hypothetical question about his daughter being pregnant and considering abortion, Bush too replied, "It would be up to her." Of all the GOP candidates, only Keyes and Bauer said that answer was unacceptable for a pro-life advocate.

7. On the World Wide Web: 63.224.30.9/issues/pro-life.html.

8. Thomas B. Edsall and Terry M. Neal, "Bush, Allies Hit McCain's Conservative Credentials," *Washington Post*, 15 February 2000, A1, 10.

9. Bush letter, quoted in "Bush Regrets Visit to Anti-Catholic School," *Washington Times*, 8 February 2000, A8. Bush's letter devotes one paragraph to regret for his own failure in this episode and then discusses at length his anger at campaign attacks on him as insensitive to Catholics and racial minorities.

10. C-SPAN broadcast of 16 February 2000 on McCain campaign rally at Furman University (observed by author). It seemed to me, watching this speech on television, that McCain appeared embarrassed by this statement.

11. On the World Wide Web: cnn.com/ELECTION/2000/primaries/SC/poll. rep.html.

12. Thomas B. Edsall, "Powerful Antiabortion Lobby Targets McCain," *Washington Post*, 22 February 2000, A6.

13. Quoted in "Who's a Bigot?" *Washington Post*, 24 February 2000, A20.

14. On the World Wide Web: cnn.com/ELECTION/2000/primaries/MI/poll.rep. html.

15. See Mark J. Rozell and Clyde Wilcox, *Second Coming: The New Christian Right in Virginia Politics* (Baltimore: Johns Hopkins University Press, 1996).

16. From McCain's standpoint, the attack on Robertson is perfectly understandable given the vitriol that the Christian Coalition founder directed at the senator and at Warren Rudman. But it is curious that McCain would include Falwell in the denunciation, given that the former Moral Majority leader had been completely silent about the GOP contest in 2000. In his own anger at being treated unfairly by Robertson and some other Christian Right leaders not mentioned in the Virginia speech, McCain unfairly tarred Falwell as one of the chief offenders.

17. Text of McCain speech, retrieved from www.mccain2000.org on 29 February 2000.

18. Quoted in Thomas B. Edsall, "Senator Risking Key Constituency," *Washington Post*, 29 February 2000, A14.

19. Two other states held GOP presidential contests on the same day as the Virginia primary. Bush easily won both the Washington State primary and the North Dakota caucuses. McCain did little to contest either state.

20. On the World Wide Web: cnn.com/ELECTION/2000/primaries/VA/poll.rep. html.

21. Nancy Gibbs, "Fire and Brimstone," *Time*, 13 March 2000, 33.

22. Quoted in Gibbs, "Fire and Brimstone," 33.

23. George Lardner Jr., "Abortion Foes Spend $200,000 to Beat McCain," *Washington Post*, 7 March 2000, A8.

24. Lardner, "Abortion Foes Spend $200,000 to Beat McCain," A8.

25. Quoted in Ralph Z. Hallow, "McCain's Religion Gambit Draws Quick Backlash in New York," *Washington Post*, 1 March 2000, A1.

26. Associated Press, "GOP Conservatives Give Bush the Edge," *Washington Times*, 8 March 2000, A12.

27. Associated Press, "GOP Conservatives Give Bush the Edge," A12.

28. On the World Wide Web: cnn.com/ELECTION/2000/primaries/NY/poll.rep. html.

29. Quoted in Tom Curry, "Christian Coalition Rates McCain Highly," on the World Wide Web: www.msnbc.com/news/412356.asp?cp1+1.

30. See Curry, "Christian Coalition Rates McCain Highly."

31. See Gary Langer, "Perception vs. Reality," on the World Wide Web: abcnews.go.com/onair/Nightline/poll0000225.html.

32. See Matthew Moen, *The Transformation of the Christian Right* (Tuscaloosa: University of Alabama Press, 1992); Rozell and Wilcox, *Second Coming*; and Mark J.

Rozell, "Growing Up Politically: The New Politics of the New Christian Right," in *Sojourners in the Wilderness: The Christian Right in Comparative Perspective,* ed. Corwin Smidt and James Penning (Lanham, Md.: Rowman and Littlefield, 1997), 235–48.

33. As scholar Donald Scruggs correctly pointed out in his comments on an earlier draft of this paper, opposition to McCain's campaign finance views had the effect of unifying the Republican establishment and the Christian Right for Bush, whereas the usual pattern was for these two GOP groups to be in combat with one another (Scruggs comments presented at the International Conference of Americanists, 14 July 2000, Warsaw, Poland).

34. See the various essays in John C. Green, Mark J. Rozell, and Clyde Wilcox, eds., *Prayers in the Precincts: The Christian Right in the 1998 Elections* (Washington, D.C.: Georgetown University Press, 2000).

35. DiIulio announced his resignation from this position in late summer 2001.

5

Catholics and the 2000 Presidential Election: Bob Jones University and the Catholic Vote

Mary C. Segers

Scholars of religion and politics regularly observe that at sixty-two million and growing, Roman Catholics constitute the largest single religious denomination in the United States. The Catholic community has a significant institutional presence in virtually every part of the nation, including almost twenty thousand parishes, 8,300 schools, 231 colleges and universities, nine hundred hospitals and health care facilities, and 1,400 Catholic charitable agencies. Indeed, the Catholic community is the largest nongovernmental provider of education, health care, and human services in the country. These institutional concerns mean that Catholic leaders have a considerable stake in the policy decisions of state and national governments on many issues, ranging from taxation and social security to health policy, employee fringe benefits, and educational funding.[1]

Moreover, the concentration of Catholics in large "swing" states (New York, California, Texas, Florida, Pennsylvania, Illinois, Michigan, Ohio, and New Jersey) is a political reality few presidential aspirants can afford to ignore. The fact that Catholics constitute 25 percent of the electorate suggests that candidates would do well to cultivate "the Catholic vote." Perhaps it is the significance of the Catholic vote in national elections that accounts for the appearance, at the funeral of Cardinal John O'Connor of New York in the midst of Campaign 2000, of every major "celebrity" politician in the country: President Bill Clinton and Hillary Clinton, Vice President Al Gore and Tipper Gore, then-Governor George Bush and Laura Bush, and of course a host of New York officials, including Gov. George Pataki, Mayor Rudolph Giuliani, and former Mayor Ed Koch.[2]

Given this potential electoral and institutional clout, one of the surprises of the 2000 presidential campaign was the appearance of anti-Catholicism as a significant issue. Although antipathy to Catholicism has a long history in American politics, this issue was considered moribund after, if not completely eliminated by, the 1960 election of John F. Kennedy as the nation's first Catholic president. Since 1960, a variety of Catholic candidates have entertained aspirations for high national office: Mario Cuomo, Edward Kennedy, Bruce Babbitt, Geraldine Ferraro, Sargent Shriver, Joseph Biden, Joseph Califano, and Alan Keyes. It was therefore unexpected that the Republican nomination contest between Arizona Senator John McCain and Texas Governor George W. Bush would revive the specter of anti-Catholic prejudice. In terms of strategy, the political reality of significant numbers of Catholics in key swing states suggested that presidential candidates in 2000 should cultivate, not alienate, Catholic voters.

Nevertheless, the accusation of anti-Catholicism was made in February 2000, in the course of the South Carolina and Michigan Republican primaries. How Catholics in general reacted to this development and how the Republican Party in particular responded to Sen. John McCain's charge that Governor Bush was insensitive to Catholics is a subject worth investigating. It tells us much about the strategic position of Catholic voters in the electorate.

This chapter first describes the political context in which McCain made his charge and the political fallout from his accusation. The second part analyzes the reaction of Catholics to this controversy as well as the reaction of the Republican Party leadership. The next part discusses the common perception of Catholics as a critical constituency in contemporary presidential elections. The chapter then reviews Catholic voting patterns in Election 2000 and concludes with general reflections on Catholics as swing voters.

MIXING GOD AND POLITICS:
THE CONTROVERSY OVER BOB JONES UNIVERSITY

Although George Bush began the contest for the GOP presidential nomination with clear advantages—many major party endorsements, Bush family connections, and a war chest of some seventy million dollars—John McCain defeated Bush in the New Hampshire primary by a whopping 49 to 30 percent margin.[3] The day after his New Hampshire loss, Bush began his next primary campaign with an address to the faculty and student body at Bob Jones University in Greenville, South Carolina. In so doing, he was merely following previous Republican candidates—Ronald Reagan, his father George H. W. Bush, and Bob Dole—who had visited the campus in search of Republican votes. There had been no controversy when these GOP leaders spoke at the university. But Bush's appearance at BJU came back to haunt him, when Senator McCain criticized him for not dissociating himself from the university's hostility to Catholicism and its ban on interracial dating.

Bob Jones Sr., a Methodist evangelist, founded BJU in 1927 in the midst of the gripping fundamentalist-modernist controversies of the 1920s. He and his successors fashioned the university as "a traditional, Bible-believing, Christian place."[4] The university, first located in Florida and then in Tennessee, relocated to Greenville in 1947. BJU currently enrolls five thousand students and has graduated thirty-four thousand, including Rep. Asa Hutchinson (R-Ark.) and South Carolina state representative Terry Haskins, the latter a McCain supporter.[5] BJU occasionally hosts Democratic speakers (e.g., Gov. Jim Hodges of South Carolina). But its bias toward Republican speakers is reflected in the honorary doctorates it has awarded to GOP luminaries John Ashcroft, Jesse Helms, and Strom Thurmond.[6]

What distinguishes Bob Jones University is its theological outlook. As a fundamentalist Christian school, BJU has always insisted on strict separatism and has refused fellowship with any group not pure in its (fundamentalist) Christianity. Hence, the Jones family has attacked Billy Graham, Jerry Falwell, and many other evangelicals and fundamentalists—not so much for their failure to accept pure biblical doctrine but because of their association with such apostates as Catholics, Mormons, mainline Protestants, Southern Baptists, and the National Council of Churches.[7] Until recently, the university banned interracial dating and criticized Roman Catholicism as a religion that emphasized good works rather than faith as the key to salvation. A visit to the BJU Website helps to explain its differences with Catholicism:

> If there are those who charge us with being opposed to the doctrines and theology of the Catholic Church, we plead guilty. But we are not Catholic-haters. . . . All religion, including Catholicism, which teaches that salvation is by religious works or church dogma is false. Religion that makes the words of its leader, be he Pope or other, equal with the Word of God is false. *Sola Scriptura.*
>
> From the time of the Reformation onward, it has been understood that there is no commonality between the Bible way, which is justification by faith in the shed blood of Jesus Christ, and salvation by works, which the faithful, practicing Catholic embraces.
>
> We love the practicing Catholic and earnestly desire to see him accept the Cross of Christ, leave the false system that has enslaved his soul and enjoy the freedom of sins forgiven that is available for any of us in Christ alone.[8]

How did Bob Jones University become the center of a major controversy over religion and politics in the 2000 primary campaign? What factors led Senator McCain to accuse Governor Bush of insensitivity to Catholics and to racial minorities because he failed to repudiate the beliefs of BJU? To understand McCain's accusation, we need to examine the political context in which it was made.

Mark Rozell has aptly summarized the negative, bitter primary contest between Bush and McCain in South Carolina (see chapter 4). McCain's defeat

of Bush in the New Hampshire primary stunned the Republican Party establishment, which had assumed that Bush's nomination was inevitable and that
he was eminently electable. To regain momentum, Bush had to win South
Carolina and end McCain's insurgent candidacy; to do this, he had to appeal
to the GOP base, the Christian Right. Hence the Bush campaign had to rely
heavily on Pat Robertson, founder of the Christian Coalition and a staunch
Bush supporter from the start.

Religious Right leaders realized that despite McCain's eighteen-year conservative voting record in Congress, his support for campaign finance reform
threatened to undercut their political effectiveness. Specifically, his sponsor-
ship of campaign finance legislation would limit their ability to run independent political advertising ("issue ads") and to contribute huge sums ("soft
money") to party campaign treasuries. As a result, Robertson, political con-
sultant Ralph Reed (former executive director of the Christian Coalition) and
such groups as the National Right to Life Committee actively campaigned for
Bush in New Hampshire and South Carolina.

Despite McCain's opposition to abortion, Robertson inaccurately charged
that McCain was actually hostile to the pro-life policy agenda. Robertson also
suggested on national airwaves that McCain lacked the temperament and
emotional stability to be president. The director of Focus on the Family, the
Rev. James Dobson, criticized McCain's moral fitness for office because of
the senator's earlier admitted adultery and the subsequent divorce that had
ended his first marriage. Dobson also criticized McCain over his votes to confirm what Dobson called "pro-abortion" Supreme Court justices. He noted
that McCain had accepted campaign contributions from the gambling and alcohol industries.[9]

In a rather antagonistic TV debate during the South Carolina campaign,
Bush, appealing to the Christian Right, quoted one of McCain's leading supporters, Warren Rudman, former New Hampshire senator and now national
chairman of McCain's campaign. "He talked about the Christian Coalition as
bigots," Bush said, turning to McCain and pausing for effect. "You don't believe that, do you?" "No," McCain replied. "But he's entitled to his own opinions."[10]

During this same debate, Alan Keyes attacked Bush for speaking at BJU
and not condemning its dating policy. "Does leadership consist of going into
BJU where serious questions, in fact, do exist about religious bigotry and
racial bigotry?" Keyes asked. "Going in, taking the applause, risking nothing
because you refuse to raise the issues? That's what G. W. Bush did." Bush responded that he did not support the university's dating policy.[11]

Here in essence were the two issues that became so inflammatory during
the early Republican primaries: Bush's critique of McCain's attitude to the Religious Right, and McCain's criticism of Bush for failing to condemn the university's anti-Catholic views and its ban on interracial dating.

The South Carolina and Michigan Primaries

On February 19, Bush defeated McCain in the South Carolina primary, 53 to 42 percent (with 5 percent for Keyes).[12] A third of South Carolina's primary voters self-identified with the Religious Right, and Bush won two-thirds of their votes. Now each candidate had won a presidential primary. The Michigan and Arizona primaries, coming three days later (on February 22), offered a chance to break the tie. Arizona was expected to vote for its native son, John McCain. But Michigan was an open battleground. Moreover, Michigan has a large Roman Catholic population (23.4 percent), especially around Detroit; it also has a conservative Calvinist concentration, in the southwestern part of the state.

On the eve of the Michigan primary, a recorded telephone message from Pat Robertson went out to conservative Christians in Michigan harshly criticizing McCain's campaign for having a top adviser (Warren Rudman) who had attacked the Christian Coalition. Robertson characterized Rudman as "a vicious bigot who wrote that conservative Christians in politics are anti-abortion zealots, homophobes and would-be censors." (He did not mention the fact that Rudman, who used those phrases in his autobiography to describe some in the Christian Right, also said there were "some fine, sincere people in its ranks.") Robertson concluded his message by urging listeners to vote for Bush to "protect unborn babies." Robertson aides said he made the calls without the knowledge of the Bush campaign. Bush advisors disavowed knowledge of the calls.[13]

In retaliation, McCain, in an appearance on NBC's *Meet the Press,* insisted that Bush should have spoken out against BJU leaders for referring to Catholicism as a "satanic cult."[14] On talk radio, he referred to BJU as a "place where I would have told them they are a bunch of idiots for having those racial policies."[15] His campaign managers targeted Catholic voters. They arranged for a telemarketing company to conduct mass phone calls to Catholic voters to alert them to Bush's appearance at BJU. At first, McCain denied knowledge of these efforts; later he acknowledged that he had known of the plans to target Catholic voters by raising the specter of anti-Catholicism in the Bush campaign.[16]

The calls to Catholic voters, made on primary day and the day before, elicited an attempt by Bush to reassure Catholics that he was their friend and that he welcomed their support. The Bush campaign electronically mailed nine news releases with statements from nine Republican governors (many Catholic) denouncing the McCain phone calls. In addition, Bush aides released a similar statement from Tom Monaghan, founder of Domino's Pizza and a Catholic conservative who is a benefactor of Catholic causes in the Detroit area. "As a Roman Catholic," Monaghan stated, "I am offended that my faith is being used as a negative smear tactic to divide people in a political campaign."[17] Finally, the Bush campaign released a script of the phone call:

> Governor George Bush has campaigned against Sen. John McCain by seeking the support of Southern fundamentalists who have expressed anti-Catholic views. Bob Jones has made strong anti-Catholic statements, including calling the pope anti-Christ, and the Catholic Church a satanic cult. Governor Bush has stayed silent.[18]

McCain won the Michigan primary, 51 to 43 percent (with 5 percent for Keyes).[19] He was also victorious in his home state of Arizona. In Michigan, voters allied with the Religious Right backed Bush, 66 to 25 percent; those not so allied backed McCain, 60 to 36 percent. As for Roman Catholics, it is difficult to tell how many Catholics voted for McCain and how many for Bush; there are no CNN exit poll data on Catholic voting, and even the Michigan newspaper polls neglected to ask detailed questions about religious affiliation that would provide data on how Catholics actually voted.[20] In any case, McCain's double victory in Michigan and Arizona on February 22, 2000, revived his campaign and suggested that Bush was not invincible.

Bush emerged from the Michigan contest on the defensive. On the evening of his defeat, he loudly proclaimed at a press conference, "Let me make it crystal clear. I reject bigotry, I reject prejudice, I repudiate anti-Catholicism and racism." Asked about the Bob Jones visit, he said, "I don't make any apologies for what I do on the campaign trail." Asked if he repudiated the recorded message that Robertson had put out against McCain, he said he did not know the content of the message, then quickly switched the focus to McCain's calls to Catholics: "I repudiate the phone calls that came in accusing me of being an anti-Catholic bigot."[21]

A curious thing was happening in these Republican primaries. Bush, the candidate of "compassionate conservatism" who could hold the center and appeal to moderates, was winning primaries by appealing strongly to the Christian Right and to anti-abortion voters. McCain, the candidate with an eighteen-year conservative record of congressional voting, was appealing to the center and winning the votes of Republican moderates, pro-choice voters, and large numbers of independents and Democrats in open primaries. It appeared that the Bush campaign had tacked so far to the right to attract conservative evangelicals that the Texas governor was in danger of losing his centrist appeal to moderates in both parties. Former Republican National Committee chairman Rich Bond lamented that Bush's rightward drift was alienating the political center: "I think he can get it back. . . . But he makes it much harder with these Bob Jones and Pat Robertson episodes, which make people from my background—Northeast, blue-collar, former Democrat, Catholic—very uncomfortable. We count, too."[22]

On Bush's major speech at Bob Jones University, Bond had this to say: "Here's what bothers me about that whole thing, and I know I'm on the record, but I feel strongly about sending this message. When George wants to be persuasive, from a conservative point of view, he talks about changing people's hearts, but when there came an opportunity to ask conservatives to change their hearts, he didn't take it at Bob Jones."[23]

Coming from a Republican Party official, this was astonishing. Other Republicans who had contributed large sums to the Bush campaign began to wonder why Bush had spent most of the seventy million dollars in his fabled war chest and yet had been unable to put this McCain insurgency down. In retrospect, of course, we might say that from this point forward, Bush would have the advantage, since most of the remaining primaries were closed (that is, open only to registered Republican party members). Closed primaries played to Bush's strength (in appealing to the party base) and to McCain's weakness.

The Remaining Primaries

One week after the Michigan contest, in late February, primaries were held in Virginia, North Dakota, and Washington. Of these, the most important was Virginia. Bush had campaigned hard in Virginia, which, of course, numbers a large contingent of Christian Right voters. With the aid of the Christian Coalition and its allies, Bush defeated McCain 53 to 44 percent (with Keyes at 3 percent).[24] For his part, McCain's speech criticizing Robertson and Falwell seems to have hurt him in Virginia, the home turf of both the Robertson and Falwell organizations—no surprise there.

But the controversy over Bush's appearance at Bob Jones University refused to go away. Concerned that Bush's vote-getting ability could be hurt in crucial primaries in states with large Catholic constituencies, the Bush campaign took steps to control the political damage. In a letter to Cardinal John O'Connor (the cardinal archbishop died on May 3), Bush expressed regret for not speaking out against racial and religious intolerance during his visit to Bob Jones. "On reflection, I should have been more clear in disassociating myself from anti-Catholic sentiments and racial prejudice. It was a missed opportunity, causing needless offense, which I deeply regret."

Much of Bush's letter, however, rejected "guilt by association," which is how he characterized the criticism of his appearance at BJU. Stating that he had "profound respect for the Catholic Church," he expressed sympathy for, and sought to ally himself with, the Catholic tradition of concern for social justice. He cited Cardinal O'Connor's "long friendship with my family" and pointed out that his brother, Gov. Jeb Bush of Florida, was a Catholic married to a Catholic.[25] There was no public response from Cardinal O'Connor, who was gravely ill with a brain tumor and could no long preside at services.

In trying to allay mounting criticism of his visit to Bob Jones, the Bush campaign was aware that Catholics in New York make up an estimated 46 percent of the Republican electorate there. As a strategist for New York Governor George Pataki (a Bush supporter) remarked, "You can't win the New York Republican primary without the Catholic vote—it can't be done."[26] The same was true in many other major primary states with large Catholic populations.

"Super Tuesday," March 7, 2000, featured eleven Republican primaries in such large states as New York, California, Ohio, Missouri, Georgia, Massachusetts, Maryland, Maine, Vermont, Rhode Island, and Connecticut. Five more states held caucuses: Minnesota, Hawaii, Idaho, North Dakota, and Washington (although the Republicans had caucuses only in Minnesota). This, in the opinion of some observers, was the closest the United States had ever come to holding a national primary to choose the major parties' presidential candidates.

Bush won decisive victories in the largely closed GOP primaries on Super Tuesday. McCain took only four small New England states. Moreover, by this time the exit polls were tracking the Catholic vote, and they showed that Bush did well among Catholic Republican voters. In California, New York, Ohio, Missouri, Maryland, and Georgia, he carried the Catholic vote. McCain took the Catholic vote in the four states he won—Connecticut, Massachusetts, Rhode Island, and Vermont. In Maine, Bush won the primary, 51 to 44 percent (with Keyes at 3 percent), but McCain won the Catholic vote, 49 to 44 percent. However, two-thirds of Maine's Republican voters were Protestant, and they voted heavily for Bush, 58 to 39 percent, thereby offsetting McCain's attractiveness to Catholic voters.[27]

In fact, comparison of the Protestant and Catholic votes in almost all the Super Tuesday Republican primaries showed significant differences in how they voted. In ten of the eleven GOP primaries, proportionately more Protestants than Catholics voted for Bush. Only in Georgia did the percentage of Catholics who voted for Bush exceed the percentage of Protestants (see table 5.1 for exit poll results).

On March 10, McCain suspended his campaign. March 14 featured six more primaries—in Texas, Florida, Louisiana, Tennessee, Oklahoma, and Mississippi. At least three of these states had significant Catholic populations: Texas (24.7 percent), Florida (13.9 percent), and Louisiana (30.6 percent). Bush won heavily in all three of these states but again attracted fewer Catholic than Protestant voters.

CATHOLIC REACTION TO THE CONTROVERSY OVER THE BUSH VISIT TO BOB JONES UNIVERSITY

Reactions of Catholics to the BJU controversy were varied. The Protestant-Catholic differential in voting, even in those states where both groups voted

Table 5.1. Comparison of Catholic and Protestant Votes in GOP Primaries on "Super Tuesday," March 7, 2000

State	Calif.	Conn.	Ga.	Me.	Md.	Mass.	Mo.	N.Y.	Ohio	R.I.	Vt.
% Catholic	21	42	13	24	30	46	26	50	25	50	31
Bush-McCain	59–38	47–49	70–27	44–49	56–36	32–65	56–37	52–43	53–41	33–65	34–61
% Protest.	64	47	80	66	57	38	65	39	65	36	55
Bush-McCain	62–32	49–44	68–27	58–39	59–33	36–59	61–31	55–39	60–35	47–51	42–54

Source: CNN exit polls. Website address: www.cnn.com/ELECTIONS/2000/primaries.
Notes: In New York, Jewish voters constituted 6 percent of GOP primary voters; they voted 28 percent Bush, 58 percent McCain.
 In Georgia, Keyes won 3 percent of the Catholic vote and 5 percent of the Protestant vote.
 In Connecticut, Jewish voters were 4 percent of Republican voters; but no breakdown of their vote was given. The overall Connecticut GOP primary results were very close. McCain won 49 percent to Bush's 46 percent (with 3 percent for Keyes). Keyes won 2 percent of the Catholic vote and 4 percent of the Protestant vote.

overwhelmingly for the same candidate, suggests that Catholics were affected to some degree by Bush's admitted error in not separating himself from the university's negative views on Roman Catholicism and interracial dating.

At the same time, many Catholics either had not heard of BJU or were unaware of its criticism of Catholicism. To some extent, the national media did a disservice to the public and to the university by quoting remarks of its current president, Bob Jones III, without explaining the theological rationale underlying the university's hostility to Catholicism.[28]

Some Catholics were surprised by the controversy and said they did not regard George W. Bush as anti-Catholic. A typical remark was that of Maureen Fiedler, a progressive Catholic nun in the Washington, D.C., area who hosts a talk-radio show, *Faith Matters*. "Where did all this come from?" she asked. "I don't for one minute think that George Bush is anti-Catholic. I don't agree with him on anything, but I don't think he is anti-Catholic."[29]

Other Catholics suggested that other issues in the campaign were more important as criteria for evaluating Bush's candidacy. Bishop Thomas V. Daily of Brooklyn said that while he considered the university's rhetoric offensive, "it's a matter of praying for them so they come to see the truth." Far more troubling, in his view, was Governor Bush's record on capital punishment. In recent years, Catholic papal and Episcopal leaders had become increasingly critical of the death penalty, largely because of unfairness in how it was administered. However, since Bush became governor in 1994, Texas had executed over 130 convicts. Bishop Daily suggested that a more meaningful way to assess Bush's qualifications for office was to look at his stance on the death penalty and on other issues of immediate concern to Brooklyn: immigration, poverty, health care, and education.[30]

Some Catholic politicians took great exception to Bush's actions. I have already noted the reaction of Rich Bond, former chairman of the Republican National Committee, to Bush's visit to BJU. Another Republican, Congressman Peter King (R-N.Y.), a Catholic from a heavily Catholic district, shifted his support from Bush to McCain. Speaking on national television about Bush's appearance at Bob Jones, King said, "To me, that shows a clear lack of judgment, and also, quite frankly, a lack of moral compass. Bush is not anti-Catholic. But he is willing to work with people who are anti-Catholics. He is willing to tolerate people who are anti-Catholic."[31] As for Democrats, a typical remark came from Sen. Joseph Biden (D-Del.): "I'm offended as a Catholic; I'm offended as a supporter of civil rights; I'm just flat out offended. It should haunt them. And it will haunt them."[32]

William Donohue, head of the Catholic League for Religious and Civil Rights, a New York–based group that fights anti-Catholic discrimination, criticized Bush for his appearance at Bob Jones. He stopped after Bush's letter to O'Connor was made public, explaining, "One of the great touchstones of

Catholicism is forgiveness for the wrongdoer who admits that he or she is wrong, and there's nothing to be gained by beating this dead horse." Nonetheless, Donohue observed that in his view, anti-Catholic bigotry was a serious problem in fundamentalist Christian circles, one that Catholic Republicans could not afford to ignore (no matter how badly they wanted the GOP to win the White House). He noted that Catholic voters generally "are up for grabs. I think Bush has alienated them."[33]

But Charles Colson, chairman of Prison Fellowship and once special counsel to President Richard Nixon during the Watergate era, wrote in a *New York Times* op-ed essay that Catholics and evangelicals "stand shoulder to shoulder together as the most significant religious bloc in America" in the battle against cultural permissiveness. While Colson did not defend the views of Bob Jones and thought Bush's visit to the school was "ill-advised," he thought the BJU controversy was the result of a divisive tactic, a calculated effort to undermine the "growing alliance" between conservative Roman Catholics and evangelical Protestants.[34]

Still other conservative commentators sought to minimize what had become an embarrassing incident for the Bush campaign. The Rev. Richard Neuhaus, editor of *First Things*, a neoconservative monthly, said he considered Bush's appearance at the university unimportant. "Everybody speaks at Bob Jones," he said. "It's a major center down there, and politicians make speeches where they have crowds." Kate O'Beirne, Washington editor for *The National Review*, called the McCain ads "shameless Catholic baiting" and said, "It's a rare Catholic who even cares about Bob Jones University."[35]

In a more thoughtful analysis, Peter Steinfels, former chief religion correspondent for the *New York Times*, wrote that "anti-Catholicism would be a worthy subject for study and debate. . . . But the place to begin is not Bob Jones University." In his view, "the Catholic Church takes more nasty hits weekly on cable television than yearly from Bob Jones." Steinfels used his biweekly column, *Beliefs,* to criticize the Democratic Party for its unqualified pro-choice position on abortion, a position that would disqualify any Catholic (and presumably pro-life) Democrat from Democratic Party nomination. He argued that the real source of contemporary anti-Catholicism in the United States was eighteenth-century Enlightenment rationalism, not sixteenth-century Reformation theology.

> The anti-Catholic animus rooted in the political polemics of the 18th-century Enlightenment and the cultural polemics of 19th-century American nativism have long since taken over all the traditional themes: The church is an authoritarian monolith; its doctrines are hopelessly premodern; its rites are colorful but mindless; its sexual standards are unnatural, repressive and hypocritical; its congregations are anti-Semitic and racist; its priests are harsh and predatory; its grip on the minds of believers is numbing. These themes still ring in some fundamentalist pulpits. But they are far more apt to be interjected into the more adult

sitcoms and late-night comedy, and to be reflected in films, editorials, art, fiction and memoirs considered enlightened and liberating.[36]

In Steinfels's view, the anti-Catholic animus of Bob Jones was relatively trivial when compared with "the constant pitter-patter of gibes, jokes, and sneers about Catholicism on television, in films, in celebrity interviews, in university and alternative newspapers." He also noted a kind of status ranking in the way Americans deal with cultural stereotypes: "If rebuking Bob Jones University is a low-cost way to oppose anti-Catholicism, the reason is that evangelical and fundamentalist Christians are farther down in the national pecking order of prejudices than Catholics." John Green, director of the Bliss Institute of Applied Politics at the University of Akron, made a similar observation, emphasizing that Protestant evangelicals see the Bob Jones controversy as an attack on them—not just as an issue involving two political candidates or as a matter of hostility to Catholicism.[37]

A recent Gallup poll tends to confirm Steinfels's view that anti-Catholicism of the Enlightenment-secular variety is more prevalent today than anti-Catholicism stemming from Reformation theology (the Bob Jones variety). Based on telephone interviews with a national sample of 1,024 adults in March 2000, Gallup found that roughly one-fourth of Americans have a negative view of the Catholic religion while nearly two-thirds view it favorably. The poll also found that contrary to widespread opinion that anti-Catholic bias exists disproportionately among evangelical Protestants, only 29 percent of born-again Christians described their opinion of Catholicism as "unfavorable." According to Gallup, "one of the biggest predictors of negative attitudes toward Catholics is an overall lack of personal religious faith or practice, rather than intense religious belief in a different religion." In other words, it is the seculars and the unchurched who view Catholicism unfavorably. Those who regard religion as unimportant, old-fashioned, or out of date tend to view Catholicism negatively.[38]

As indicated by the Catholic comments quoted here, Catholics were indeed surprised and offended by the Bob Jones controversy—although they also tended to minimize the long-term impact of the whole affair. However, Republicans generally and the Bush campaign in particular could not afford to be frivolous with Catholic expectations or with the Catholic vote. As we shall see, they scrambled to shore up support in the American Catholic community.

THE GOP REACTION TO THE BOB JONES CONTROVERSY

During the 2000 presidential campaign, the Republican Party consistently took steps to woo Catholic voters. In the wake of the Bob Jones controversy, Bush campaign handlers fell all over themselves trying to reassure Catholics that Bush was Catholic-friendly. They sought out Catholic forums and photo-ops, replete with church banners and Roman-collared clerics, to assure everyone that his presidency would not be an instrument of a dominant religious group—conservative evangelicals.[39] They set up a Catholic Task Force within the Republican National Committee to concentrate on winning "the Catholic vote" in the election.[40] The Republican-controlled Congress passed a resolution honoring the contributions of Catholic schools and voted to award the Congressional Gold Medal to Cardinal John O'Connor for his sixteen-year tenure as archbishop of New York. After charges of anti-Catholicism were raised in a bitter controversy over a new chaplain of the House of Representatives, Speaker Daniel Hastert (R-Ill.) appointed Father Daniel Coughlin of Chicago as chaplain, the first Roman Catholic priest ever to hold that post.[41]

For his part, George Bush repeatedly reminded voters that "my little brother and my sister-in-law are Catholic." He sent the letter to Cardinal O'Connor admitting that the visit to Bob Jones was a regrettable mistake. He also went on record opposing any downgrading of the Vatican's permanent-observer status at the United Nations.[42] He stressed his opposition to abortion, reminding listeners that he opposed "partial-birth" abortions, public funding of abortion, and *Roe v. Wade*.[43] He indicated that he would not permit any change in the Republican Party platform on abortion, which called for a ban on the practice, without exception, and for the appointment of judges who respect "the sanctity of innocent human life." Whenever the subject of school choice arose, Bush made sure to mention parochial schools as possible recipients of vouchers.

In short, the Bush campaign and the Republican Party made a major effort to attract Catholic voters. The establishment of the task force was particularly interesting. This unit, headed by Thomas P. Melady, former president of Sacred Heart University in Connecticut and ambassador to the Vatican in the Bush administration, began with a budget of four hundred thousand dollars, one full-time staff member, and a college intern. Founding members included such prominent Catholic Republicans as former Secretary of State Alexander Haig, Congressman Christopher Smith (R-N.J.), Bowie Kuhn (former baseball commissioner), Tom Monaghan, and co-chair Bonnie Robichaux Livingston (wife of former Rep. Robert Livingston, R-La.). The task force initially focused on the campaign to downgrade the Vatican's status at the United Nations from permanent observer to nongovernmental organization. Ultimately the group's goal was to bring back "Reagan Democrats" (those 57 percent of Catholics who voted for Ronald Reagan in the 1984 election) to the Republican Party.[44]

Melady's strategy was to emphasize the GOP's position on key Catholic issues such as school choice and abortion. Eliminating the right to abortion might be unrealistic, he recognized, but Republicans could keep trying to ban "partial-birth" abortion. Melady thought school choice was another area of agreement between the GOP and Catholic voters—whether through vouchers, charter schools, or more aid to parents who wish to send their children to private or parochial schools. Melady also emphasized Bush's approach to charitable giving and social action—the idea, endorsed by both Gore and Bush, that some health, educational, and welfare functions could be handed over to private, faith-based groups, who would receive federal subsidies.

Another Catholic businessman associated with the Republican effort to woo Catholics was Brian Tierney, an advertising executive from Philadelphia. Tierney owned a major public relations and advertising firm, Tierney Communications, which had designed and deployed the official Website for the Republican National Convention in Philadelphia. In late June, he joined the Catholic Task Force to do fund-raising and grassroots campaigning. Tierney, whose firm handled public relations for the Philadelphia archdiocese, got Philadelphia Cardinal Anthony Bevilacqua on stage in prime time at the Republican Convention and sprinkled the crowd with priests and nuns. Beginning with the convention, Tierney raised $1.7 million for the task force. He used that money for polling, direct mail, and phone banks in twelve states, including Florida. In the final weeks of the campaign, Tierney boarded his private plane to barnstorm for Bush, arguing that Bush's policies, including his tax cut, matched those of the church. According to one account, Tierney helped Bush win almost two million more Catholic votes than Bob Dole got in 1996 and rallied over a hundred thousand new Catholic votes for Bush in Florida.[45]

Republicans also tried to argue that Bush's big campaign theme, "compassionate conservatism," was rooted in Catholic social thought. Sen. Rich Santorum (R-Pa.) insisted that Bush's proposal for government funding of social service programs run by churches and other faith-based organizations exemplified the Catholic concept of *subsidiarity*—the idea that social problems are best understood and solved by the organizations and people closest to them. In his speeches, Bush often invoked *solidarity* and *the common good*, two other phrases central to Catholic social thought. Even Marvin Olasky, the evangelical University of Texas academic who wrote the 1992 book *The Tragedy of American Compassion*, noted: "Catholic social teachings and subsidiarity have been a strong strain in the shaping of compassionate conservatism. . . . [I]t has provided a structural framework."[46]

However, there were points of contrast between Catholics and the Republican Party. An obvious one was capital punishment, which Catholics oppose as part of a consistent ethic of respect for life. As Bishop Daily pointed out, Texas had executed a number of convicts since Bush became governor in 1994. When Bush addressed Catholic audiences, he was asked about abortion, but he was also questioned about the death penalty. For example, at the annual conference of the Catholic Press Association in May 2000, Bush was quoting papal encyclicals to the effect that "a truly welcoming society must be a culture of life" when a questioner raised the issue of the death penalty in Texas. Bush replied that capital punishment "sends a chilling message" that deters crime, and that he knew of not one innocent person whom the state of Texas had executed.[47]

UNPREDICTABLE CATHOLIC VOTERS

Several observations about the Catholic vote in presidential elections have become truisms. Political scientists remind us that Catholics do not vote as a bloc, that there really is no such thing as "the Catholic vote." As Appleby remarked, "Catholics are not monolithic voters unless faced by an appalling instance of anti-Catholic bigotry."[48] (It is questionable whether Bob Jones was such a case.) Catholics are pluralistic in their political allegiances and loyalties—as might be expected in such a large community.

A second truism is that Catholics have become "the quintessential swing voters" in American presidential elections. The majority of the Catholic vote is up for grabs in any given election; it cannot be taken for granted. One of the reasons Catholics have become such a critical constituency is the distinctiveness of the Catholic electorate. Unlike Jews, who are heavily Democratic, or evangelicals, who are heavily Republican, Catholic voters are an unusual mix of liberal and conservative. They tend to support simultaneously an activist government in economic matters (a Democratic tendency) and in moral matters (a Republican tendency). A Catholic citizen may vote Republican on the issue of abortion yet vote Democratic on social justice concern for the poor and minorities. So Catholic voters are conflicted voters, and it is hard for political professionals to know which issues are salient for Catholics or how best to tailor campaign appeals.

Catholics have become less partisan as they have assimilated into all areas of American society: politics, business, education, law, and the professions. The old New Deal identification of Catholic ethnic workers with the Democratic Party eroded over time to be replaced with a more fluid sense of political allegiance among white Catholics (Hispanic and African American Catholics remain more highly identified with the Democrats). A high-water mark for the Democratic Party was the 83 percent Catholic vote for Kennedy in 1960 (for obvious reasons); a high-water mark for the GOP was the 57 percent Catholic vote for Reagan in 1984. The fact is that, as illustrated by the career of former Pennsylvania Governor Robert Casey, many Catholic views do not fit neatly with those of either of the two major American political parties. Casey, a Democrat, was liberal on many social policy issues (education, health care, and welfare) but conservative or pro-life on abortion. As a result of his anti-abortion stance, he was denied an opportunity to address the 1992 Democratic convention.[49]

What all this means is that, in general, "Catholics as a group now seem more susceptible to candidate-centered and issue-specific appeals than they were when their partisan identification was stronger."[50] This has made it difficult for party strategists like Thomas Melady. GOP laissez-faire policies on the economy and health care may alienate just as many Catholics as do liberal views on abortion. Pro-life Catholics may gravitate to the GOP yet be put off by Bush's attitude toward the death penalty—which makes him appear to be a harsh, rather than a compassionate, conservative.

To complicate matters further, there are racial, ethnic, generational, and gender cleavages among the Catholic electorate. African Americans (6 percent of the 1996 Catholic vote) and Hispanic Catholics (10 percent of the 1996 Catholic vote) vastly preferred Clinton and Democratic congressional candidates to Dole and the GOP. Except for Cuban Americans, Hispanics traditionally vote Democratic, and they are the fastest-growing bloc of ethnic voters in the United States today, having increased from 22.4 million in 1990 to 35.3 million in the 2000 census.[51]

Generational differences may also affect Catholic voting. Older Catholics are more likely to vote Democratic, while younger Catholics are more willing to vote Republican in many cases. But, as David Leege has shown, while these younger Catholics may be drawn to the GOP on economic issues, they tend to hold much more "permissive" social and moral views than do most Republicans, especially Christian Coalition members. On issues of sexuality and reproduction, for example, these young Catholics are more pro-choice and more pro–gay rights than evangelicals, and they tend to flee to the Democratic Party if Republican rhetoric about "family values" gets too strident. Younger Catholics also tend to be irregular churchgoers who are less knowledgeable than their elders about the church's social teaching.[52]

Gender differences clearly affect the Catholic electorate. Since the 1984 election and the vice-presidential candidacy of Congresswoman Geraldine Ferraro, many Catholic women have remained firmly in the Democratic Party. Young Catholic women today tend to be highly educated, working in professional and managerial jobs; they have benefited from equal pay and affirmative action policies; and they tend to vote Democratic. As Leege notes, Catholic women have developed a political voice different from that of young Catholic men (who tend to gravitate toward the GOP).[53]

Recently, in an effort to better understand the Catholic electorate, researchers have distinguished churchgoing Catholics from self-identified but less observant Catholics. This research was prompted by the need to understand the decline among Catholics in Democratic Party identification, the movement of some Catholics to the Republican Party, and the greater flow of Catholics to the independent column. In fact, exit polls now routinely ask all voters about frequency of church attendance in order to gauge how intensity of religious observance influences voter choice.[54]

In the 2000 campaign, researchers studying Catholic voting behavior produced some interesting analyses. According to a 1999 national survey conducted for *Crisis* (a conservative Catholic monthly) by the Washington firm QEV Analytics, religiously active Catholics tended to be conservative, vote Republican, and be ripe for political alignment with born-again, evangelical Christians. Analysts for *Crisis* also distinguished "social justice Catholics," who believe government has a positive role and duty to care for the poor and vulnerable, from "social renewal Catholics," who believe that America is deteriorating morally and that federal government policies like welfare have exacerbated that moral decline. In Campaign 2000, where presidential character was one of the important issues, QEV Analytics suggested that religiously active, social-renewal Catholics were ripe for political mobilization by the Bush campaign and the Republican Party.[55]

Other researchers disputed this analysis, suggesting that issues of race and the economy accounted for Catholic voters' support of Nixon in 1972 and Reagan in 1984, and that, in any case, it is very difficult to show that religion predicts how one will vote.[56] Still others suggested that sociological changes among Catholics who became affluent, and moved to the suburbs, and away from ethnic urban neighborhoods, might account for changes in Catholic partisan identification as well as for the volatility of Catholic voting patterns.[57]

All this suggests how pluralistic and diverse the American Catholic electorate is. In fact, the political complexity of Catholic voters reflects, to some extent, internal divisions within the American Catholic community. Disagreements over the legacy of reforms of the Second Vatican Council (an ecumenical council of the world's Catholic bishops that met in Rome from 1962 to 1965 and introduced major changes in liturgy and other areas) continue to influence church life. Issues of abortion, contraception, sexuality, and the role of women in the church remain controversial. Liberal Catholics tend to emphasize the church's teachings on social justice in state and society, while conservative Catholics tend to stress issues of personal morality.

These divisions within the American Catholic community surfaced briefly in the midst of Campaign 2000 when two opposing groups ran full-page advertisements simultaneously in the *New York Times*. Liberal Catholics signed on to an ad sponsored by Catholics Speak Out (CSO), a Maryland-based organization supporting church reform. The Catholic League for Religious and Civil Rights, a Manhattan-based office whose program opposes anti-Catholicism in the arts (cinema, drama, museum exhibits), ran an op-ed, quarter-page advertisement on the op-ed page in opposition to the CSO's item.

The CSO's "Open Letter to Candidates for Office from Roman Catholic Voters" was accompanied by the names of 2,700 individual and sixty-seven organizational signers and 150 non-Catholics. The open letter called for campaign finance reform, an increase in the minimum wage, universal health care, arms control, reform of Social Security and Medicare, a moratorium on the death penalty, fair immigration policies, full civil rights for gays and lesbians, gun control, and cancellation of developing nations' debts. The letter declared that as Catholic voters, the signers did not agree with the Catholic bishops on certain issues, notably abortion and contraception. It called on candidates to "support programs that make contraceptives, including emergency contraception, easily available to women and men here and in poor countries." The ad noted that the "signers . . . hold a range of views on the morality and legality of abortion, but we all seek to reduce its frequency. Catholic opinion is not monolithic on this subject."[58]

The Catholic League's own quarter-page item, entitled "Who Speaks for Catholics?" and signed by Donohue alone, called CSO a "radical fringe group" of dissenters who "seek to define an alleged Catholic diversity by boasting that it is legitimate Catholic teaching to be either pro-life or pro-abortion." "It is not," the ad said. "Just as there are not diverse Catholic teachings on genocide or racial discrimination, there is no legitimate diversity in Catholic teaching on abortion. All three are social evils." Calling CSO an intellectually dishonest organization, Donohue stated, "I think they have a tremendous amount of arrogance to speak with such an authoritative voice for the Church."[59]

The fact that one group chose to question the orthodoxy of another group in this intramural exchange is an indication of the extent of disagreement within the American Catholic community, a disagreement that influences politicians' efforts to attract Catholic votes.

OFFICIAL CHURCH ACTIVITY IN THE 2000 PRESIDENTIAL CAMPAIGN

Catholic church leaders were also active in Campaign 2000. The National Conference of Catholic Bishops issued its quadrennial statement of political responsibility, which discussed the many issues of the election.[60] Individual bishops also spoke out: Cardinal Bevilacqua appeared on stage at the Republican Convention, while Cardinal Roger Mahoney of Los Angeles appeared at the Democratic Convention, where he condemned abortion.

As Election Day neared, Archbishop Edward Egan sent a letter to the 413 parishes of the New York archdiocese bluntly urging 2.4 million Catholic parishioners to vote for candidates in local, state, and national races who "share our commitment to fundamental rights for the unborn."[61] He also urged Catholics to support candidates who favored school vouchers. In a New Jersey parish on the Sunday before Election Day, bishops' statements were inserted in parish bulletins urging Catholics to vote and singling out "protecting the life of the unborn child as a priority that requires special attention and wholehearted effort."[62]

But while Catholic voters respect their bishops' advice on moral issues, many Catholics reserve to themselves the right and the duty, in a democracy, to make responsible judgments about sound public policy. This was evident in a letter to the editor of the *New York Times* that appeared the day after Archbishop Egan's statement. Frank McNeirney of Bethesda, Maryland, wrote:

> Many Roman Catholics, myself included, agree with Archbishop Edward M. Egan of New York that working to stop abortions should be a priority. But we are convinced that simply voting for politicians who want to outlaw abortions may not be the best strategy.
>
> The history of Prohibition has shown us what happens when we enact laws that are certain to be ignored by a large segment of the population. A more effective way for Catholics to achieve their goal may be to elect candidates whose economic and social policies are likely to deter women from seeking abortions in the first place.[63]

Despite the desire of priests and bishops to issue voting instructions, the church has stopped short in most cases of endorsing or denouncing particular candidates (endorsement of political candidates could mean the end of the church's tax exemption). So the statements of clergy on a broad range of issues are strictly advisory. As Scott Appleby remarks, "In fact, Catholics are left with quite complicated decisions to make as to which candidates would be the true champion of the whole range of Catholic social and moral concerns."[64]

To summarize, what seems clear about the political behavior of American Catholics is the complexity of this large, diverse electorate and the volatility of Catholic voters. Yet no one underestimates the significance of "the Catholic vote." American Catholics are important in presidential elections, because these elections are won and lost in the Electoral College. Geographically and demographically, voting Catholics live mainly in states with large electoral votes, states where close elections are decided: California, New York, Texas, Florida, Pennsylvania, Ohio, Michigan, Illinois, New Jersey, Massachusetts, Wisconsin, Missouri. Most of these states have significant Catholic pluralities (see table 5.2). So, of course, the Bush campaign and the Republican Party—as well as the Democratic Party—had to worry about the Catholic vote. As Bush campaign manager Karl Rove put it, "Catholics [were] this year's soccer moms—the essential swing voters to whom rhetoric must be tailored."[65] Nevertheless, the question remains: How effective were Republican efforts to woo Catholic voters?

Table 5.2.   States with Highest Percentage of Catholics in Population

State	% Catholic	Electoral Votes	1996 Vote	2000 Vote
Rhode Island	63.7	4	Democratic	Gore
Massachusetts	48.9	12	Democratic	Gore
New Jersey	41.8	15	Democratic	Gore
Connecticut	40.9	8	Democratic	Gore
New York	39.8	33	Democratic	Gore
Wisconsin	31.7	11	Democratic	Gore
Illinois	31.5	22	Democratic	Gore
Louisiana	30.6	9	Democratic	Bush
Pennsylvania	29.6	23	Democratic	Gore
New Hampshire	28.1	4	Democratic	Bush
California	27.8	54	Democratic	Gore
Minnesota	26.4	10	Democratic	Gore
Texas	24.7	32	Republican	Bush
Michigan	23.4	18	Democratic	Gore
Ohio	19.7	21	Democratic	Bush
Missouri	16.1	11	Democratic	Bush
Florida	13.9	25	Democratic	Bush

Total: Seventeen states, with a total of 312 electoral votes.
Source: Matthew Brunson, ed., *2000 Catholic Almanac* (Huntington, Ind.: Our Sunday Visitor, 1999).

THE CATHOLIC VOTE IN THE 2000 ELECTION

In the 2000 presidential election, Catholics accounted for 26 percent of the electorate. Nationally, they voted for Gore by a margin of 50 percent to 47 percent (with 1 percent for Buchanan and 2 percent for Nader). Table 5.2 shows seventeen states with large Catholic pluralities and large numbers of electoral votes. Roughly 48 million Catholics, or 74 percent of the total population of sixty-two million American Catholics, live in these seventeen states. In the 1996 election, President Clinton won all these states except Texas. In 2000, Gore won eleven of these states, and Bush took six. Gore won California, New York, Illinois, Pennsylvania, Michigan, New Jersey, Minnesota, Massachusetts, Wisconsin, Connecticut, and Rhode Island—with a total of 210 electoral votes. Bush took Texas, Louisiana, Ohio, Missouri, New Hampshire, and eventually Florida—giving him 102 electoral votes.

One cannot assume, of course, that Catholic voters in a particular state voted the way a majority of the state's total population voted. For example, one cannot assume that New Jersey's Catholics voted mostly for Gore simply because a majority of New Jerseyans voted for Gore (56 to 41 percent). In fact, if we look at the exit polls for each state, we find that in the case of New Jersey, Catholics constituted 40 percent of the voters in 2000 and broke for Bush over Gore (51 to 47 percent).[66] Catholic voters in Michigan and Minnesota also preferred Bush to Gore by slim margins, even though statewide, both were in the Gore column. The opposite was true in New Hampshire; Bush won the popular vote and the electoral vote, but Gore won the New Hampshire Catholic vote (49 to 47 percent).[67]

In fact, if we look at the Catholic vote in the same seventeen states, the exit polls show that Gore won the Catholic vote in nine of these states while Bush took a majority of Catholic votes in eight states (three by thin margins). Approximately thirty-seven million Catholics reside in the eleven states won by Gore, while about eleven million Catholics live in the six states won by Bush. Although Bush did well among Catholics in Texas, Florida, Missouri, and Ohio, Gore won the Catholic vote overall and took most of the states with large Catholic populations.

Voter News Service exit polls analyzing the 2000 vote by religion show that Protestants (54 percent of the electorate) voted for Bush over Gore, 56 to 42 percent. Catholics, a quarter of the electorate, voted for Gore over Bush, 50 to 47 percent. Jews (4 percent of the electorate) voted overwhelmingly for Gore. Gore also took a sizable majority of the votes of "other" religious Americans and of nonreligious, secular voters, 60 to 30 percent (with the remaining votes going largely to Nader).

Christian conservatives constituted 14 percent of the electorate and voted overwhelmingly for Bush. African Americans, 10 percent of the electorate, backed Gore by a margin of nine to one. At 7 percent of the electorate, Hispanics, who are 80 percent Catholic, supported Gore two to one. With Bush winning a majority of Protestant voters but losing to Gore among all other categories, we see how close the election was.

In the 2000 election, whites constituted roughly 80 percent of the electorate, with the other 20 percent composed of African Americans, Asians, Hispanics, and other minorities. As Andolina and Wilcox show (in chapter 6), Bush carried a majority of regular churchgoing white mainline Protestants, white evangelical Protestants, and Catholics. The white Catholic vote was close, with Bush winning 52 percent and Gore taking 45 percent. By contrast, Hispanic Catholics went overwhelmingly for Gore, 76 to 24 percent.[68]

CONCLUSION: CATHOLICS AS QUINTESSENTIAL SWING VOTERS

While Al Gore won a majority of the Catholic vote nationwide, George Bush and the Republican Party made some inroads among white Catholic voters. Whether this is temporary or lasting only time will tell. Bush attracted only one of every four Hispanic votes, and Hispanics are becoming an increasingly larger portion of the American Catholic community; we know from the 2000 census that they now exceed African Americans as the largest minority in the country.[69] Some have said that while Gore had a slim edge nationally, the Catholic vote in the 2000 election was pretty evenly divided between Bush and Gore.[70] If so, then once again Catholics had proved themselves to be a bellwether constituency within the American electorate. Their split perhaps mirrored the closeness of the general election—a tight race in both the Electoral College and in the popular vote, although in the end Gore led in the national poll by 540,000 votes and Bush led in the Electoral College by four votes. In the aftermath of the 2000 election, Catholic voters remain quintessential swing voters.

It is clear that the controversy over Bush's appearance at Bob Jones University did not have much resonance with Catholic voters. In a national poll of likely Catholic voters conducted in October 2000 by Belden, Russonello & Stewart, a public opinion research firm in Washington, D.C., analysts found that only 9 percent of Catholic voters worried "very much" that "candidates for office this year are anti-Catholic," and that another 19 percent worried "somewhat." Seventy-two percent did not worry at all about anti-Catholic candidates. Thus, although concerns about anti-Catholicism had been raised during the primaries, it was not on the minds of Catholics by October.[71]

The same public opinion poll found that despite the efforts of bishops and priests to influence Catholic laity to vote for candidates who were antiabortion and pro-vouchers, only 5 percent of Catholic voters said the views of the bishops were "very important" to them in deciding whom to vote for in the 2000 election. "Another 20 percent said they were somewhat important, and 75 percent said the views of the bishops were unimportant."

In this poll, taken three weeks before the general election, Catholic voters prioritized the issues as: protecting Social Security and Medicare (46 percent), improving the health care system (45 percent), improving public education (39 percent), fighting crime (35 percent), protecting American jobs (31 percent), and promoting moral values in the country (31 percent). They were less influenced by moral issues important to the church hierarchy; for example, majorities of Catholic voters in this survey held pro-choice views on abortion, supported the death penalty, and believed that physician-assisted suicide should be allowed for terminally ill patients. The survey analysts concluded that while American Catholics identify with the Catholic church for religion, the vast majority of Catholic voters do not look to the church or the bishops for political guidance.[72]

Without question, Catholics continue to dominate numerically in the U.S. Congress. Of the 535 members of the 107th Congress, 150 are Roman Catholic, followed by seventy-two Baptists and, in third place, sixty-five Methodists. Catholic members of Congress declined by one but remain by far the largest religious group in Congress (they have been the largest religious bloc since 1964). Despite Republican campaign efforts aimed at Catholic voters, the Catholic delegation numbers ninety-one Democrats and fifty-nine Republicans.[73]

In the last four decades of presidential elections, American Catholics have been a bellwether of the nation's voting. Candidates who win the Catholic vote seem to win the White House as well. According to exit polls, a majority of Catholics voted for Richard Nixon in 1972, Jimmy Carter in 1976, Ronald Reagan in 1980 and 1984, and Bill Clinton in 1992 and 1996. (The figures for the 1988 election of George H. W. Bush are conflicting; Gallup showed Dukakis the winner, 51 to 49 percent, while a *New York Times*/CBS poll showed Bush the winner, 52 to 47 percent.)[74] In 2000, Catholics favored the Democratic candidate, Al Gore, by the margin of 50 percent to 47 percent. Once again the Catholic vote proved to be a marker. This time, the closeness of the Catholic vote reflected the tightness of the race generally. Catholics favored Gore, who won the most popular votes. But in this extraordinary election, Bush prevailed in the Electoral College.

POSTSCRIPT: CATHOLICS AND THE BUSH ADMINISTRATION

Distinctions between liberal and conservative Catholics were reflected in the 2000 election campaign in the ads run by Catholics Speak Out and the Catholic League. With Bush's victory, conservative Catholics now have access to the White House, just as liberal Catholics—Bishop Joseph Sullivan of Brooklyn, Sister Maureen Fiedler of the Quixote Center in Maryland, and Bishop Walter Sullivan of Richmond, Virginia—had it during the Clinton administration. Conservative and neoconservative Catholics advised Bush during the very early stages of his campaign. Richard Neuhaus of *First Things,* Deal Hudson of *Crisis,* and John DiIulio, whom Bush appointed to head his new White House Office of Faith-Based and Community Initiatives, tutored Bush in Catholic social doctrine in the period leading up to the Iowa caucuses and the New Hampshire primary.

The access of conservative Catholics and conservative evangelicals was clear in the nomination of John Ashcroft to be attorney general. Bush's original choice for the post was Montana Governor Marc Racicot, a Bush friend and spokesman during the Florida recount. While conservatives were pleased that Racicot was a self-described "pro-life Catholic" who bragged of signing regulatory reforms of abortion in Montana, they objected to "his criticism of Henry Hyde's Judiciary Committee during the impeachment hearings, his apparent disdain for the Religious Right, and his proposal to add sexual orientation to Montana's hate-crimes law following the murder of Matthew Shepard." Religious conservatives, both Catholic and Protestant, lobbied intensively against Racicot's nomination. According to the *Weekly Standard,* "They recruited pro-life Princeton professor Robert George to draft a paper on Racicot. George's dispatch was on its way in 24 hours to Bush political adviser Karl Rove in Austin. . . . In a conference call with Rove, nearly every social conservative on the line turned thumbs down on Racicot. He still probably could have had the job, but facing strong conservative objections [he] decided he didn't want it. Ashcroft . . . was the clear favorite of the religious conservatives. Bush went along, turning out to be more responsive than social conservatives had dreamed possible."[75] Neoconservative Catholics clearly have direct access to the White House in the Bush administration.

NOTES

1. National Conference of Catholic Bishops/United States Catholic Conference, "Faithful Citizenship: Civic Responsibility for a New Millennium," A Statement on Political Responsibility by the Administrative Board of the U.S. Catholic Bishops (Washington, D.C.: United States Catholic Conference, 1999), 28, note 6. See also Mitchell Benson, ed., *2000 Catholic Almanac* (Huntington, Ind.: Our Sunday Visitor, 2000). Prior to the quadrennial presidential elections, the American Catholic bishops issue a "Statement of Political Responsibility" discussing the many issues of the campaign. "Faithful Citizenship" is the Statement for the 2000 elections.

2. At the installation of Cardinal O'Connor's successor, Archbishop Edward Egan, on 19 June 2000, there was a similar gathering of high public officials: governors, mayors, Supreme Court Justice Antonin Scalia, former New York governors and mayors, such as David Dinkins and Ed Koch.

3. On the World Wide Web: www.cnn.com/ELECTION/2000/primaries/NH/results.html.

4. Interview with Dr. Bob Jones III, *Larry King Live,* March 3, 2000. See www.cnn.com/TRANSCRIPTS/0003/03/lkl.00.html.

5. Gustav Niebuhr, "On the Campus in the Center of the Storm, Life Goes On," *New York Times,* 5 March 2000, National Report, 22.

6. *The Star-Ledger,* 14 March 2000, 7. This is the old *Newark Star-Ledger.* It styles itself "the Newspaper for New Jersey" and addresses national issues as well as all statewide and county news (as well as local news in daily "special editions"). It is the newspaper of record in New Jersey. Ashcroft's appearance at Bob Jones University came back to haunt him during Senate hearings on his confirmation as attorney general in the new Bush administration. See Neil A. Lewis, "Much-Sought Speech by Ashcroft Found: Senate Panel Will Get Copy of Comments at Bob Jones University," *New York Times,* 12 January 2001, A18.

7. Private communication with James Guth, professor of political science, Furman University, Greenville, South Carolina. See also James Guth, "Letter from Greenville: Living with Bob Jones," *The Christian Century,* 22–29 March 2000, 328–29. Also see his essay on the congressional elections of 1994 in Mark Rozell, ed., *God at the Grassroots: The Christian Right in the 1994 Elections* (Lanham, Md.: Rowman & Littlefield, 1995).

8. From the Website of Bob Jones University, www.bju.edu.

9. Frank Bruni and Alison Mitchell, "Bush and McCain Scurry toward Showdown," *New York Times,* 18 February 2000, A25. Officially, Dodson did not endorse anyone in the South Carolina GOP primary.

10. John Hassell, "A Bristling Bush and McCain Flash Anger in South Carolina Debate," *The Star-Ledger*, 16 February 2000, 1.

11. David Fireston and Alison Mitchell, "In Debate, McCain and Bush Clash over Tactics," *International Herald Tribune*, 17 February 2000, 3. Alan Keyes did appear at BJU and did take exception to the two BJU views and policies in question. See Guth, "Letter from Greenville: Living with Bob Jones," 329.

12. On the World Wide Web: www.cnn.com/ELECTION/2000/primaries/SC/results.html.

13. James Bennet, "Evangelist Goes on the Attack to Help Bush," *New York Times*, 22 February 2000, A1. For Rudman's reaction to the Robertson ad, see Carey Goldberg, "Advising McCain, Rudman Is Happily Back in the Fray," *New York Times*, 26 February 2000, A9.

14. Alison Mitchell with Frank Bruni, "Bush and McCain Swap Strategies for Next Battle," *New York Times*, 21 February 2000, A12.

15. "McCain Minces No Words in Attacks," *New York Times*, 22 February 2000, A17.

16. David Barstow, "Bush Aide Says McCain Misled Public on Calls," *New York Times*, 27 February 2000, 33. According to this report, the McCain phone calls originated in this way. "Aides for McCain said inspiration for the calls came from a handful of political amateurs. Five days before the Michigan primary[,] . . . a group of McCain volunteers began calling Catholic friends and neighbors, telling them that Mr. Bush had given a speech at Bob Jones University. Within days, immediately after Mr. Bush had defeated Mr. McCain in a bitter South Carolina primary battle with the help of Christian Coalition and anti-abortion phone banks, the McCain campaign recognized the effectiveness of the Michigan phone calls and decided to expand on them. Aides drafted a telephone script, bought lists of Catholic voters and contracted with a telemarketing company, Conquest Communications of Richmond, Virginia, that on Monday, the day before the primary, called 24,000 Roman Catholic households in Michigan. The campaign spent $8,000 on the calls."

17. Frank Bruni, "Bush Angry over Calls to Michigan Catholics," *New York Times*, 23 February 2000, A17.

18. Bruni, "Bush Angry over Calls to Michigan Catholics."

19. On the World Wide Web: www.cnn.com/ELECTION/2000/primaries/MI/results.html.

20. On the World Wide Web: www.cnn.com/ELECTION/2000/primaries/MI/poll.rep.htm. For information about Catholic voting in Michigan and the failure of polling organizations to ask questions about denominational affiliation in the Michigan exit polls, I am grateful to Mark Rozell and John Green (private communication).

21. Frank Bruni, "Right-Wing Baggage Puts Drag on Bush Caravan," *New York Times*, 24 February 2000, A22. Earlier, Bush was asked whether voters might conclude that he was not an ardent foe of racial and religious intolerance. Bush replied, "Don't you judge my heart based upon giving a speech at a university." *New York Times*, 18 February 2000, A25.

22. Bruni, "Right-Wing Baggage Puts Drag on Bush Caravan."

23. Bruni, "Right-Wing Baggage Puts Drag on Bush Caravan."

24. On the World Wide Web: www.cnn.com/ELECTION/2000/primaries/VA/results.html.

25. Frank Bruni with Nicholas D. Kristof, "Bush Rues Failure to Attack Bigotry in Visit to College," *New York Times*, 28 February 2000, A1. The full text of Bush's letter to Cardinal O'Connor is on A12.

26. Richard L. Berke, "Regrets Well Placed, If Questionably Timed," *New York Times*, 28 February 2000, A12.

27. For statistics in this paragraph, see www.cnn.com/ELECTION/2000/primaries.

28. Notable exceptions to media superficiality about Bob Jones University were few. Gustav Niebuhr of the *New York Times* wrote informative, balanced articles about the university, and Larry King of CNN interviewed Bob Jones III, president of BJU, on March 3, 2000. For another balanced account, see Guth, "Letter from Greenville: Living with Bob Jones," 328–29.

29. Interview with Maureen Fiedler, S.L. (Sisters of Laretto), at the Quixote Center in Hyattsville, Maryland (near Washington, D.C.), 7 April 2000. Fiedler, a progressive Catholic and feminist nun, is a political activist who has a Ph.D. in political science from Georgetown University. She has been a national commentator for NPR and now hosts *Faith Matters*, a religious talk-radio program that airs weekly.

30. Diana Jean Schemo, "Catholics Minimize Impact of Bush Visit to Bob Jones," *New York Times*, 2 March 2000, B5.

31. The *Lehrer News Hour*, PBS, 29 February 2000. See also Randal C. Archibold, "New York Lawmaker Switches to McCain," *New York Times*, 21 February 2000, A12.

32. Berke, "Regrets Well Placed, If Questionably Timed."

33. Diana Jean Schemo, "Catholics Minimize Impact of Bush Visit to Bob Jones," *New York Times*, B5.

34. Charles W. Colson, "Dividing the Faithful Won't Work," *New York Times*, 2 March 2000, A27.

35. For the Neuhaus comment, see Diana Jean Schemo, "Catholics Minimize Impact of Bush Visit to Bob Jones," B5. Kate O'Beirne is quoted in Francis X. Clines, "Mixing God and Politics and Getting Burned," *New York Times*, 5 March 2000, sec. IV, 1.

36. Peter Steinfels, "Beliefs," *New York Times*, 4 March 2000, A13.

37. Steinfels, "Beliefs." John Green is quoted in Clines, "Mixing God and Politics and Getting Burned," 5.

38. "Anti-Catholic Bias Deepest among Unchurched," *The Catholic Advocate*, 12 April 2000, 12. This paper is the weekly publication of the Newark Roman Catholic archdiocese. The article was an Associated Press release.

39. Frank Bruni, "Using Signals and Cues to Project Bush's Image," *New York Times*, 19 March 2000, sec. I, 32.

40. "Republicans Scramble to Shore Up Pivotal Support among Catholics," *CQ Weekly*, 4 March 2000, 459–62. See also *The Catholic Advocate*, 12 April 2000, 12.

41. For a detailed chronology of this controversy, see "Republicans Scramble to Shore Up Pivotal Support among Catholics," 460–61.

42. Alison Mitchell, "Bush Sides with Vatican on Its Status at the UN," *New York Times*, 27 May 2000, A10. The Vatican (or the Holy See, as it is properly called) is not a member state of the United Nations but a nonmember with permanent observer status. No other world religion has this status; Switzerland is the only other permanent observer at the UN. Although the Holy See does not have voting power in the General Assembly, it has been given a vote in international conferences, such as the 1994 International Con-

ference on Population and Development in Cairo and the 1995 Fourth UN World Conference on Women in Beijing. The current controversy over the Vatican's status at the UN stems, in large part, from its political activism at these conferences on issues of family planning, sexuality, and abortion. Nearly four hundred organizations, including the nongovernmental organization Catholics for a Free Choice, and the International Planned Parenthood Federation, have asked UN Secretary-General Kofi Annan to review the status of the Holy See as a permanent observer. They argue that the Holy See is not a state but rather a religious headquarters. See M. C. Segers, "The Catholic Church as a Transnational Actor," paper presented at the Annual Conference of the American Political Science Association, Boston, 1998.

On February 16, 2000, Rep. Christopher H. Smith (R-N.J.) introduced a resolution (H Con Res 253) expressing Congress's opposition to any moves to end the Vatican's permanent observer status at the UN. Sen. Robert C. Smith (R-N.H.) introduced a similar "sense of Congress" resolution in the Senate. (Both are Catholic.) Vice President Al Gore and the Clinton administration supported permanent-observer status for the Holy See. See *Catholic New York* (weekly publication of the New York archdiocese), 2 March 2000, 9; also "Republicans Scramble to Shore Up Pivotal Support Among Catholics," 462.

43. According to Bush, the Supreme Court in *Roe v. Wade* "stepped across its bounds and usurped the right of legislatures." But when asked by a reporter whether he thought the Court's decision should be overturned, Bush said, "It should be up to each legislature." Despite the 2000 GOP platform's wording on abortion, Bush indicated that he supports exceptions to a ban on abortion in cases of rape, incest, and when the mother's life is at stake; and he also refused to vow that any judges he might nominate to the Supreme Court would be opposed to abortion. Bush seemed to be adopting in his public statements a carefully calibrated position on abortion, one designed to placate the Right and not alienate the Center. See Frank Bruni with Leslie Wayne, "Bush Firms Up 'Soft' Anti-Abortion Stance," *New York Times*, 22 January 2000, A1. See also Robin Toner, "Bush About to Walk Abortion Tightrope," *New York Times*, 12 June 2000, A26.

44. In the final weeks of the presidential campaign, the GOP spent four million dollars on mailings aimed at Catholics in blue-collar towns such as Flint, Michigan; Green Bay, Wisconsin; and Scranton, Pennsylvania. See Peter Spiegel, "Candidates Put Their All into Battle for Catholic Hearts," *Financial Times*, 31 October 2000, 5. See also "Republicans Scramble to Shore Up Pivotal Support among Catholics," 459–62, and *The Catholic Advocate,* 12 April 2000, 12.

45. Maximillian Potter, "Life of Brian," *Philadelphia Magazine* 92, no. 2 (February 2001): 88–97. See also Joe Nicholson, "Stop the Press," *Editor and Publisher,* 5 February 2001, 14–20; also Raymond A Schroth, "Stopping the Press," *National Catholic Reporter,* 2 March 2001, 10–11.

46. Franklin Foer, "Spin Doctrine: The Catholic Teachings of George W.," *The New Republic,* 5 June 2000, reprinted in *Conscience* 21, no. 3 (Autumn 2000): 18–23. According to Foer, Bush was tutored in Catholic social doctrine by Richard John Neuhaus, Deal Hudson, and John DiIulio. See also "Republicans Scramble to Shore Up Pivotal Support among Catholics," 459–62.

47. Alison Mitchell, "Bush Sides with Vatican on Its Status at the UN," *New York Times*, 27 May 2000, A10.

48. R. Scott Appleby, quoted by Clines, "Mixing God and Politics and Getting Burned," 5.

49. Mark Shields, "A Conservative in Name Only," *Washington Post*, 5 June 2000, A17. See also Steinfels, "Beliefs," B6. Former Governor Robert P. Casey of Pennsylvania died on 30 May 2000. See the obituary by Irvin Molotsky, "Former Gov. Robert P. Casey Dies at 68; Pennsylvania Democrat Opposed Abortion," *New York Times*, 31 May 2000, A20.

50. Stephen J. Wayne, *The Road to the White House 2000: The Politics of Presidential Elections* (New York: Bedford/St. Martin's, 2000), 90.

51. Eric Schmitt, "New Census Shows Hispanics Are Even with Blacks in U.S.," *New York Times*, 8 March 2001, A1. See also Michael Janofsky, "Candidates Courting Hispanic Vote," *New York Times*, 25 June 2000, Sunday national section, 14. In the 2000 election, exit polls showed that the vote by race was: 81 percent white, 10 percent African American, 7 percent Hispanic, 2 percent Asian, and 1 percent other. On the World Wide Web: www.cnn.com/ELECTION/2000/epolls/US/P000.html.

52. David C. Leege, "The Catholic Vote in '96: Can It Be Found in Church?" *Commonweal*, 27 September 1996, 11–18. See also the editorial in the same issue of *Commonweal*.

53. Leege, "The Catholic Vote in '96," 12 and 15. Leege restates this thesis in his "Divining the Electorate: Is There a Religious Vote?" *Commonweal*, 20 October 2000, 16–19.

54. John Green, Lyman Kellstedt, James Guth, and Corwin Smidt, "Who Elected Clinton: A Collision of Values," *First Things*, no. 75 (August–September 1997): 35–40; Leege, "Divining the Electorate," 16–19. Voter News Service exit polls asked, do you "attend religious services: more than weekly, weekly, monthly, seldom, never?" For a sample, see www.cnn.com/ELECTION/2000/epolls/US/P000.html.

55. Steven Wagner, "Catholics and Evangelicals: Can They Be Allies?" *Crisis* (January 2000): 12–17. This was part of a series on the Catholic vote in America; previous issues included "The Mind of the Catholic Voter" in *Crisis* (November 1998) and "The Heart of the Catholic Voter" in *Crisis* (June 1999). The editor of *Crisis*, Deal Hudson, is an informal adviser to the Bush campaign.

56. Leege, "Divining the Electorate," 16–19.

57. Gerald M. Pomper, *The Election of 1996: Reports and Interpretations* (Chatham, N.J.: Chatham House, 1997), 182. Pomper also suggests that the changing character of the Democratic Party was probably another reason for the erosion of Catholic support. "As the party placed less emphasis on economic and class issues, and more on matters of race, gender, and individual expression, it began to lose support among Catholics, who have always been relatively conservative on social issues such as personal morality, sexuality, and patriotism." For a general analysis of Catholic partisan identification, see William B. Prendergast, *The Catholic Voter in American Politics: The Passing of the Democratic Monolith* (Washington, D.C.: Georgetown University Press, 1999).

58. "An Open Letter to Candidates for Office from Roman Catholic Voters," sponsored by Catholics Speak Out, *New York Times*, 23 October 2000, A7.

59. Catholic League for Religious and Civil Rights, "Who Speaks for Catholics?" *New York Times*, 23 October 2000, Op-Ed, A23. See also John Burger, "Catholic

League Counters Catholics Speak Out Ad on Election," *Catholic New York*, 26 October 2000, 14.

60. "Faithful Citizenship: Civic Responsibility for a New Millennium." See also Benson, ed., *2000 Catholic Almanac*.

61. Eric Lipton, "Egan Delivers Blunt Message for Elections," *New York Times*, 30 October 2000, B1.

62. The 5 November 2000 Sunday service bulletin of St. Teresa of Avila Parish in Summit, New Jersey, for example, included an insert from Bishop James T. McHugh, "Bringing Respect for Human Dignity to Politics." The insert also included Bishop McHugh's "Choosing the Lesser Evil," a reflection on the dilemma of choosing between an unequivocally pro-choice candidate and a candidate who supports a woman's "right to choose" with qualifications. Catholics were urged to vote for the second candidate as the lesser evil. Bishop McHugh had been bishop of Camden, New Jersey, and at the time of the election was bishop of Rockville Centre, New York. Applying his distinction to the New York and New Jersey Senate races in 2000, the lesser evil would have been Republican Rick Lazio over Democrat Hillary Clinton, and Republican Bob Franks over Democrat Jon Corzine.

63. Frank McNeirney, "How Catholics Vote," letter to the editor, *New York Times*, 31 October 2000, A26.

64. Eric Lipton, "Archbishop Egan Urges Votes for Candidates Opposed to Abortion," *New York Times*, 30 October 2000, B4.

65. Franklin Foer, "Spin Doctrine: Bush's Debt to Catholicism," *Conscience* 21, no. 3 (Autumn 2000): 23.

66. On the World Wide Web: www.cnn.com/ELECTION/2000/epolls/NJ/P000.html. According to the Voter News Service, Catholics were the only religious group identified in the New Jersey exit poll of 1,573 respondents who voted mostly for Bush. Protestants, Jews, other believers, and seculars all voted mostly for Gore.

67. For New Hampshire, see www.cnn.com/ELECTION/2000/epolls/NH/P000.html (November 16, 2000). For Minnesota, see www.cnn.com/ELECTION/2000/epolls/MN/P000.html (16 November 2000). For Michigan, see http://www.cnn.com/ELECTION/2000/epolls/MI/P000.html (3 March 2001).

68. Voter News Service national exit poll of 13,130 respondents: see www.cnn.com/ELECTION/2000/epolls/US/P000.html. Religiously active white Catholics favored Bush, 57 to 43 percent. Less religiously active Catholics voted for Gore, 59 to 41 percent. See George Weigel, "Analysis of Voting Pattern Shows Church Attendance Makes Difference," *The Catholic Advocate*, 28 February 2001, 11. (Weigel is citing John Green's statistics for Election 2000.)

69. Susan Sachs, "Redefining Minority," *New York Times*, 11 March 2001, sec. IV, 1 and 4.

70. Andrew Sullivan, "Two Nations, Undivided," *New York Times Magazine*, 26 November 2000, sec. VI, 23–24.

71. John Russonello and Katya Balasubramanian, "Winning the Catholic Vote," *Conscience* 21, no. 4 (Winter 2000–2001): 2–5.

72. See John Russonello and Katya Balasubramanian, "Winning the Catholic Vote," 2–5. A second preelection survey of likely Catholic voters reached similar findings; this was conducted by the Center for Applied Research in the Apostolate at

Georgetown University, in collaboration with the Commonweal Foundation and the Faith and Reason Institute. See "Catholics in the Public Square," *Conscience* 21, no. 4 (Winter 2000–2001): 6.

73. Newsbriefs, *National Catholic Reporter,* 19 January 2001, 13. See also Albert Menendez, "Religion and the 107th Congress," *Conscience* 21, no. 4 (Winter 2000–2001): 7–9.

74. Wayne, *The Road to the White House 2000,* 86–89 and 280–81.

75. *The Weekly Standard,* 1 January/8 January 2001, 2. See also *The Weekly Standard,* 11 December 2000, 2. Bob Davis and David Cloud reported that Racicot withdrew from consideration for attorney general primarily for financial reasons; see their "O'Neill, Friend of Greenspan, Is Named Treasury Secretary," *Wall Street Journal,* 21 December 2000, A20.

6

Stealth Politics: Religious and Moral Issues in the 2000 Election

Molly W. Andolina and Clyde Wilcox

Presidential elections often hinge on the state of the economy. When the economy is good, the party of the president wins; when it is poor, the opposition party triumphs.[1] In 1980, with the economy in recession and inflation high, Ronald Reagan asked voters if they were better off than they had been four years before, and he handily defeated incumbent Jimmy Carter. Four years later, in the midst of an economic recovery, he asked the same question and was easily reelected. In 1992, Clinton exploited Americans' frustrations with a faltering economy to unseat George Bush from the White House. The Clinton campaign focused its message with a reminder on its office bulletin board that "It's the Economy, Stupid," and most exit polls showed that economic considerations dominated the election.[2]

In 2000, Al Gore sought to capitalize on a strong economy but managed only a very narrow victory in the popular vote and ultimately lost the election. Political scientists have developed aggregate statistical models to predict the vote share of parties in presidential elections, and all of these models predicted a relatively easy Gore victory.[3] Instead, the election was essentially a draw. What happened? In the aftermath of Gore's defeat, many professional politicians and pundits argued that Gore had suffered from the panoply of scandals surrounding the presidency of Bill Clinton and that moral, social, and religious issues had been critical, supplanting traditional economic concerns.

The pundits are not alone. Research has shown that such issues do matter, even in years when polls reveal a public focused primarily on the economy. In 1992, for example, abortion was a major determinant of vote choice, albeit a far less important one than economic attitudes.[4] In the 2000 presidential election, the two major-party candidates focused their campaigns on traditional domestic and economic issues, such as education, Social Security reform, health care, and taxes, but religious, moral, and social issues were also quite salient to many voters. In this chapter we will examine the context of these issues, describe how each campaign dealt with the issues, and explore whether each issue appears to have mattered in vote decisions. We will conclude with some observations about how these issues have manifested themselves in Bush's early actions as president.

Although the list of religious and moral issues that matter to at least a few voters is very large, we will focus in this chapter on four: abortion, gay rights, the death penalty, and some broader church-and-state issues. In general, both candidates sought to blur distinctions on these issues to appeal to the moderate majority. Yet Bush managed to do so without alienating his base of religious conservatives: Bush carried a majority of regular church-attending white mainline Protestants, white evangelical Protestants, and Catholics.[5]

THE ELECTORAL CONTEST: THE CANDIDATES

The 2000 presidential election was extremely important to the GOP, which had been frustrated by its inability to unseat Clinton in 1996 and its failure to remove him from office in 1998. Party leaders from all factions wanted a candidate who could beat a sitting vice president in a booming economy, and they settled early on Governor George W. Bush of Texas. Never in modern times had so many party activists endorsed a single candidate so early in the process.

That Bush would be an early consensus choice was surprising. Bush had relatively little experience in public office. He had served only six years as governor of Texas, perhaps the weakest executive position in all fifty states.[6] Unlike his father, who had been the head of the Central Intelligence Agency and ambassador to China, the younger Bush had little experience in foreign affairs, had seldom traveled outside the United States, and appeared to know little about world history or geography.

Bush won the nomination for many reasons, but he could not have won without the early and energetic support of the Christian Right.[7] Many movement activists got behind Bush quite early, which was surprising given the lukewarm support they had given to him in his bid for governor in Texas just six years earlier. Moreover, Gary Bauer, head of the Family Research Council, was an active candidate, as were movement favorites Alan Keyes and Patrick Buchanan.

Bush ultimately won the support of the movement for several reasons. First, by amassing a substantial campaign war chest and voluminous endorsements, he appeared to be a train ready to leave the station, and movement activists wanted access to a president. Second, most Christian conservatives viewed Clinton as a moral catastrophe and believed that it was vital to elect a "true Christian" to the White House. Third, Bush spent a significant amount of time courting movement leaders at the national, state, and even local levels and provided them with an apparently powerful testimony of his personal born-again experience. Finally, Bush signaled that he would support key Christian Right goals, such as appointing conservative justices to the Supreme Court, pushing for vouchers for private schools and providing government help for religious charities, and perhaps most importantly, testifying publicly to his faith.[8]

During the primaries the Bush campaign attacked John McCain as too moderate on abortion and other social issues, but in the general election Bush moved back to the center on social and moral issues. Although he campaigned on a promise to restore morality to the White House, he focused primarily on education, health care, tax cuts, and smaller government. In 1996, the Robert Dole campaign had taken a lot of flak for running toward the center on social issues, but social conservatives allowed Bush the leeway of a moderate campaign because they wanted so much to win. Like Clinton, Bush tried to win issues traditionally associated with the other party (education) and sought to appear ideologically ambiguous.

Gore won his nomination by running to the right of Bill Bradley, and he stayed to the center during the general election campaign. His campaign emphasized his experience: he had served in both the House and Senate before his stint as vice president, and he had been quite active in this latter role—focusing on streamlining and reforming the bureaucracy, cleaning up the environment, and contributing to foreign policy. Gore sought to capitalize on the strong economy, with a booming stock market and record low unemployment and inflation. Moreover, he reminded voters that trends in difficult social problems were moving in the right direction—teenage pregnancies and abortions were less common, crime rates were at a twenty-five-year low, and school test scores were rising.

Polls showed that the public saw Gore as the most experienced candidate. On election day, two-thirds of voters saw Gore as knowledgeable, compared to just 54 percent who said so of Bush. Similarly, 65 percent of voters saw Gore as capable of handling a world crisis; only 55 percent viewed Bush this way. Voters also believed that the economy was doing well. Fully 65 percent of voters said the country was moving in the right direction, a marked contrast to the 53 percent who had said so in 1996 and only 39 percent in 1992. Yet 57 percent also indicated that the country was on the wrong track morally.[9]

On the day of the election, only 18 percent of voters indicated the economy was the most important issue in determining their vote—down sharply from 43 percent in 1992. Other key issues included education (15 percent), taxes (14 percent), and Social Security (14 percent). In a notable testimony to the nature of the campaign, the Voter News Service (VNS) exit polls did not give voters abortion as a choice when it asked them to select the key issue in deciding their votes.

The public was largely satisfied with the economy, and indeed many did not remember the poor economic conditions of eight years ago.[10] In the absence of pressing economic concerns, did religious, moral, and social issues decide the election?

ABORTION: THE MOTHER OF ALL MORAL ISSUES

No issue has inspired as much political activism, as much political passion, and as much political confrontation as abortion.[11] Abortion is a strong influence on vote choice,[12] and it has been a source of secular realignment in partisanship.[13] For twenty years presidential candidates have used symbolic rhetoric, policy promises, and platform planks to appeal to abortion activists for votes, volunteers, and contributions. Although polls have consistently shown that a plurality of voters support abortion rights, the pro-life minority has historically been more likely to cast their votes on this single issue.[14]

Americans' attitudes toward abortion have been relatively stable over the past thirty years. Since 1972, the General Social Survey (GSS) has asked respondents to react to hypothetical circumstances under which they might support abortion. Citizens are given the opportunity to support abortion under each of six situations—when the health of the mother is in danger, when the pregnancy is the result of rape, when the fetus is severely defective, when the family is too poor to support another child, when the mother is unmarried, and when a married woman wants no more children. In each year the survey has been conducted, the average number of circumstances approved has been, in round numbers, four of six.

Yet this stability does not mean that the abortion issue always helps Democrats or Republicans, or that it is always debated in the same way. A majority of Americans are neither strictly pro-life nor purely pro-choice but instead favor abortions under certain circumstances. One survey in the 1990s showed that 25 percent of the public believed both that abortion was murder and that it was sometimes the best choice.[15] More recently, a *Los Angeles Times* poll from June 18, 2000, showed that 57 percent of respondents thought that abortion was murder but that more than half also thought that it should be allowed anyway. Morally conflicted voters are often up for grabs in election campaigns, and parties and campaigns strive to define and frame the abortion issue to appeal for their votes, but without losing the enthusiasm, volunteers, and contributions of their activist bases.

Party advantage on the issue has ebbed and flowed. During the mid-1980s, Republicans sought to focus attention on parental notification and consent—both policies with very high levels of approval. But after the Supreme Court allowed state regulation of abortion in 1989, in the *Webster v. Reproductive Health Services* case, Democrats focused the public's attention on the possibility that *Roe v. Wade* might be reversed. In both cases, there was a slight change in public opinion on abortion as a result of this issue framing,[16] and also a shift in the way the issue helped and hurt candidates.[17] In the late 1990s, Republicans focused attention on a late-term abortion procedure that came to be popularly known as "partial birth" abortion, and gruesome descriptions of it allowed Republicans to debate the issue on stronger ground. Gallup polls conducted in January and March 2000 showed that 65 percent of the public opposed partial-birth abortions, except for the purpose of saving the life of the mother.

Going into the 2000 election, there was some evidence that the continuing debate on "partial birth" abortions had resulted in a small shift away from the pro-choice position. The *Los Angeles Times* survey described above found that only 43 percent of the public supported the *Roe* decision, compared with 56 percent who had taken this stance four years earlier. Similarly, Gallup polls indicated that the number of Americans who called themselves pro-choice had fallen to 48 percent in 2000, down from 56 percent in 1995.

This presented the campaigns with a complex strategic environment. Bush needed the active support of the pro-life community in order to win a nomination, but he could not stake a strict pro-life position and expect to do well among Republican moderates and independents during the general election. Gore wanted to stress his pro-choice credentials in urban areas and in the Northeast and on the West Coast, without spending time defending the "partial birth" procedure.

Over the final weeks of the campaign, the National Abortion Rights Action League and Planned Parenthood ran issue advertisements in battleground states for Gore and on behalf of Democratic Senate and House candidates. The National Right-to-Life Committee did some less visible voter contacting, and the Christian Coalition distributed voter guides, albeit fewer than in previous years.

The Bush Box and Weave

Bush began his campaign by indicating a support for life and emphasizing his intention to appoint strict constructionists to the Court, but he delivered no strong rhetoric about banning abortions or overturning *Roe*. When John McCain emerged as a significant challenger, Bush moved to the right on the issue; his campaign and its surrogates attacked McCain for being "soft" on abortion. McCain had an almost perfect pro-life voting record in Congress on abortion, but he had voted to authorize the use of fetal tissue in research on Parkinson's disease soon after his friend Morris Udall died of the illness. The

National Right-to-Life Committee and the Christian Coalition joined the attack, making millions of phone calls and sending mailings to GOP voters featuring a baby who "endorsed" Bush.[18] The abortion issue cut sharply in that primary and in those that followed; in South Carolina Bush won 67 percent of the strongly pro-life vote and 58 percent of the moderately pro-life vote but won only 43 percent of the moderately pro-choice vote and 40 percent of the pro-choice vote.[19]

The price for this support was that Bush was bound to nominate a strongly pro-life running mate and to back the pro-life platform plank without a conscience exception. A *Los Angeles Times* Poll in June showed that Bush would lose support among his base by choosing a pro-choice running mate and that his gains among moderates would be small. Bush's choice of Richard Cheney and his support for the pro-life platform plank bought him the freedom to ignore the issue during the convention.

During the general election Bush danced back to the center. He sought to send subtle signals of support to the pro-life community without making overt commitments to litmus tests for judges or to a push to criminalize abortion. There was a great deal at stake: The *Los Angeles Times* poll found that 34 percent of voters would change their votes if they learned that their candidates' views on abortion were in conflict with their own. Bush needed moderately pro-choice Republicans and independent votes to win, but he also needed the activism of the pro-life movement.

Bush boxed his way around the abortion issue in a classic "bob and weave," avoiding a discussion of the particulars while swearing fealty to the pro-life position. Mostly he ignored the topic altogether. The Bush/Cheney 2000 Website listed the candidate's positions on thirty-one different issues, among which abortion was notably absent. In fact, a search for "abortion" under the issues platform on the site drew no "hits."

Instead of discussing the larger question of *Roe v. Wade* and abortion in general, Bush sought to frame the issue in terms of subsidiary issues, such as the abortion pill RU-486, and a possible ban on partial-birth procedures. In the summer of 2000, after twelve years of studies, the FDA approved the use of RU-486 in the United States. Bush condemned the decision but did not directly address how he would change it, simply arguing that "as President, I will work to build a culture that respects life." When pushed to clarify his stance during the first debate, he stated that a president could not overturn the FDA approval—"Once the decision's made, it's been made"—but he left the door open for action by offering the caveat "unless it's proven to be unsafe for women."[20]

On partial birth abortions, Bush's position was clearer. After the Supreme Court ruling overturning a Nebraska law banning partial-birth abortions, Bush released a press statement expressing his "disappointment" in the decision, offering to "come up with a law that meets the constitutional scrutiny," and, in a direct promise, pledging to "fight for a ban on partial-birth abortion." He reiterated his pledge to appoint judges who were "strict constructionists," and he held up Justice Antonin Scalia as his idea of a perfect appointment.

Not surprisingly, in the first debate, when Bush was questioned about his stance on RU-486, he used his time to highlight his opposition to partial-birth abortions.

Gore: It's the Supreme Court, Stupid

Gore took a solidly pro-choice position throughout the campaign.[21] He sought to frame the debate more broadly, around the threat to abortion rights posed by potential Bush appointees to the Court. The Supreme Court's five-to-four split over the constitutionality of Nebraska's partial-birth abortion ban suggested that one or two retirements could dramatically affect the future of *Roe*. Pro-choice groups joined with the Gore campaign in an attempt to mobilize their constituencies to meet this threat.

In first debate, Gore quickly pushed aside the question of partial-birth abortions, explaining that "the main issue is whether or not the *Roe v. Wade* decision is going to be overturned" and warning viewers that the next president would appoint "three, maybe even four justices of the Supreme Court." Indeed, although Bush attempted to downplay the significance of this issue, Gore repeatedly hammered his message home: "It is on the ballot in this election, make no mistake about it."

Abortion and the Electorate

In 1992 and 1996, many analysts believe, the abortion issue helped the Clinton-Gore ticket win votes from independents and from moderate Republicans. In 2000, the Bush campaign neutralized the Democratic advantage and probably came out ahead on the issue. Many voters were torn between a desire to keep first-trimester abortions legal and an antagonism toward partial-birth abortions. Moreover, the public was divided on RU-486, with 50 percent favoring the FDA decision and 44 percent opposing it.[22] When asked in October in a Pew Research Center poll to pick the candidate who best represented their views on abortion, 41 percent opted for Bush and 38 percent picked Gore, a virtual tie.[23]

The National Election Study (NES) asked respondents their opinions on abortion and on the importance of the issue. Only 13 percent of respondents wanted a ban on abortions, but fully half of those 13 percent indicated that abortion was extremely important to them. In contrast, 40 percent of the public wanted abortion to be always legal, but only 35 percent of them said that abortion was extremely important. This "intensity gap" was evident in

Pew Research Center polls as well: More Bush supporters mentioned abortion as an important issue than did people who favored Gore.[24]

The NES surveys also showed that Gore was perceived as somewhat more extreme on abortion than Bush. When asked to place the candidates on a four-point abortion scale, more than half put Gore in the most pro-choice position, whereas only 22 percent put Bush in the strongly pro-life position. Moreover, voters were somewhat more likely to be certain that they knew where Gore stood on the issue. Thus, Bush successfully blurred his position on the issue, allowing him to appeal to a wider audience.

In VNS exit polls, Gore's margin among the slight majority (54 percent) who favored legal abortions was not as pronounced as Bush's margin among the 38 percent who favored restricting or outlawing abortions altogether. Our multivariate analysis of exit poll data shows that pro-choice voters were 5 percent more likely to vote for Gore than other voters with the same partisanship, ideology, gender, race, marital status, age, and other social characteristics. Pro-life voters, in contrast, were 10 percent more likely to support Bush.

The real difference was among the moderate middle—the majority of voters who favored abortion under some but not all circumstances. Here, Bush did 10 percent better among those who favored significant restrictions on abortion than he did among other voters, but Gore did not pick up votes among those who favored allowing abortions under many but not all circumstances. Since there are many more pro-choice than pro-life voters, the net impact of Bush's stronger showing was somewhat limited. Nevertheless, the exit poll data suggest that Bush gained as much as 2 percent of the vote net over Gore because of the abortion issue, primarily by winning the votes of those who wanted some restrictions on abortion.

GAY RIGHTS: A MOVE TOWARD TOLERANCE

If the public has become slightly more conservative on abortion over the past few years, it has become much more liberal on gay rights. This change has transformed the issue from one in which Democratic liberals were on the defensive to one on which Bush resisted strong appeals from the Christian Right to stake out more conservative positions. Yet on this issue as well, the candidates sought to blur their differences while sending clear signals to their activist bases.

Attitudes toward gays and lesbians have been changing rapidly since the late 1980s, and attitudes toward public policy issues have been moving since 1992.[25] In 1988, fully 35 percent of respondents to the National Election Studies rated gays and lesbians at zero degrees—the coldest possible rating—on a "feeling thermometer" that ranged up to a hundred degrees. By 1992 that

Bush's Stance: Don't Talk, Don't Tell

As with abortion, Bush sought to convey an ambiguous position on gay and lesbian rights. The Republican nominee hoped to attract social conservatives by staking a more traditional position than Gore, but his campaign was clearly cognizant of changing attitudes. When asked by reporters during the primaries if he shared Pat Robertson's views on homosexuality, his answer did not contain the words "gay" or "homosexual." Instead, Bush tried to deflect the issue to John McCain, arguing that McCain was "trying to pit one group of people against another," and then repeating his mantra of being a "uniter, not a divider."[27]

Later in the summer, Bush met with the Log Cabin Republicans, a group of conservative gays and lesbians active in GOP politics. Although the meeting did not lead to any policy changes, Bush reported that it made him a "better man." This encounter was highly symbolic, for Christian Right leaders had urged Bush to refuse the meeting. (In 1996 Bob Dole had fumbled his interactions with the group. He first accepted a contribution from them, quickly returned it, and then indicated that if it were offered again, he would accept it.) In an interview with Barbara Walters, Bush did not condemn homosexuality as a sin, but he also refused to condone it as an orientation with which one is born.

In the second debate, when asked if he would support a federal law that protected gays and lesbians against firing based on their sexual orientations, Bush deferred, claiming that he did not know the particulars of the act and asserting his personal tolerance of other individuals. Bush stated that he was for "equal rights, not special rights" but failed to clarify how he would differentiate between the two terms. "Special rights" has been a phrase used by the Christian Right to signify protections from discrimination in housing and employment, among other issues.

Some of the Bush/Cheney campaign's softest language in this area came from the vice presidential candidate, whose daughter is a lesbian. During his debate with Lieberman, Cheney advocated a fairly laissez faire attitude toward gay relationships. He stated that "people should be able to enter into any kind of relationship they want to enter into. It's really no one else's business in terms of trying to regulate or prohibit behavior in that regard."

While Cheney didn't endorse gay marriage—or an official sanction of homosexual unions—he did not condemn them outright either, arguing that the matter is best left up to the states. In the next presidential debate, Bush moved the ticket rightward, stating forcefully that he was against gay marriages and that marriage is "a sacred institution between a man and a woman."

Gore's Stance: Only a Dime's Worth of Difference

Although Bill Clinton had spent some of his early popularity on a gay rights issue and consistently endorsed antidiscrimination laws, Gore avoided a strong stand on gays rights and, like Bush, sought to convey an ambiguous position on this issue. The vice president announced his support for "civil unions" for gays and lesbians but did not explain that position, nor did he emphasize it. Moreover, in the second debate, instead of distancing himself from Bush, Gore echoed his opponent's sentiment about the sanctity of heterosexual marriages. On the other hand, Gore did speak strongly on behalf of the Employment Non-Discrimination Act, legislation that would protect gays and lesbians from being fired for their sexual orientation, and for hate crimes legislation. It is possible that the mathematics of the Electoral College may have led Gore to downplay the issue. The "swing states" were generally morally conservative ones; in fact, Gore's losses in Florida, West Virginia, and Tennessee were to be central to his defeat.

Gay Rights and the Electorate

The exit polls did not ask citizens their views on gay rights. According to VNS, openly gay and lesbian voters made up 4 percent of the electorate nationwide, and they cast their votes for Gore by a 70 to 25 percent margin. Gay and lesbian voters were significantly more pro-Gore than even their partisanship, ideology, and other characteristics would predict. Of course, gay rights issues affect many more Americans than those who are openly gay or lesbian—they affect gays and lesbians who remain closeted, and also their friends, families, and colleagues. Moreover, the gay rights issue influences the votes of many Christian conservatives, who constituted 14 percent of the electorate in 2000 and who voted overwhelmingly for Bush.[28]

The campaign itself shows how quickly political parties shift their positions as issues change and how quickly both parties move to middle ground on most issues. Both Bush and Gore made a point of stressing their "tolerance" and of forthrightly rejecting discrimination. Although Gore took a more liberal position, he still emphasized his opposition to gay marriage. In the end, gay rights in the 2000 campaign may be most remembered for what was absent: Gone were Pat Buchanan's attacks on "deviant lifestyles."

CHURCH-AND-STATE ISSUES: ACCOMODATIONISM REIGNS

A more general constellation of issues involves questions of church and state. In the 2000 campaign most of this debate revolved around establishment issues—school prayer, government vouchers for religious schools, allowing faith-based organizations to receive public money, and public endorsements of religion. Both Bush and Gore portrayed themselves as deeply religious men, but Bush was far more open in his faith. In the primary election debates Bush named Jesus as his favorite philosopher and the Bible as his favorite book, and he made quiet but public testimonies to his conversion at regular intervals. Bush clearly sent a signal to religious conservatives that he would hold up his faith in public.

America is an intensely religious nation. An overwhelming majority of Americans believe in God, a somewhat smaller but still solid majority indicates that religion is important to their lives, and about 40 percent claim to attend church services at least once a week.[29] Many Americans believe that religious faith is an essential moral compass for political leaders. Seven in ten say it is important for presidents to have strong religious beliefs, but they are wary of those who trumpet their beliefs too loudly. Half of the public says they are uncomfortable when politicians draw attention to how religious they are.[30]

Public opinion on church-state issues has traditionally favored accommodationist policies. One study found that large majorities of both the mass public and cultural elites support prayer in public schools, displays of the Nativity scene on public lands, and other public endorsements of Christianity. Yet this support is generally unreflective. In focus groups, as participants consider the impact of religious diversity on school prayer, many abandon their support for the practice.[31] However, the public distinguishes sharply between public symbolic endorsements of religion (even if they involve small outlays of money) and the use of tax money to support religious schools. In the early 1990s only a minority supported public funding of religious schools.

In past campaigns, Republicans have enthusiastically endorsed accommodationist practices, while Democrats have been more likely to support separationist positions. The electoral advantage has depended on how the issues were framed.

School prayer was a minor issue in the campaign, primarily after the Supreme Court declared that student-led prayers at football games were unconstitutional. The case had originated in Texas, and many Texas school districts announced that they would defy the court ruling. An ABC poll conducted in March 2000 showed that 67 percent of the public supported student-led prayer at football games.

The voucher issue was more central to the 2000 campaigns, primarily as a centerpiece of Bush's educational plan. The GOP nominee proposed allowing students in "failing" school districts to take their shares of federal funding for that school district as vouchers to purchase educations in private schools, including religious schools. The public knew little about the details of Bush's plan or how vouchers might work, but a narrow 53 to 44 percent majority supported their use. Vouchers are especially popular among Christian conservatives, as well as among some Democratic constituencies, including Catholics, Hispanics, and African Americans.[32]

The final church-and-state issue was that of faith-based initiatives—allowing religiously based organizations to receive government funding so that they can provide social welfare services, many of which have been traditionally provided directly by government. Support for these initiatives reflects support for vouchers; 54 percent of voters favor programs in which the government provides funds to religious organizations for such programs as job training or drug treatment. Significantly more voters (67 percent) support allowing "such groups to *apply for* government funding, along with other organizations, for these purposes."[33] Interestingly, many conservative religious leaders are ambivalent about this proposal, fearing that government money would be an enticement for religious organizations to become entangled in government regulations and bureaucracy.

Bush's Carefully Worded Support

The Supreme Court decision on prayer at football games gave Bush a chance to position himself on church and state without substantial cost. He roundly criticized the decision but failed to articulate a mechanism for action. Also, despite his focus on education (it was the first issue listed on his Website), he omitted a discussion of school prayer from his detailed educational proposal.

Nor did Bush highlight his support for vouchers, which he referred to as "educational opportunities" and which he buried beneath other elements of his education platform, such as yearly testing. Yet, when Bush did discuss these vouchers, he made a point of including religious schools, mentioning Catholic or parochial schools as eligible for funds.

Bush was more explicit and vocal in his support for faith-based initiatives. He spoke often of the need for "armies of compassion" and "charitable choice." In his stump speeches and on his Website Bush emphasized the importance of encouraging groups, including religious organizations, to replace a void left by the scaling back of government services. He had advocated such programs in Texas and repeatedly lauded them on the campaign trail.

Gore's Muffled Response

The Gore campaign was silent about prayer in schools. Gore (backed by a strongly worded platform) was a harsh critic of Bush's education plan, but his criticism avoided concerns about the separation of church and state, criticizing instead the taking of "taxpayer money away from public schools."[34] The vice president concentrated most of his criticism on the specifics of the plan, such as allowing schools that received federal funds to deny entrance to some applicants, and failing to offer enough money actually to pay for parochial school tuition.[35]

Finally, Gore joined in Bush's call for provision of public money to faith-based social service agencies. He did not emphasize the issue or provide many details of his plan, but he did seek to negate Bush's advantage on the issue.[36]

Church-State Issues in the Electorate

After the initial media focus on the Court school-prayer decision, the issue never really surfaced in the campaign. The voucher issue, however, did attract a lot of attention—from both candidates and the news media. Republican strategists hoped that it would help them unify the GOP coalition; Christian conservatives supported the plan because it would allow them to withdraw their children from public schools without financial cost, and social moderates backed it to introduce competition among schools. Moderates also hoped that the issue would help them attract devout Catholics and minority voters like Hispanics and African Americans.

Vouchers and faith-based programs are especially popular among African Americans, a constituency that has been loyal to the Democratic Party since the 1960s. Early in the campaign, it looked like Bush's position on these issues, along with a Republican convention that highlighted diversity, might allow the GOP to make inroads into this voting bloc. Bush never closed the sale, however; on November 7, blacks stayed with Gore by a margin of nine to one, and Hispanics backed Gore two to one. Bush did carry the votes of Catholics who were frequent church attendees, however.

THE DEATH PENALTY: THE DOG THAT DIDN'T BARK

We conclude with an issue that was never part of the campaign but that might have been a powerful issue for Gore. The public has been strongly supportive of the death penalty since the early 1970s, when the murder rate skyrocketed. Polls have consistently shown large majorities of Americans in favor of the death penalty, making the United States an outlier in both world opinion and public policy. The issue has traditionally helped Republican presidential candidates, including George H. W. Bush in 1988.

Yet events over the past year have begun to erode public support for capital punishment. The drop in the rate of violent crime has been part of this story, but far more important has been the development of DNA evidence. Over the past several years, anti–death penalty advocates have sought to demonstrate the innocence of men and women on death row, with startling results. Illinois freed thirteen people in a relatively short period of time, primarily because of the focused efforts of one professor of law whose class investigated a case each term, and also a series of investigative reports by the *Chicago Tribune*. In response, Illinois's Republican governor declared a moratorium on executions, a move supported by 63 percent of the public.

Illinois is not alone. Across the nation defendants who had served long terms on death row and sometimes had come within days or even hours of execution have been freed as new evidence proved their innocence. Accordingly the media has focused more attention on the nature of the legal process that could produce such errors. Many of those freed had had inadequate legal representation—lawyers who had slept through trials, had failed to call eyewitnesses who could establish alibis, or had neglected to challenge improper evidence or file proper motions of their own.

The issue had potential significance, because Texas executes more people annually than the other forty-nine states combined, and in his six years as governor George W. Bush had presided over more executions than any governor in U.S. history. In 2000 the state broke the national record (previously held by Texas a few years earlier) for executions in a single year. In the spring, one especially dubious case caught the media's eye. There was no physical evidence in the case, only one eyewitness who, until the police provided hints, had failed to identify the suspect in two consecutive trials, and two witnesses who placed the suspect at another location. The quality of legal representation was low. Bush denied all appeals, and the defendant was executed. In this and other cases, religious leaders from Pat Robertson to the pope called on Bush for clemency.

The Texas appeals process is burdened by requirements that serve to speed cases through the system. A majority of people executed in Texas had been represented by lawyers who had been sanctioned or cautioned by the state bar. It would seem that Gore could have made an issue of the death penalty, calling for mandatory DNA evidence and perhaps a suspension of the practice pending further investigation. Even Pat Robertson, head of the Christian Coalition, had called for a suspension of the death penalty in the late 1990s.

Bush and "The Ultimate Punishment," and Gore's Echo

In the second debate, defending his position on hate crimes, Bush argued that additional legislation was unnecessary since those who committed high-profile hate crimes in Texas were given "the ultimate punishment." His comments were delivered with such relish that they drew an additional question in the third and final debate, posed by an audience member. The questioner challenged Bush to clarify his response, noting that he seemed to take particular pleasure in executions. The question resonated because of widespread rumors that Bush had taunted at least one death row inmate who made a final call to appeal for clemency. Bush defended his support of the death penalty and declared that he took his responsibility gravely.

Bush also asserted, with absolute certainty, that none of those executed during his term as governor had been innocent—despite the facts that he had denied all appeals and that DNA evidence was freeing prisoners convicted in the Texas legal system.

Gore also supported the death penalty, and he did not use either debate to push for a moratorium on executions or to challenge Bush's administration of justice in Texas. Accordingly, the death penalty was not an issue in the 2000 campaign, and it is impossible to know how it would have played. In 2001, several groups, including national newspapers and the Catholic Church, are suing across the country to recover DNA evidence on people who have been executed. If one of these cases uncovers a suspect wrongly executed, the issue might go back on the national agenda.

RELIGIOUS AND MORAL ISSUES AND THE VOTE

The 2000 National Election Study allows us to see how these issues influenced the vote. In table 6.1 we have estimated a logistic regression equation predicting two-party vote. We used a number of models, controlling for demographic and social characteristics, evaluations of the national economy, ideology, and partisanship, with generally consistent results. The model presented here includes a measure of support for vouchers, for the death penalty, for antidiscrimination laws for gays and lesbians, and for overall abortion. Other models substituted attitudes on partial-birth abortion and parental consent laws, gays in the military, and gay adoption.

The results show that partisanship, ideology, and evaluations of the economy were the strongest predictors of voting behavior. Those who lived in the South were markedly more likely to vote for Bush, and blacks were more likely to vote for Gore. Yet, both abortion and gay rights were highly significant predictors of vote choice, even after controlling for these more proximate factors. This is especially striking in that these issues have already led some citizens to change their partisanship, a change that is hidden in these models by controlling for party identification. Vouchers and the death penalty were not significant predictors of vote choice.

We estimated additional models that allowed us to estimate the probability that a person with a particular position on each of these issues would cast a ballot for Bush. The data show that a voter who took the most pro-life position was 16 percent more likely to vote for George W. Bush than one who took the pro-choice position, even after controls for partisanship, ideology, evaluations of the economy, and social characteristics. Our interpretation is that the abortion issue appears to have been largely a draw—with perhaps a tiny edge to Bush, primarily because of his extra appeal to those who favored significant restrictions on abortion but not an outright ban. Bush gained 8 percent more of the vote among that set of voters than he won

Table 6.1. Religious and Moral Issues in the 2000 Campaign: Logistic Regression Predicting Two-Party Vote: NES 2000

Variable	B	S.E.
Sex	.145	.297
Race	−1.98	.888*
South	.795	.326*
Education	−.082	.067
White evangelical	.418	.640
Catholic	−.116	.176
Church attendance	.071	.095
Partisanship	1.023	.096**
Ideology	.538	.128**
National Economy	−.463	.137**
Abortion	.417	.160**
Gay rights	.383	.136**
Vouchers	.055	.099
Death Penalty	.171	.137
Constant	−.121	1.443
Predicted Correctly:		
Gore = 89%		
Bush = 89%		
Nagelkerke R-square = .787		

*a strong indicator.
**the strongest indicator.

among other voters with the same partisanship, ideology, and demographic characteristics.

Surprisingly, the gay rights issue had a greater impact on predicted vote. A voter who strongly opposed antidiscrimination laws was fully 31 percent more likely to cast a Bush ballot than was a similar voter who strongly supported them. The gay rights issue appears to have helped Gore slightly, primarily because there were more voters who favored these laws than voters who opposed them. The strong impact of an issue that was hardly prominent during the campaign and on which the GOP candidate took a vague position suggests that social and moral issues matter to voters even when they are not stressed by candidates.

THE BUSH ADMINISTRATION: INITIAL POLICY RESPONSE

In Bush's first month in office, the economy was suddenly an issue again. The Federal Reserve met twice—once in special session—to lower interest rates. The news media reported large-scale layoffs. Also, the new president immediately argued for significant, across-the-board tax cuts in order to jump-start economic growth. He also lost little time addressing his father's former foe, Saddam Hussein, authorizing air strikes in mid-February.

Despite this focus on economic and foreign policy, Bush did not forget the Religious Right. Even before his electoral victory was declared, he moved quickly with cabinet appointments and policy pronouncements that placated social conservatives. He chose Christian Right favorite John Ashcroft as attorney general and pro-life Governor Tommy Thompson of Wisconsin to head the department of Health and Human Services. Not long after he was sworn in, Thompson announced that the Food and Drug Administration would initiate a review of RU-486, an action at which Bush had hinted during the campaign. Finally, in a policy that echoed that of his father and reversed a Clinton initiative of 1993, Bush ordered a halt in federal funding of international family-planning programs that provided either abortion services or counseling. Christian conservatives had asked for a more sweeping set of executive orders, but even this less extensive action instigated an outcry from liberal abortion-rights groups.

On gay rights, Bush walked a middle ground, clinging tightly to the status quo. He apparently passed over Dan Coates for secretary of defense because the senator was opposed to the military's current "don't ask, don't tell" policy. The military had made peace with this policy, and in fact had expelled more gays and lesbians during the past eight years than during the previous eight years.[37]

Although Bush devoted significant energy to his tax cut proposal, the first program the new president sent to Congress was an education reform package that included provisions for vouchers, reflecting his campaign position. But in the face of growing opposition among liberal groups and teacher's unions, Bush signaled a willingness to bargain on this and other elements of the plan.

In a more conservative vein, after a December meeting with religious leaders, Bush created a White House Office of Faith Based and Community Initiatives, headed by political scientist John J. DiIulio Jr. Bush promised to make these initiatives a key part of his administration, despite protests from the American Civil Liberties Union that such plans violate the line between church and state. As of the first months of the administration, it was unclear precisely what programs the administration would propose or how such proposals would fare in the Supreme Court.

Finally, Bush oversaw the first national execution in a generation, that of convicted Oklahoma bomber Timothy McVeigh on June 11, 2001. Meanwhile, however, Congress was considering a bill that would require the national government to provide access to DNA testing for anyone convicted in federal court of a capital crime.

For many of these issues, however, the most important policy consequence of Bush's victory would be not his legislative proposals, executive orders, or cabinet choices but his Supreme Court appointments. It is highly likely that the president will nominate at least two justices in his first term. With Democrats in control of the Senate after the defection of James M. Jeffords of Vermont, the nomination battles threaten to be contentious and partisan. But if Bush's victory with Ashcroft is any indication of his success rate, the former Texas governor will leave an imprint on abortion, gay rights, the death penalty, and church-state issues that will endure for many years to come.

NOTES

1. Robert S. Erikson, "Economic Conditions and the Presidential Vote," *American Political Science Review* 83 (1989): 567–73. See also Gregory B. Markus, "The Impact of Personal and National Economic Conditions on the Presidential Vote: A Pooled-Cross-Sectional Analysis," *American Journal of Political Science* 32 (1988): 137–54, and Ray C. Fair, "The Effects of Economic Events on Votes for President: A 1984 Update," *Political Behavior* 10 (1988): 168–79.

2. Paul R. Brewer, "Public Opinion, Economic Issues, and the Vote: Are Presidential Elections 'All about the Benjamins?'" in *Understanding Public Opinion,* ed. Barbara Norrander and Clyde Wilcox, 2d ed. (Washington, D.C.: Congressional Quarterly Press, forthcoming).

3. Michael S. Lewis-Beck and Thomas W. Rice, *Forecasting Elections* (Washington, D.C.: Congressional Quarterly Press, 1992). For a general review of these models, see James E. Campbell and Thomas E. Mann, "Forecasting the Presidential Election: What Can We Learn from the Models?" *Brookings Review* 14, no. 4 (Fall 1996): 26–31. For the 2000 election, see Adam Clymer, "The 2000 Campaign: Political Memo; The Winner Is Gore, If They Got the Math Right," *New York Times,* 4 September 2000.

4. Alan Abramowitz, "It's Abortion, Stupid," *The Journal of Politics* 57 (1995): 176–86; Alan Abramowitz, "The Cultural Divide in American Politics: Moral Issues and Presidential Voting," in *Understanding Public Opinion,* ed. Barbara Norrander and Clyde Wilcox, 1st ed. (Washington, D.C.: Congressional Quarterly Press, 1997).

5. John C. Green, "Religion and Voting in the 2000 Elections," paper presented at conference on Religion in the 2000 Elections, Rice University, February 2001. This pattern did not hold for black Christians, who voted overwhelmingly for Gore.

6. The powers of the state government in Texas are limited, and the powers of the governor are dwarfed by those of the lieutenant governor. By law, the Texas legislature only meets 140 days every two years. The governor of Texas has no cabinet and directly oversees only about two hundred state employees; by contrast, the mayor of Chicago, Richard Daley, is responsible for over forty thousand. Nicholas Lemann, "The Redemption: Everything Went Wrong for George W. Bush, Until He Made It All Go Right," *The New Yorker,* 31 January 2000, 48–63.

7. See chapter 4 in this book, Mark J. Rozell, "The Christian Right in the 2000 GOP Presidential Campaign."

8. Clyde Wilcox, "The Christian Right in the 2000 Elections," paper presented at conference on Religion in the 2000 Elections, Rice University, February 2001.

9. Exit poll data collected by the Voter News Service is available from several Websites, including CNN.com and MSNBC.com, www.cnn.com/ELECTION/2000/epolls/US/P000.html (7 February 2001).

10. Brewer, "Public Opinion," and David Moore, "Booming Economy No Advantage for Gore," Gallup Poll releases, 16 August 2000, www.gallup.com/poll/releases/pr000816.asp (19 February 2001).

11. Sidney Verba, Kay Lehman Schlozman, and Henry E. Brady, *Voice and Equality: Civic Voluntarism in American Politics* (Cambridge, Mass.: Harvard University Press, 1995).

12. Abramowitz, "It's Abortion, Stupid."

13. Greg D. Adams, "Abortion: Evidence of an Issue Evolution," *American Journal of Political Science* 41, no. 3 (July 1997): 718–38.

14. Elizabeth Adell Cook, Ted G. Jelen, and Clyde Wilcox, *Between Two Absolutes: Public Opinion and the Politics of Abortion* (Boulder, Colo.: Westview, 1992).

15. Cook, Jelen, and Wilcox, *Between Two Absolutes.*

16. Clyde Wilcox and Barbara Norrander, "Policy Mood and Social Issues," in *Understanding Public Opinion*, ed. Norrander and Wilcox, 2d ed.

17. Elizabeth Adell Cook, Ted G. Jelen, and Clyde Wilcox, "Issue Voting in Gubernatorial Elections: Abortion and Post-Webster Politics," *The Journal of Politics* 56 (1994): 187–99.

18. Rozell, "The Christian Right" (chapter 4 of this book).

19. VNS exit polls, www.cnn.com/ELECTION/2000/primaries/SC/poll.rep.html (7 February 2001).

20. Transcripts from the three presidential debates and the sole vice-presidential debate can be found at the Websites of major cable and network news outlets. See, for example, www.msnbc.com/news/472353.asp (2 February 2001).

21. This despite evidence that earlier in his political career (as a representative from Tennessee) Gore struggled with the morality of abortions, ultimately voting against federal funding of abortions.

22. The Gallup Poll, October 2000, on the World Wide Web at www.gallup.com/poll/indicatiors/indabortion.asp (18 January 2001).

23. Pew Research Center for the People and the Press, "Presidential Debate Clouds Voters' Choice," Washington, D.C., 10 October 2000, available on the World Wide Web at www.people-press.org.

24. Pew Research Center, "Presidential Debate."

25. Clyde Wilcox and Robin Wolpert, "Gay Rights in the Public Sphere: Public Opinion on Gay and Lesbian Equality," in *The Politics of Gay Rights*, ed. Craig A. Rimmerman, Kenneth J. Wald, and Clyde Wilcox (Chicago: University of Chicago Press, 2000).

26. The Gallup Poll, on the World Wide Web at www.gallup.com/poll/indicators/indhomosexual.asp (18 January 2001).

27. "Bush Answers Reporters' Questions in Bellevue, Washington," 28 February 2000, www.vote-smart.org/index.html (11 February 2000).

28. Wilcox, "The Christian Right."

29. Andrew Kohut, John C. Green, Scott Keeter, and Robert Toth, *The Diminishing Divide: Religion's Changing Role in American Politics* (Washington, D.C.: Brookings Institution, 2000).

30. Pew Research Center for the People and the Press, "Religion and Politics: The Ambivalent Majority," Washington, D.C., September 20, 2000, available on the World Wide Web at www.people-press.org.

31. Ted G. Jelen and Clyde Wilcox, *Public Attitudes on Church and State* (New York: Sharpe, 1995).

32. Pew Research Center for the People and the Press, "Issues and Continuity Now Working for Gore," Washington, D.C., September 14, 2000, available on the World Wide Web at www.people-press.org.

33. The Pew Research Center, "Issues and Continuity: Now Working for Gore."

34. See transcript from the first debate, cited above.

35. The national government provides less than 10 percent of the funding for public schools, so portability of national government funding would allow poor children to pay for private schools entirely.

36. One observer called Gore's endorsement of faith-based programs his "Sister Souljah" speech, referring to Clinton's 1992 condemnation of the rap singer's lyrics. In subsequent interviews, however, Gore's staff attempted to soften the candidate's position.

37. Francine D'Amico, "Sexuality and Military Service," in *The Politics of Gay Rights,* ed. Rimmerman, Wald, and Wilcox.

7

A Historic First:
The Lieberman Nomination

Mary C. Segers

The 2000 presidential election had many surprises, the most astonishing of which was the contested race in Florida that extended the election by more than a month. But a similarly historic moment occurred on August 7, 2000, when Al Gore selected Sen. Joseph I. Lieberman to be his running mate on the Democratic ticket. Lieberman was the first Jew ever to run for national office on the ticket of a major political party. Gore's bold decision in naming Lieberman as his running mate was another step toward genuine equality of opportunity in American public life. As the Rev. Jesse Jackson remarked, "With this selection, another barrier falls and another opportunity rises. Surely this makes America better. We all benefit when ceilings are lifted that limit talent because of religion, race, gender or sexual orientation."[1]

Lieberman brought to the Democratic national ticket a wealth of experience in legislative and executive politics. A graduate of Yale College and Yale Law School, Lieberman was elected to the Connecticut state senate in 1970; there he served for ten years, six of them as senate majority leader. He then served as the Connecticut attorney general for six years, during which he reorganized the office as a consumer defender. In 1988 he ran for the U.S. Senate, defeating a three-term incumbent, Sen. Lowell Weicker. He was elected to a second term in 1994 and to a third term in 2000 (Lieberman ran simultaneously for Senate and for vice president, as did Lloyd Bentsen in 1988 and Lyndon Johnson in 1960).

In the Senate, Lieberman built a reputation as a moderate and a centrist. He supported President Bill Clinton's efforts to fashion a more centrist "New Democratic" Party and in 1995 was named chairman of the Democratic Leadership Council. Although he was a strong supporter of President Clinton (who, incidentally, as a Yale law student, had worked in Lieberman's first political campaign in 1970), Lieberman did not hesitate to condemn Clinton's behavior in the Monica Lewinsky case in 1998. While he did not vote to remove Clinton from office, Lieberman was the first prominent Democrat to denounce Clinton's conduct as not only inappropriate but flatly immoral.

Lieberman is a religious man, an observant Orthodox Jew. According to Rabbi Barry Freundel, who heads Lieberman's congregation in Washington, "His religious values shape the way he functions as a Senator." He and his family follow kosher dietary rules, and he neither works nor rides in cars, trains, or planes on the Sabbath. Exceptions are made for vitally important work, however, and Lieberman's five-mile Saturday walks from his Washington home to the Senate chamber in order to vote on pending legislation are legendary. Lieberman belongs to the branch of Judaism known as "Modern Orthodox," which refers to Jews who are steeped in biblical studies yet are more inclined than the ultra-Orthodox to believe in living thoroughly in the here and now.

The choice of a vice-presidential candidate is interesting for what it tells us about the man who made the selection. Gore's choice of Lieberman as the first Jew on a major party ticket was historic and courageous. The choice spoke of tolerance more than tactics. Lieberman himself called "Al's selection of me an act of chutzpah," using the familiar Yiddish word for audacity. Gore had refused to poll the question of the possible effect of having a Jew on the ticket. He had apparently concluded that win or lose, it was a risk worth taking.

If the decision was principled and courageous, the choice nonetheless redounded favorably to Gore and made him look bold and decisive. The selection of Lieberman, who was known for his moral rectitude and for his Senate speech denouncing Clinton's scandalous conduct, enabled Gore to distance himself from Clinton on the issue of presidential character. Moreover, Lieberman's observant faith was a strength, not a weakness, because it trumped the Republicans on values and religion.

There were other tactical advantages to the choice of Lieberman. Pundits thought that extreme anti-Semites in the country either would not vote at all or would vote for Patrick Buchanan, the Reform Party candidate. Many such anti-Jewish voters lived in Southern states that Gore probably would not win anyway. Moreover, Lieberman's candidacy and pro-Jewish sentiment could make a difference in key states like California, Florida, and New York, where Jews were concentrated.

In addition to these tactical advantages of choosing Lieberman, Gore's timing was exactly right. His selection of Lieberman for vice president completely upstaged the Republicans on the issue of diversity. The GOP had just held a party convention emphasizing themes of diversity, toleration, inclusiveness, and compassion. The Republicans featured many Hispanic and African American entertainers, but they performed for convention delegates who were largely white, middle class, and upper middle class—a fact not lost on the TV viewing audience. Coming immediately after the GOP convention, Gore's choice of Lieberman reinforced the idea that the Republicans might talk about diversity but it was the Democrats who "walked the walk" and practiced diversity.

To appreciate the historic character of Lieberman's nomination as the first Jew on a major party ticket, it helps to set things in context and review briefly the history of anti-Jewish prejudice in the United States. Accordingly, the first part of this chapter will provide an overview of the legal, political, and social discrimination American Jews have faced through much of this country's history. The second section examines Lieberman's political career and his centrist views on the issues, including issues about which he and Gore differed. The third section analyzes Lieberman's performance as the Democratic vice-presidential candidate in the 2000 campaign, including his debate with Republican vice-presidential candidate Dick Cheney, and other noteworthy aspects of the race. The fourth section is a detailed examination of the controversy Lieberman triggered with his speeches about the role of religion in public life. Finally, the chapter concludes with an evaluation of Lieberman's candidacy and some tentative conclusions about his political future.

ANTI-JEWISH DISCRIMINATION IN AMERICAN PUBLIC LIFE

Gore's choice of Lieberman as his vice-presidential candidate must be seen in the context of the struggle against unjustifiable discrimination and for expansion of genuine equality of opportunity in American public life. Like the 1960 election of John F. Kennedy as the first Catholic president, or the 1984 nomination of Geraldine Ferraro as the first woman to run for vice president, Lieberman's nomination broke down barriers to full political participation. As Jesse Jackson remarked, "Each time a barrier falls for one person, the doors of opportunity open wider for every other American."[2]

Barriers to Jewish participation in public life certainly existed in colonial times and during the history of the early republic. Religious tests for public office were common in the American colonies and persisted in the states of the new nation despite the banning of such tests in Article VI of the Constitution. North Carolina and Maryland were two examples of Jewish opposition to this form of religious discrimination. In North Carolina, the 1776 state constitution both promised citizens "the natural and inalienable right to worship Almighty God according to the dictates of their own conscience" and restricted non-Protestants from holding "any office or place of trust or profit in the Civil Department within this State." No one protested when Jacob Henry, a Jew from Carteret County, was elected to the state legislature in 1808. But in 1809, when Henry sought to reassume his seat, his right to it was challenged on constitutional grounds, and a move was made to declare his seat vacant. In response, Henry gave an eloquent speech in the North Carolina House of Delegates defending liberty of conscience and his own religious creed. Pointing to the inconsistency between the protection of religious views in the North Carolina bill of rights and the constitutional restriction of office holding to Protestants, Henry persuaded his colleagues that he should keep his legislative seat.[3]

A similar situation prevailed in Maryland, where the state constitution required anyone assuming "an office of trust or profit" (including lawyers and jurors) to execute a "declaration of belief in the Christian religion." This religious test barred Jews not only from public office but from the legal profession as well. A campaign against the restriction, based on the argument that Jews should have "the same civil privileges that are enjoyed by other religious sects," began as early as 1797. The restriction was not removed, however, until January 5, 1826, when the Maryland legislature passed a bill permitting Jews to substitute a declaration of belief "in a future state of rewards and punishments." Later that same year two Jews won election to the Baltimore city council.[4]

Jonathan D. Sarna describes the struggle of Jews against religious discrimination as a struggle for civil equality based on the provisions of the Constitution and on Jewish patriotism. In seeking equal rights for themselves on the state level, they appealed to principles shared by Americans of all faiths. They sought to live under a government where all religious societies were "on an equal footing."[5] For instance, in protesting a Christological test oath for public office in Pennsylvania in 1783, a delegation of prominent Philadelphia Jews said the test deprived them "of the most eminent rights of freemen" and was particularly unfair since they had fought and suffered in the Revolution. These arguments were ultimately persuasive, and in 1790 Pennsylvania issued a new state bill of rights that omitted this religious test oath.

The two thousand Jews present in the United States at the time of the American Revolution faced other restrictions besides test oaths, including blasphemy laws, Sunday laws, church taxes, and restrictions on voting. Gradually, these restrictions were eliminated. Initially, Jews simply argued for equal treatment and accommodation of all religions on an equal basis. They were not hostile to religion; they recognized the need for religious education in schools as the basis for the morality necessary in a democratic republic. However, as the nineteenth century wore on and the Christian Bible and prayers were introduced into the new public schools, Jews began to gravitate toward a more separationist stance. Sunday closing laws, prayer in the schools, and the Protestant claim that America was "a Christian Nation" moved American Jews to emphasize church-state separation and to ally themselves with nonreligious secularists in a struggle to make public schools and other government undertakings religiously neutral.[6]

It is noteworthy that while American Jewish thought on church-state relations in the twentieth century in the face of these perceived threats has been largely separationist, it has never been monolithic—either in the nineteenth or twentieth century. For example, on the issue of state aid to religious schools (Christian or Jewish), the opinions of Jewish leaders and community groups are complex. Advocates of Jewish day schools often find themselves sympathetic with their Catholic counterparts who favor public aid to parochial schools. At the same time, most Jewish organizations in the twenty-first-century United States remain vigilantly separationist, wary of any laws favoring particular religious groups and disadvantaging religious minorities.

American Jews faced social as well as legal and political discrimination throughout much of American history. The Ku Klux Klan in the 1880s, and especially in the 1920s, railed against Jews, Negroes, and "papists." During the postwar twenties and the Depression-era thirties, Jews and other minorities suffered from nativist exclusionary and anti-immigration sentiments. David Wyman points to anti-Semitic attitudes among members of Congress and the public as one factor explaining the failure of the American government to open the gates to Jewish refugees fleeing Nazi persecution in Europe during the 1930s and 1940s.[7] Although many who opposed refugee immigration felt no antipathy toward Jews and were motivated chiefly by concerns about high unemployment, much restrictionist and anti-refugee sentiment was closely linked to anti-Semitism. Wyman notes that during the 1930s hate propaganda was pumped throughout American society by more than a hundred anti-Semitic organizations, led by groups such as Father Charles Coughlin and his Social Justice movement, William Dudley Pelley's Silver Shirts, the German-American Bund, and the Rev. Gerald B. Winrod's Protestant fundamentalist Defenders of the Christian Faith. These groups were effectively silenced once the Second World War began, but a wave of anti-Jewish actions continued throughout the war itself. In northeastern cities such as Boston and New York, Jewish cemeteries were vandalized, synagogues were damaged or defaced with swastikas, anti-Semitic literature was widely distributed, and teenaged street gangs beat Jewish schoolchildren.[8]

According to Wyman, the pervasiveness of anti-Semitism in the United States during the late 1930s and the war years is confirmed by contemporary national public opinion polls. "The results of polls done from 1938 to 1946 indicated that over half the American population perceived Jews as greedy and dishonest and that about one-third considered them overly aggressive."[9] Even on Capitol Hill, some congressmen expressed anti-Jewish views for the record. Rep. John Rankin (D-Miss.) referred to a Jewish news columnist as "that little kike" and frequently lashed out against the Jews.

Moreover, ordinary citizens wrote hate-filled letters to members of Congress and government officials objecting to Jewish refugees' being permitted to enter the country.[10]

During the Second World War, a particularly insidious kind of anti-Semitism circulated in pamphlets and posters, and as jokes and rhymes. One recurrent theme accused Jews of cowardice and of shirking military service, staying home and prospering, while Christian boys were sent off to fight and die. A typical example was a piece called "The First American," which was widely circulated in oral and written form:

> First American killed in Pearl Harbor—*John J. Hennessy*
> First American to sink a Jap ship—*Colin P. Kelly*
> First American to sink a Jap ship with a torpedo—*John P. Buckley*
> Greatest American air hero— *"Butch" O'Hare*
> First American killed at Guadalcanal—*John J. O'Brien*
> First American to get four new tires—*Abraham Lipshitz*[11]

Wyman notes that these anti-Jewish attitudes raised real obstacles to the development of any American initiative to save European Jewish refugees during the Second World War. The prevalence of these negative attitudes toward Jews at mid-century provides a benchmark for understanding the progress signaled by Joe Lieberman's nomination fifty years later. Again, public opinion polling confirms this. For example, in 1937, only 46 percent of voters surveyed by Gallup said they would vote for a qualified Jewish candidate for president. By 1999, 92 percent of voters said they would; only 6 percent said they would not; and the rest had no opinion.[12]

Lieberman himself has said that "I cannot remember a single instance of anti-Semitism in my youth."[13] He noted that he was lucky to have grown up in a multiethnic, multiracial, multireligious community (Stamford, Connecticut), and he was optimistic that people would judge his candidacy fairly and apart from the old anti-Semitic attitudes. The public reaction to his nomination did feature some anti-Semitic slurs on Internet chat rooms and a complaint from a local NAACP leader in Texas.[14] But by and large, expressions of anti-Jewish sentiment were marginal during the presidential campaign.

It is conceivable that prejudice against Jews in public life had all but disappeared by the 2000 election. At the time Lieberman was nominated, American Jews numbered six million, or 2 percent of the population. There were eleven Jewish senators and twenty-three Jewish representatives in the 106th Congress, which met during 1999–2000. American Jews were also readily identifiable in the ranks of party leaders, campaign managers, pollsters, campaign contributors, and interest-group leaders. In a sense, then, anti-Jewish sentiment had abated to the point that the nomination of the first Jew to a major party ticket was becoming possible. Still, it took a combination of Gore, Lieberman, and circumstance to make this a reality.

LIEBERMAN: MODERATE AND CENTRIST

As a senator, Lieberman was known for his thoughtful position on many is-sues and for his willingness to work with bipartisan coalitions for passage of legislation. He brought to the Senate ten years of experience as a state legis-lator, including six years as majority leader in the Connecticut state senate. He learned to reach across the aisle and forge alliances with opposition lead-ers to pass legislation. He gradually built a reputation as the Senate's voice of reason, moderation, and civility.

Lieberman also brought to national office a philosophy of democratic cen-trism. Like Al Gore (and unlike the left wing of the Democratic Party), Lieber-man supported the 1991 Persian Gulf War resolution authorizing President George H. W. Bush to use military force in Kuwait. He favored American support of Israel in the Middle East, but he also voted for military aid to Saudi Arabia. He consistently supported international trade measures opposed by organized labor, such as the North American Free Trade Agreement (NAFTA); yet he took labor's side on other issues of primary importance to unions, like increases in the minimum wage and prohibitions against em-ployers' hiring permanent replacements for striking workers.[15]

As part of this moderate, centrist agenda favored by Clintonian "New Democrats" and the Democratic Leadership Council (which he chaired from 1995 on), Lieberman described himself as "pro-business, pro-trade and pro-economic growth." As a senator from Connecticut, Lieberman supported measures important to that state's large industries such as insurance, health care, and military technology. But his pro-business attitude appeared to go beyond local constituency service and to reflect a genuine belief that both the Democratic Party and the nation's economy would flourish when government promoted international trade, business entrepreneurship, and technological innovation. As Lieberman put it, "You can't be pro-jobs and anti-business."[16]

At the same time, Lieberman was a vigorous advocate of campaign finance reform and had supported legislation banning unregulated donations ("soft money") to political parties. Like Gore, he supported abortion rights, strong measures to protect the environment, gun control, gay rights, consumer pro-tections, and civil rights legislation. Unlike Gore, however, Lieberman sup-ported school vouchers on an experimental basis for District of Columbia inner-city schools, was critical of some affirmative action programs, and at one time considered privatizing a small portion of Social Security. Once se-lected as the Democratic vice-presidential nominee, Lieberman downplayed these differences with Gore and stressed a basic Democratic commitment to diversity and to equal opportunity for all citizens. At the Democratic Con-vention, he received the support of black congressional representatives once they realized that he was the only one of the four national candidates (Bush,

Cheney, Gore, and Lieberman) to have gone South in the 1960s to work for voting rights for African Americans.[17]

To summarize, Lieberman may have been an Orthodox Jew, but he was no orthodox Democrat. He was known as a senator of independence and integrity, as a legislator who deliberated carefully over policy options. He described his approach this way: "I'm going to do what I think is right on every issue, and not feel obliged to vote a particular way because it is the party line or because people expect me to."[18]

LIEBERMAN AS CAMPAIGNER

The national reaction to Gore's historic choice of Lieberman for vice president provided Lieberman with a kind of honeymoon period in which all factions could rejoice at his selection. Lieberman's own reaction to the news was to say, "Miracles happen" and to thank the Almighty unabashedly in his speech at the formal announcement of his candidacy in Nashville, Tennessee, on August 9. Jewish citizens took great pride in this unexpected nomination and celebrated it, though some expressed concern that Jews might be blamed if the Democrats were defeated.[19] The *New York Post*'s headline on August 8, 2000, simply said, "Oy vey"—loosely translated from the Yiddish as "Woe is me, such a problem!" Republicans acknowledged that it was difficult to condemn Lieberman directly, because of his reputation for moral rectitude and his historic standing as the first Jew ever to run on a major party ticket. Indeed, his candidacy energized the Gore campaign and abruptly ended the Bush campaign's momentum (or "bounce") coming out of the Republican Convention held the previous week.

Lieberman proved to be an able campaigner. Although he is not an electrifying orator, he has a genial manner, and his speeches demonstrated his own thoughtful approach to the issues. He was a good number-two on the ticket, frequently introducing Gore to audiences with glowing testimonials to his virtues.[20]

When not praising Gore, Lieberman was criticizing the policies of the Republicans, denouncing Bush's record on children's health care in Texas and attacking his economic proposals. Indeed, he took the lead in attacking the opposition, allowing Gore to remain above the fray. His approach was not to make personal attacks on Bush and Cheney but to criticize GOP strategies and policies. He was the Gore campaign's favorite spokesman on the NBC *Today Show,* ABC's *Good Morning America,* and on the Sunday morning talk shows. Lieberman was also able to promote the achievements of the Clinton administration in a way that Gore was not. Partly because Lieberman had already criticized Clinton's conduct in his 1998 Senate speech, he was free in the 2000 campaign to praise the Clinton presidency's "extraordinary record" on the economy and on reducing crime. Gore apparently felt that he could not campaign on the basis of the Clinton/Gore administration's achievements without being tainted by Clinton's scandalous behavior.

Both Lieberman and his Republican counterpart, Cheney, acquitted themselves well in the vice-presidential debate on October 5. In contrast to three Bush-Gore presidential debates, which were characterized by posturing and tense one-upmanship, Lieberman and Cheney conducted, before a TV audience of 28.5 million people, an honorable exchange on the issues. Their debate was marked by an easy cordiality between two seasoned professionals who stuck to the issues and answered the questions. Some described their exchange as "a rarity in contemporary presidential politics: a thoughtful, informative debate free of rancor."[21] The public was generally pleased with the vice-presidential debate, so much so that in comments and letters to the editors of daily newspapers voters frequently expressed regret that Lieberman and Cheney were not presidential rather than vice-presidential candidates.[22]

In retrospect, one of Lieberman's more interesting campaign forays was to Florida. Gore and Lieberman appeared together in southeast Florida at the end of August, visiting largely Jewish community centers and asserting that they would compete aggressively for the state's twenty-five electoral votes. Democrats had won the state in 1996 and narrowly lost it in 1992. Although Jews accounted for only 6 percent of Florida's voters in 1996, local Democrats in 2000 said that Joe Lieberman was regarded as "a rock star, like Barbra Streisand," in south Florida and that his ability to turn out votes would make the Democrats surprisingly competitive. Lieberman's mother, Marcia Lieberman, also campaigned in Jewish communities in south Florida.[23]

Despite Republican control of the governorship and the state legislature, the Gore campaign devoted significant resources to the campaign in Florida; it ran its first television advertisements in the Tampa, Orlando, and West Palm Beach markets, and it sent Lieberman there several times. During his first visit, Lieberman told a large crowd at a largely Jewish community center, "I can't tell you how important Florida is. I honestly believe that Al Gore and I are going to win Florida and as a result are going to win the election in November."[24] Given Florida's contested election, these remarks seem somewhat prescient.

CRITICISM OF LIEBERMAN ON THE CAMPAIGN TRAIL

Once the novelty of his vice-presidential candidacy had worn off, Lieberman had to weather criticism from a variety of different groups. He was criticized by the Republicans, certainly, but also by some Democrats and independents. Left-wing Democrats like Rabbi Michael Lerner, editor of *Tikkun,* a liberal magazine on Jewish affairs, criticized Lieberman's centrist "New Democrat" views as insufficiently attentive to issues of social justice.[25] African American leaders such as Congresswoman Maxine Waters (D-Calif.) were concerned that Lieberman not underrate the importance of affirmative action. At the Democratic Convention in Los Angeles, Lieberman and Gore made a major effort to reassure the Democratic Left on these issues.

Lieberman also came under fire for being a bit of a moralizer. For several years, he had criticized the Hollywood movie industry for violence and explicit sex in its films. He and a former Republican drug czar, William Bennett, had given "Silver Sewer" awards to production companies that featured salacious films. Although some actors, such as Martin Sheen, said Lieberman was right in his critique of the entertainment industry, some critics accused him of being sanctimonious and hypocritical—he owned investments in some of the companies he was criticizing, and Hollywood moguls were prominent contributors to the Democratic Party and the Gore/Lieberman campaign.[26]

Others criticized Lieberman for not withdrawing from his Connecticut race for a third term in the Senate. Neither Connecticut law nor federal law prevented Lieberman from running simultaneously for vice president and for reelection to the Senate. Connecticut Democratic Party leaders said it was too late to hold a primary and that if Lieberman withdrew, a replacement would have to be chosen at a special party convention. But Lieberman decided to stay on the ballot for the Senate, following the precedent of two senators and vice-presidential nominees from Texas, Lloyd Bentsen in 1988 and Lyndon B. Johnson in 1960.

Nevertheless, both the *New York Times* and the *Washington Post* suggested that Lieberman end his Senate campaign. The *Times* argued that his dual candidacy was unfair to his Connecticut constituents and "undercut his own image as a person who puts principle above political convenience."[27] As the race for control of the Senate tightened, the pressure on Lieberman to withdraw increased. The dilemma for Democrats was that if Lieberman won both elections (the vice presidency and his Senate seat), he would have to resign his Senate seat, thus clearing the way for Connecticut Governor John Rowland, a Republican, to choose his replacement. As the *Times* editors stated, "That choice would surely be a Republican, an even greater distortion of fairness if a majority of Connecticut voters want a Democrat to represent them." Moreover, Lieberman's fail-safe approach to the election dilemma seemed to undermine the national Democratic party's argument about the importance of returning control of the Senate to the Democrats, and to betray a lack of confidence in Gore's winning potential.

Lieberman addressed these questions about his dual candidacy plainly and directly. He cited polls showing that the people of Connecticut were roughly evenly divided about his decision to run simultaneous campaigns yet overwhelmingly favored his reelection. He had decided to remain on the ballot, explaining that he and the people of Connecticut had "agreed to disagree" on that issue. Ultimately, of course, Lieberman lost the race for vice president but won reelection to the Senate with 65 percent of the vote. His gamble worked: he remains in the Senate, and his victory contributed to the Democratic Party's gain of four additional seats to reach a fifty-fifty split (before the defection of James M. Jeffords) in the new Senate.[28]

Lieberman received by far the most criticism of the campaign for his frequent comments about the role of religion in public life. Since this became a national debate, special attention is given here to Lieberman's remarks and to the opinions of his critics.

LIEBERMAN ON RELIGION AND POLITICS

In Joseph Lieberman, the Democrats got a vice-presidential candidate who talked about God as eagerly as did any evangelical Republican. Lieberman's public utterances about religion and politics surprised liberals, delighted conservatives, and caused a fair amount of controversy.

Three weeks into his campaign, Lieberman gave a Sunday-morning address at the Fellowship Chapel Church in Detroit, one of the city's largest African American congregations. Declaring that belief in God is the basis of morality and of the nation, he called for a greater role for religion in American public life. He urged Americans to "renew the dedication of our nation and ourselves to God," and he cited George Washington's admonition never to suppose that "morality can be maintained without religion."

Lieberman insisted that the religious faith of believers is not inconsistent with the freedom of nonbelievers, and he emphasized the importance of tolerance and compassion. "I want to talk to you this morning about another barrier that may fall, as well, as a result of my nomination. I hope it will enable people, all people who are moved, to feel more free to talk about their faith and about their religion. And I hope that it will reinforce the belief that I feel as strongly as anything else, that there must be a place for faith in America's public life." He added that "we know that the Constitution wisely separates church from state, but remember: the Constitution guarantees freedom *of* religion, not freedom *from* religion."

As evidence for his argument, Lieberman pointed to the historical role of religion in American public life, noting that religious "awakenings" had led to such liberal achievements as the Declaration of Independence and the Bill of Rights in the eighteenth century, the abolition of slavery and various progressive social reforms in the nineteenth century, and the civil rights movement of the twentieth century. He suggested that perhaps a fourth "awakening" of religion in American was necessary, as an antidote to violence, promiscuity, vulgarity, and the degradation of family values.[29]

Lieberman, of course, was no newcomer to debates about the role of religion in politics and public discourse. Practically every stump speech and campaign stop featured references to his Jewish faith. He had argued long and eloquently that a general decline in moral values, particularly in popular culture, must be reversed by a reaffirmation of religion. As a candidate, he presented himself to the voters as an observant Orthodox Jew who took his religion seriously. Yet his remarks in Detroit were remarkably similar to themes and phrases commonly voiced by conservative Republicans. As one commentator noted, "His words, if spoken by a conservative Christian, would probably be received with alarm by many factions in Lieberman's own party—including many Jews—who are wary of the political activism of the religious right."[30]

In a sense, that is exactly what happened. The day after Lieberman's Detroit speech, the Anti-Defamation League called upon Lieberman to stop making "overt expressions" of religious belief on the campaign trail. In a letter signed by Abraham H. Foxman, national director of the ADL, and Howard P. Berkowitz, its national chairman, the league declared to Lieberman that in a political context, such expressions of faith risk alienating people and run "contrary to the American ideal." Foxman and Berkowitz also said that although the organization believed that candidates "should feel comfortable explaining their religious convictions to voters," there was "a point at which an emphasis on religion in a political campaign becomes inappropriate and even unsettling in a religiously diverse society such as ours."[31]

Foxman and Berkowitz took particular issue with Lieberman's reference to George Washington's view that morality cannot be maintained unless it is rooted in religion. "To even suggest that one cannot be a moral person without being a religious person is an affront to many highly ethical citizens," they wrote. "The United States is made up of many different types of people from many different backgrounds and different faiths, including individuals who do not believe in any god, and none of our citizens, including atheistic Americans, should be made to feel outside of the electoral or political process."[32]

The irony of the ADL's criticism of Lieberman was not lost on most observers. This clash pitted the nation's oldest battler against anti-Semitism against the first Jew named to a major party presidential ticket. But it also fostered other unusual alliances. The ADL found itself supported by atheists and opposed by some rabbis. Conservative Christians supported Lieberman but also used the occasion to complain that the media had held their favored candidates to a double standard. Richard D. Land, president of the Ethics and Religious Liberty Commission of the Southern Baptist Convention, put it this way: "For people to applaud Sen. Lieberman for taking his Judaism seriously but then to diss Gov. Bush for saying in reply to a question that Jesus Christ was the philosopher who influenced him the most is a double standard."[33]

Land urged the media to be consistent and to get over its "extreme prejudice against evangelicals who are seen as threatening."[34]

For his part, Lieberman clarified his call for a greater role for religion in public life, saying that he meant it as a matter of public discourse, not public policy. He insisted, in response to the ADL's criticism, that he did not consider those who are not religious to be amoral or unfit for public office. Asked if he would object to an atheist's being president, he said, "Personally, no, if I thought it [sic] was a good person." He also said he respected former Senator Bill Bradley's refusal to discuss his religious views during the 2000 presidential primary campaign. These qualifications suggested that Lieberman's advocacy of faith in public life was more subtle and nuanced than originally seemed to be the case. "Religion in my opinion can be, and in my opinion usually is, a source of good behavior. But two things: I know religious people who I consider not to be moral, and I also know people who are not religious who I consider to be extremely moral. So, you know, I'm talking here about probabilities."[35]

At the same time, Lieberman's aides went to great lengths to distinguish between his comments and efforts by Christian conservatives to mingle religion and politics—noting, for example, that Lieberman supported abortion rights and opposed prayer in public schools. Conservative evangelicals, by contrast, invoked religion to justify their opposition to abortion and gay rights and their support for school prayer. The fact that faith can be used to justify any number of political positions—even opposing positions— suggests the difficulties of drawing specific policy conclusions even from similar religious premises. Lieberman himself cautioned against using faith to justify any measure that is considered politically divisive. "I think there's a difference here between respecting faith and feeling free to talk about the way in which it informs and benefits American life, and talking about it in a way that may make some people feel excluded."[36]

Probably the most important difference between Lieberman and the Religious Right over the role of faith in politics was that as a member of a minority religion, Lieberman could speak about faith in a way that did not raise the specter of coercion. By contrast, the very nature of their religion—with its emphasis upon conversion—makes Christian evangelicals potentially more threatening. Conservative Christians believe that their mission is to spread the "good news" of the gospel of Jesus to all nonbelievers. Indeed, the Southern Baptists Convention's Website describes a "strategy for evangelizing the world" by "aggressively pursuing converts." At times, Southern Baptists have invoked their evangelical call to justify campaigns for the conversion of American Jews. Such views are very different from those of Lieberman, who, as a Jew, has no sectarian mandate to proselytize.

As Lieberman explained his remarks on religion and politics, his position became clearer. He was not saying that citizens cannot be moral if they are not religious. Nor was he saying that specific policy preferences follow automatically from basic religious beliefs. He certainly was not arguing that faith-based views should be introduced into public life in order to shape or enact exclusionary, coercive public policies. But he was arguing that the nation's political discourse could benefit from attention to the religious beliefs and moral ideals of citizens and leaders. From concerns about the moral tenor of popular entertainment to fundamental issues of social justice, religion can shape the public debate for the better and help keep that debate civil and tolerant. In a free society, Lieberman argued, religiously motivated views should be given an equal hearing. Even the public expression of religious views by candidates gives us a sense of their vision for the polity and should be heard so that citizens may properly evaluate their candidacy.

Lieberman also thought that more God-talk could be a kind of learning experience. As he put it, "I understand that some people who are particularly sensitive to religious discrimination may get uncomfortable when people talk about their faith, but I find it both informative and encouraging." When religious Christians discuss their faith, Lieberman said, "I don't feel excluded by it." In seeking to encourage public expression of religion, Lieberman tied his call for more talk of religion in public life to the growth of vulgarity and violence in popular culture. He argued that an absence of religion in public life had created a void, filled in part by that popular culture that conveys meanness, not meaning. He did not see this as a gain but as a loss.[37]

It is interesting to note how Lieberman's views resemble those expressed by American Jews in the eighteenth and nineteenth centuries before they moved toward a more strict separationism. The Jewish position then was religious liberty and equal treatment before the law, so that all religions would be on an equal footing. Jews also expected schools to convey the moral norms necessary for a democratic citizenry to function, and they saw the connection between religion and morality. In a sense, Lieberman echoes these earlier views. While he strongly supports tolerance and separation of church and state, he also thinks religion has a role to play in public affairs. He appeals to the nation's Framers, who valued both faith and religious freedom. They saw that in a society in which government does not tightly control people, "it's helpful to have other sources of good behavior, and so religion is one of those. So in that sense, it is an ally of government in trying to create a good society."[38]

DEBATE AND CRITIQUE OF LIEBERMAN'S VIEWS ON RELIGION AND PUBLIC LIFE

Lieberman's remarks set off a lively debate about the role of religion in politics, raising concerns in some quarters about maintaining the separation of church and state. One commentator saw Lieberman's call for "a new spiritual awakening" in America as a call for the rebirth of a nationally prominent religious Left in the United States. Lamenting a divisive standoff between religious conservatives and liberal secularists who are hostile to religion, this observer argued that if Lieberman "succeeds at reuniting morality and political liberalism, he will have revived one of the most powerful movements in American history—a potent force in the abolition of slavery, labor reforms and the civil rights movement." She thought Lieberman was important because he "has severed the connection between religious devotion and political conservatism," and because he "demonstrates that people of religious faith can, and do, disagree on important political issues that imply deeply held moral beliefs."[39]

Another commentator suggested that in stressing the religious foundation of American society and government, Lieberman was advocating what has been called the country's "civil religion," the spiritual and nonsectarian ties that bind America's majority of believers, of whatever faith. Civil religion in the United States encompasses, for example, the basic beliefs that led the Framers to proclaim that the Creator had endowed persons with certain "inalienable rights."[40] Civil religion is useful in the American context as a basic set of beliefs or common values that unites Americans, thereby promoting some measure of social stability. The tenets of civil religion tend to be general, vague, and almost bland—and to lack any cutting edge or prophetic critique of existing society. Nevertheless, proponents of civil religion contend that it is useful in providing a common language and common values in American public life.

How did ordinary citizens react to this lively debate? Lieberman's defense of American civil religion was, after all, one in a lengthy series of expressions of faith by various presidential candidates throughout the long campaign. Ordinary voters were understandably skeptical about all this God-talk, although they tended to think that of all the candidates, Lieberman was the most sincere in his expressions of faith. "He doesn't just say it," one voter said, "he lives it."

At the same time, many voters wanted to hear more about the issues than about nominees' professions of faith. One Denver woman said, "I've heard enough from the candidates about how they pray. I want to hear about how they're going to keep the economy going." People also worried that the religious pondering of politicians was just another form of pandering to voters. "It's just a way to try to get votes, it's got nothing to do with running the country," one California man said. "It just doesn't have any relevance, and they ought to stop talking about it."[41]

But media pundits could not resist discussing the issues Lieberman raised. *Commonweal*, a lay Catholic journal of opinion, editorialized that Lieberman's God-talk was useful in reminding citizens "of the irreducible moral dimension of politics." They recognized that religion could be exploited for political ends, but they trusted that "Americans are not easily duped by showy piety." In supporting the public expression of religion, they argued that "demagoguery is always a danger. It does not follow, however, that the danger is best combated by quarantining the suspect. Religious claims must be subject to the same scrutiny and criticism as any other voice seeking to influence public policy."[42]

Washington Post columnist E. J. Dionne wrote that Lieberman's comments about religion tested everyone's consistency—that of liberals, conservatives, the ADL, and the Religious Right. He too pointed to the risks of such public God-talk by politicians: the dangers of pandering to voters and using political positions to proselytize. But, on balance, he welcomed Lieberman's public statements as an expression of, rather than a threat to, religious liberty. And he offered voters a way to evaluate politicians' expressions of faith. While Dionne thought it good for a politician to explain the extent to which his or her political views are rooted in religious commitments, he argued that in a free and pluralistic society that includes nonbelievers, politicians must explain themselves in terms accessible to those who do not share their faith. Dionne thought Lieberman had passed this test of rational accessibility but that Bush clearly had not. As he wrote, "The problem with Bush's naming Christ as his favorite philosopher was not the invocation itself but Bush's response to a request for elaboration: 'Well, if they don't know, it's going to be hard to explain.' A politician in a free society has to explain why he's bringing God and faith into a campaign—or not drag God into politics at all."[43]

While Dionne and the editors of *Commonweal* applauded Lieberman's talk of religion and the debate it provoked, other media commentators still worried about undue mixing of religion and politics. Since Lieberman had declared strong support for church-state separation, this was not an issue. But the worries of these pundits indicated how difficult it is for Americans to distinguish between constitutional clauses calling for church-state separation and the broader question of the relation between religion and politics in American history and in contemporary American politics. The *New York Times* editorialized that Lieberman "seemed to cross the boundaries of tolerance" in citing Washington's rejection of the idea that morality can be maintained without religion. As we have seen, Lieberman, in response to this criticism, made the necessary qualification that, of course, people *can* be moral without being religious.

The *Times* welcomed Lieberman's condemnation of the movie industry for its disdain of moral values and his call for greater government funding for faith-based organizations that deliver services to the poor and the homeless. But the editors warned that there should never be any compromise with the Constitution's ban on government establishment of religion. "Exhorting Hollywood to make different movies cannot veer into government censorship, and government funding of 'faith-based' organizations should never be used to support religious proselytizing by these groups." Struggling to make the necessary distinctions, the *Times* editors concluded, "It is fine to call for more religion in American public life. But supporting the constitutionally based separation of religion from public policy or favoring limits on the role of government in promoting religious values should not be denigrated as immoral or anti-religion. In the end, tolerance and understanding of the boundaries between church and state are what have allowed religion to flourish in the United States as it has in few other countries in history."[44]

Not to be outdone in this lively exchange, Abraham Foxman clarified the Anti-Defamation League's criticism of Lieberman in an interview with a *New York Times* journalist. Foxman made two important points. First, he noted that the Republican primaries had been filled with "competition over who loves God more, who's more faithful to Jesus and his principles." He said he found this kind of talk disturbing. While it no doubt comforts many people, "it also frightens a lot of others," he said, and hearing repeated professions of faith from a Jewish candidate did not make him feel any better. "What troubled a lot of people is that he [Lieberman] used the line that the Constitution provides for freedom *of* religion and not *from* religion. That's a religious-right line. And it's not true, because it does protect us from religion."

Secondly, Foxman commented upon Lieberman's assurances that the goal of God-talk in the public sphere is not imposed religiosity. "That's the rationale," he said. "It's O.K. if he does it. But it reinforces and legitimizes that type of talk. The reason the Falwells and Robertsons come to his defense is because they understand that he softens the turf. They are a majority, and they do want their Christian—what they now say is Judaeo-Christian—religion as *the* religion." Foxman thought this was treading on very dangerous ground.[45]

In perhaps a final word, former Senator Eugene McCarthy also expressed strong reservations about politicians' expressions of religious faith. "Perhaps God does not object to political appropriation. But, in some sense, such tactics mock God. They also muddle politics." McCarthy insisted that the president is *not* the moral leader of his people but the premier political leader—"one hopes with some sense of morality." Furthermore, McCarthy urged that while religious belief may well be good for democracy, its politicization is not. "Religifying politics tempts politicians to messianic delusion. And politicizing religion cheapens and corrupts the spirit. If we return to the wisdom of the founders on this point, excessive public expressions of religious piety will be regarded with suspicion. Our motto should be: 'By their *deeds* shall we know them.'"[46]

EVALUATION

What are we to make of this debate? If less dramatic than the extraordinary Florida recount, it was one of the more interesting aspects of the 2000 presidential campaign. The following points may be drawn from this lively exchange about the role of religion in American public life.

First, Lieberman made the case that general discussion of religious beliefs is valuable in public life. He suggested that at the very least, religion should not be excluded from political discourse. Religiously motivated views should be given an equal hearing in our public dialogue. Public debate is impoverished if we remove all references to religious belief and God-talk from the public square.

Lieberman pointed to American history for examples of the role of religion in shaping democracy, particularly in social reform movements such as the abolitionist movement of the nineteenth century or the civil rights movement of the twentieth century. But he also contended that religion could be valuable in reaffirming the moral foundation of the country and appealing to common, widely shared values. In an age of moral relativism, such a civil-religion approach could enhance the country's national dialogue.

Lieberman also argued that a politician's discussion of religion could tell us something about a candidate's personal values and vision for the country. Lieberman's display of obvious pride in his faith and heritage was not an attempt to proselytize but an effort to encourage others to reach within their beliefs for the common good and betterment of all. Even nonbelievers recognized the validity of what Lieberman was doing, at the same time that they accused him of moral overreaching. Ron Barrier, the national spokesman for American Atheists, founded by Madalyn Murray O'Hair, said, "Someone running for elective office . . . has every right to share with us how they derive their ethics. But we feel Senator Lieberman has crossed a line by actually implying that morals without religion are impossible. . . . We find that to be a bit alienating."[47] Lieberman did acknowledge that there is no necessary connection between religion and morality. But that still leaves us with the valid possibility of candidates explaining to voters how they derive their ethics. Indeed, as Dionne stressed, candidates who are religious believers have particular obligations to explain in plain language how their beliefs influence their conceptions of public morality and public policy.

Lieberman spoke of the greatness of America, where one can be a proud Jew and an American simultaneously. As a religiously observant person known for speaking frankly and eloquently about the ways in which his faith informs his public life, Lieberman did fellow Americans a service and stimulated a serious exchange about faith and politics, one in which several important clarifications were made.

Among these important clarifications are the following. First, there are risks and dangers in all this talk of religion by political candidates. Hypocrisy and pandering to voters are ever-present dangers. Demagoguery is another risk. Piety can be mistaken for political acumen. There is always the danger that citizens and clergy may impose a religious test on people seeking public office. Religious language may become a code for a controversial political agenda that candidates support but would rather not discuss for fear it would alienate prospective voters. Moreover, if religion can corrupt politics, there is also the attendant risk that politics can corrupt religion. In advocating a "wall of separation between the garden of the church and the wilderness of the world," Roger Williams of colonial Rhode Island was reminding us of that possibility.[48]

Nevertheless, Lieberman's reasoned discussion of the role of religion in public life was one of the more memorable aspects of the 2000 election campaign. By speaking so openly about religion and his own faith commitments, he may have broken the monopoly of religious discussion held by the Religious Right. In saying that public life has more to gain than to lose from attending to the religious concerns of citizens, Lieberman initiated a lively debate and made a real contribution to the national dialogue.

CONCLUSION

Thomas Marshall, Woodrow Wilson's vice president, observed of the vice presidency, "Once there were two brothers: one ran away to sea, the other was elected vice president—and nothing was ever heard from either of them again."[49] Marshall's comments epitomize the traditional view of the number-two spot on the ticket. The office of vice president has no real power; its duties are largely ceremonial. Moreover, in the end, people vote for presidents, not vice presidents.

But the election of 2000 upset this conventional wisdom. Both Cheney and Lieberman were men of experience, seasoned politicians who brought heft and substance to their respective tickets. Both acquitted themselves well in the vice-presidential debate. Their friendly, humorous exchange provided a needed respite from the awkward tenor of the three Bush-Gore debates. Their cordial professionalism augured well for possible cooperation in the new Senate, where the initial fifty-fifty split meant that Cheney would cast tie-breaking votes and Lieberman's reasoned bipartisanship would be needed more than ever.

Lieberman did a good job as Gore's number-two on the Democratic ticket, and he was especially supportive and helpful to Vice President Gore during the five-week-long Florida recount. Lieberman then returned to the Senate for a third term—but this time with a difference: he was one of the nation's best-known senators and a hero of the Democratic Party. His thoughtful approach to the issues, his legislative leadership, and his cordial relations with Senate colleagues virtually guaranteed that Lieberman would remain in the national spotlight. Some mention has already been made of a possible presidential candidacy in 2004. For the moment, this is sheer speculation. For now, Lieberman must be content with a strong performance in the 2000 campaign and a candidacy that made history—not only because he was the first Jew ever nominated for national office by a major party, and not only because he was on the losing end of one of the closest presidential elections in the nation's history, but also because his eloquent statements about the role of religion in public life were real contributions to American political discourse.

NOTES

1. Jesse L. Jackson Sr., "Mission from the Moral Center," *Washington Post,* 10 August 2000, A29.

2. Jackson's remark is from Lieberman's speech in Nashville on joining the Democratic ticket. See Joseph L. Lieberman, "Lieberman on Joining the Democratic Ticket: 'I Am Humbled and Honored,'" *New York Times,* 9 August 2000, A16.

3. For Henry's speech, see John E. Semonche, *Religion and Constitutional Government in the United States* (Carrboro, N.C.: Signal, 1986), 109–11. See also Jonathan D. Sarna, "American Jews and Church-State Relations: The Search for 'Equal Footing,'" in Jonathan D. Sarna and David G. Dalin, *Religion and State in the American Jewish Experience* (Notre Dame, Ind.: University of Notre Dame Press, 1997), 82–85. As Sarna notes, Jacob Henry was permitted to retain his seat on the doubtful grounds that the words "Civil Department" in the state's constitution excluded the legislature. In 1835, an amendment awarded Catholics full rights commensurate with Protestants, but the exclusion against non-Christians was retained. Jews won complete equality in North Carolina only in 1868. See Sarna, "American Jews," 82–83.

4. Semonche, *Religion and Constitutional Government,* 111–15. See also Sarna and Dalin, *Religion and State,* 94–97.

5. These are the words of Jonas Phillips, a German Jewish immigrant merchant from Philadelphia, who petitioned the 1787 Constitutional Convention to change Pennsylvania's religious test for public office. See Sarna, "American Jews and Church-State Relations," 1.

6. In 1892, the U.S. Supreme Court in *Church of the Holy Trinity v. United States* declared that the United States actually was a "Christian Nation." Sarna, "American Jews and Church-State Relations," 13–14.

7. See David Wyman, *The Abandonment of the Jews: America and the Holocaust 1941–1945* (New York: New Press, 1984).

8. Wyman, *The Abandonment of the Jews,* 9–11.

9. Wyman, *The Abandonment of the Jews,* 14–15.

10. Wyman, *The Abandonment of the Jews,* 12–14.

11. Wyman, *The Abandonment of the Jews,* 11–12. In reality, as Wyman notes, the proportion of Jews in the U.S. armed forces was at least as great as the proportion of Jews in the American population.

12. Laurie Goodstein, "To Many Social Conservatives, an Ally," *New York Times,* 8 August 2000, A23.

13. Richard Lacayo, "Walking the Walk," *Time,* 21 August 2000, 33.

14. Lisa Guernsey, "Choice of Jewish Candidate Is Noted in Slurs on Internet," *New York Times*, 9 August 2000, A18. Also, Ruth E. Igoe, "Anti-Semites Online: 'It's Ugly Out There,'" *Star-Ledger*, 9 August 2000, 9. (The *Star-Ledger* is a newspaper of record and the largest-circulation daily in the state of New Jersey.) Interestingly, exchanges within mainstream political chat rooms contained phrases like "Jew in power," "allegiance to Israel" and "influence in banking." One commentator noted, "It's the same type of old canards that we were seeing in the 1960s with John F. Kennedy and how people thought he could not be independent of the pope. The same is true in the discussions we are seeing about Lieberman and Israel. It's the same myth of dual loyalty, that a Jew cannot be a good American."

15. David E, Rosenbaum, "The Record: Senator Often Stands to Right of His Party," *New York Times*, 8 August 2000, A21.

16. Leslie Wayne and Don Van Natta Jr., "As a Senator, Lieberman Is Proudly Pro-Business," *New York Times*, 27 August 2000, 1 and 22.

17. Kevin Sack, "Trip South in '63 Gave Lieberman a Footnote, and Hold, in History," *New York Times*, 26 September 2000, A21. See also Paul Zielbauer, "A Grave Young Man at Yale," *New York Times*, 2 October 2000, B1.

18. Robert D. McFadden, "A Man of Steady Habits: Joseph Isador Lieberman," *New York Times*, 8 August 2000, A22.

19. Clyde Haberman, "Sense of Pride among Jews Is Tempered with Concern," *New York Times*, 8 August 2000, A23. See also David Margolick, "For American Jews, Hope and Uncertainty," *New York Times*, 12 August 2000, A15.

20. Richard Perez-Pena, "Best Crowd-Pleaser for Gore Is Lieberman," *New York Times*, 13 September 2000, A18.

21. Richard Perez-Pena and Michael Cooper, "Running Mates, Ready to Fight, Kept Gloves On," *New York Times*, 7 October 2000, A1.

22. William Safire, "Two Kangaroo Tickets," *New York Times*, 10 August 2000, A21; see also "The Race for No. 2: A Debate with a Difference," letter to the editor, *New York Times*, 2 October 2000, A14.

23. "Campaign Briefing," *New York Times*, 2 November 2000, A28.

24. Kevin Sack, "Gore and Company Making a Serious Play for Florida," *New York Times*, 24 August 2000, A23.

25. Haberman, "Sense of Pride among Jews Is Tempered with Concern."

26. "Sheen Backs Lieberman's Take on Tinseltown," *Star-Ledger*, 16 September 2000, 3. See also Bernard Weinraub, "The Hollywood Factor: Moguls Rattled by Gore's Choice of Critic of Entertainment Industry," *New York Times*, 11 August 2000, A17; Katharine Q. Seelye, "Before a Hollywood Crowd, Democrats Lower the Volume," *New York Times*, 20 September 2000, A1; Richard Perez-Pena, "Lieberman Is Criticized on Violent Entertainment," *New York Times*, 21 September 2000, A26; and Jacques Steinberg, "Parents Say Censoring Films Is Their Job, Not Politicians'," *New York Times*, 28 September 2000, A1.

27. Editorial, *New York Times*, 5 October 2000, A34.

28. Lieberman won 828,902 votes to 448,077 for his opponent, Republican candidate Phil Giordano. Source is on the World Wide Web, www.sov-sots.state.ct.us.

29. Richard Perez-Pena, "Lieberman Seeks Greater Role for Religion in Public Life," *New York Times*, 28 August 2000, A14. See also Cathleen Decker, "Lieberman Mix of Faith, Politics Sets Off Clash," *Los Angeles Times*, 30 August 2000, A1.

30. Richard Perez-Pena, "Lieberman Seeks Greater Role," A14.

31. Gustav Niebuhr, "Lieberman Is Asked to Stop Invoking Faith in Campaign," *New York Times*, 29 August 2000, A19.

32. Decker, "Lieberman Mix of Faith, Politics Sets Off Clash," A1.

33. Decker, "Lieberman Mix of Faith, Politics Sets Off Clash," A7.

34. Laurie Goodstein, "What Hath God Wrought? Lieberman and the Right," *New York Times*, 3 September 2000, sec. 4, p. 5.

35. Richard Perez-Pena, "Lieberman Defends His Call for Bigger Role for Religion," *New York Times*, 30 August 2000, A21.

36. Perez-Pena, "Lieberman Defends His Call," A21.

37. Perez-Pena, "Lieberman Defends His Call," A21.

38. Perez-Pena, "Lieberman Defends His Call," A21.

39. Eleanor Brown, "Lieberman's Revival of the Religious Left," *New York Times*, 30 August 2000, A23.

40. Goodstein, "What Hath God Wrought? Lieberman and the Right," 5. Robert Bellah first explained the concept of "civil religion" in a noted 1967 essay in *Daedalus*. See Robert Bellah, "Civil Religion in America," in *Religion in America*, ed. W. McLoughlin and Robert Bellah (Boston: Houghton Mifflin, 1968), 3–23.

41. Dirk Johnson, "Hearing about God but Wondering about Issues," *New York Times*, 5 September 2000, A23.

42. The Editors, "God Talk," *Commonweal*, 22 September 2000, 5.

43. E. J. Dionne, "Lieberman's Invoking of Religion Is Reason to Rejoice," *Star-Ledger*, 5 September 2000, 11.

44. "Mr. Lieberman's Religious Words," editorial, *New York Times*, 31 August 2000, A24.

45. Clyde Haberman, "Whose God Is It, Anyway?" *New York Times*, 6 September 2000, B1.

46. Eugene J. McCarthy and Keith C. Burris, "The Singular Piety of Politics," *New York Times*, 31 August 2000, A23.

47. Decker, "Lieberman Mix of Faith, Politics Sets Off Clash."

48. Roger Williams, "Mr. Cotton's Letter Lately Printed, Examined and Answered," London, 5 February 1644, reprinted in Perry Miller, *Roger Williams: His Contribution to the American Tradition* (Indianapolis: Bobbs-Merrill, 1953), 89–100 (the quote is on 98).

49. Quoted in Adam Clymer, "Choosing a Running Mate Matters. Or Mattered," *New York Times*, 20 August 2000, sec. 4, p. 4.

Two

Religious Liberty in a Pluralistic Society:
The *Smith* Case

8

Evolving Standards under the Free Exercise Clause: Neutrality or Accommodation?

George E. Garvey

The First Amendment of the U.S. Constitution provides that "Congress shall make no law respecting an establishment of religion, or prohibiting the free exercise thereof."[1] There is, I believe, a popular belief that the law of church and state relations in the United States is clear and fixed. To many, the controlling principle is embodied in the phrase, generally attributed to Thomas Jefferson, "wall of separation."[2] In legal analysis, however, slogans or formulas seldom provide the certainty they promise. Difficult issues generate a complex jurisprudence, and, to be sure, the relationship between citizen, state, and church in the United States is most complicated. Constitutional interpretation, in the area of religious liberty as elsewhere, involves a synthesis of many factors, including the original intent of the Framers, historical patterns and traditional relationships, modern exigencies, issues of federalism and separation of powers, and, as the legal realists remind us, perhaps what the deciding judges ate for breakfast. The flippant reference to the morning meal, of course, reflects a deeper insight, that the beliefs and experiences of judges will influence their perceptions about the fair and just outcome in any case. This is likely to be particularly true where religion is concerned, since religious values generally command an abiding allegiance from those indoctrinated in any faith.

Several basic themes can be identified in the literature and jurisprudence related to the relationship between church and state in the United States. One commentator, for example, lists separation, equality, and noncoercion (liberty) as major values implicit in the Constitution's religion clauses.[3] When a government enactment violates all three principles, the outcome should be readily apparent should the offending law be challenged. The legal establishment of a favored sect, for example, particularly if coupled with the imposition of disabilities on members of disfavored religions, surely violates any conception of separation, equality, or liberty. Laws, however, are seldom so crude; a particular law or policy may simultaneously foster one or more goal, such as equality or liberty, while impeding others, such as separation. The challenge of selecting between competing principles—separation, equality, and liberty—has contributed to a complex and seemingly erratic body of law.

Scholars disagree about the relationship between the establishment and free exercise clauses. Some argue that they embody two distinct concepts, while others contend that they reflect a single, unified principle. The case law also occasionally treats these two pillars of U.S. church/state policy as a unity, and as quite distinct at other times. This chapter will not engage that issue directly, other than to acknowledge that the concepts seem so often to blend that at some level they surely share a common foundation. At the very least, the antiestablishment norm and the free exercise ideal reflect a common commitment to religious liberty, freedom of conscience, and noncoercion.

This chapter explores some of the most critical and controversial modern constitutional developments relating to the religion clauses. The principal focus is on the truly extraordinary, continuing struggle between the judicial and legislative branches of the federal government regarding the appropriate meaning of the free exercise clause.[4] Analysis of the free exercise clause is complicated by issues related to federalism and separation of powers, as well as by concerns about religious liberty. At some risk of oversimplification, the critical contemporary issue is whether the free exercise clause requires neutrality or accommodation. The Supreme Court has reversed its position regarding this matter in recent years,[5] prompting a legislative response,[6] which, in turn, has produced a judicial rebuff to Congress.[7]

This chapter explores the circumstances leading to the legislative enactment and subsequent judicial rejection of the Religious Freedom Restoration Act of 1993[8] (RFRA), as an example of the unresolved stresses that exist in the interpretation and application of the free exercise clause of the First Amendment, a tension experienced at every level and in every branch of government. The controlling constitutional principles have naturally evolved over time and they evidence an inner conflict reflected in diverse and sometimes bewildering judicial decisions. Multiple concurring and dissenting opinions in significant cases demonstrate the depth of the divisions among Supreme Court justices. The challenge of reconciling the sometimes-conflicting constitutional norms of disestablishment and religious liberty has been, and continues to be, daunting.

The stresses evident in the free exercise jurisprudence are rooted in the experience of colonial Americans. The competing views of that era regarding the relationship between religious and civil authority must naturally influence modern interpretations of the meaning of the First Amendment. This chapter, therefore, begins with a brief introduction to that historical foundation. It then argues that in spite of the prohibitions of the First Amendment, much of the history of the United States has been characterized by a cultural, legal, and social order that has been quite overtly Protestant. Early constitutional law related to the religion clauses will be briefly surveyed and, ultimately, the chapter will focus on the contemporary intragovernmental dispute regarding the proper interpretation of the free exercise clause and the implications for a pluralistic society.

My conclusion is that the tension reflected in judicial, legislative, and executive actions related to religion is inherent, and healthy, in a society where the polity's commitment to religion, however that is defined, is notable but where religious viewpoints are extremely diverse. Striking the balance between the freedom to exercise one's religious preference, including the freedom to have no preference or traditional religious belief at all, and ensuring that tolerance or accommodation does not "establish" any single sect or broader religious belief system, such as Christianity, will be a perpetual challenge. In light of the conclusion that tension is a healthy reflection of the religious diversity of the United States, Congress generally seems to have the better part of the current dispute. For reasons developed later in more depth, I question the standard of review established by RFRA—"a compelling state interest"[9]—but support Congress's conclusion that this is a particularly unfortunate area for the courts to opt for a rigid formula and defer excessively to the democratic majority.

HISTORICAL BACKGROUND

The complex relationship between citizen, state, and religion is surely as old as organized society. Rulers have sought legitimacy by uniting with the priestly classes throughout history. Priests, for their part, have sought protection and support from secular rulers. At times the secular and religious elites have cooperated, and at times they have clashed. A comprehensive listing of the various historical patterns of church and state relations, or a weighing of the social utility of those unions and disunions, is beyond the scope of this chapter and author. The point is simply that the study of any social or political order would be incomplete without considering the role that religion has played in the culture.

Attempting to understand the U.S. constitutional ordering of the role of church and state in society does not require a comprehensive search through ancient history. European religious wars and persecutions provided the framework for the colonial American experience. Established religions and official intolerance had spawned migration to many of the

American colonies. Within the English colonial world, this largely reflected intolerance by the Church of England toward minority Protestant sects, such as the Puritans and Quakers. A superficial approach to history might lead intuitively to the conclusion that the roots of the American vision have been found: Those fleeing religious intolerance would naturally seek two goals, disestablishment and freedom of conscience. The story, however, is more complicated.

The colonists seeking relief from intolerance did not practice tolerance. The new land provided the colonists an opportunity to establish their own faiths, and those who did not share their beliefs were often not welcome. Moreover, commercial interests that brought with them the established Anglican Church colonized many of the southern territories. There were some experiments in toleration: Roger Williams in Rhode Island; Pennsylvania and New York practiced some forms of religious tolerance; and there was even a Catholic incursion in Maryland. The bigger picture, however, reflected a mosaic of established churches and varying levels of intolerance and persecution. The American experience, therefore, cannot be explained or understood as a clean colonial break from the European practices of established religions, intolerance, and persecution. Rather, to borrow a religious metaphor, the Founders of the United States did not merely reject the sins of their European fathers, but rather, they began a process of political conversion for their own failings. Even if we reject notions of U.S. triumphalism rooted in myths about the "Founding Fathers," the American experiment in religious pluralism is most impressive and interesting when seen for what it has been, an evolving and flawed human endeavor.

It is not possible to identify any single principle that captures the intent of the men who drafted, enacted, and ratified the First Amendment.[10] A recent book by John Witte,[11] however, has distilled the several dominant and competing approaches to religion at the time the First Amendment was adopted into four themes that help explain why the religion clauses were destined to promote an ongoing constitutional dialectic rather than to establish a well-defined wall between church and state. Witte identifies two significant theological views and two parallel political perspectives that influenced the thinking of Americans when the United States was established. The theological themes are categorized as the "Puritan view"[12] and the "evangelical view."[13] The Puritans, represented primarily by the Congregationalists of New England, had a clear vision of separate *but cooperative* realms of church and state:

> Although church and state were not to be confounded, they were still to be "close and compact." For, to the Puritans, these two institutions were inextricably linked in nature and in function. Each was an instrument of Godly authority. Each did its part to establish and maintain the community. . . . The Puritans,

therefore, countenanced both the coordination and the cooperation of church and state.[14]

The evangelicals, including Baptists and Anabaptists, had been the minority religions in the American colonies, as they had been in Europe. Theological beliefs, represented by Roger Williams's concern that the secular world invariably corrupts the religious, as well as a history of repression, resulted in a strong commitment among the evangelicals to disestablishment, separation, and freedom of conscience.

The parallel political perspectives are, in Witte's categories, "Enlightenment views"[15] and "republican views."[16] Like their theological counterparts, these political viewpoints differed with regard to the extent and necessity of separation between church and state. The Enlightenment thinkers sought strict separation, sharing with evangelicals a belief that the union of civil and religious authority corrupts both. Moreover, they placed little value on organized religion. Religion was a matter of personal conscience, and the communal aspects of religion were of secondary interest. The "Enlightenment view" was that law should protect the realm of individual conscience and maintain strict separation between civil and religious authorities. James Madison and Thomas Jefferson most notably represented this viewpoint among the nation's founders.

The political counterparts to the Puritans were the "civic republicans." The republicans sought a community of shared values, civic virtues that were fostered by religion. "Republican writers sought to imbue the public square with a common religious ethic and ethos—albeit one less denominationally specific and rigorous than that countenanced by the Puritans."[17] The republican position on religion is often associated with George Washington and John Adams.

There were, of course, some widely shared views at the time that the First Amendment was adopted. All camps were committed to freedom of conscience, and although there were still established churches in New England, even the Puritans/Congregationalists were becoming less committed to the maintenance of their religious establishments. There was, however, a fairly sharp division at some level between those who sought very strict separation (evangelicals/Enlightenment thinkers) and those who believed that religion should enjoy the cooperation and support of the state (Puritans/republicans). While modern judicial rhetoric tends to accept the primacy of the Enlightenment viewpoint—which is not surprising, given Madison's and Jefferson's involvement in the creation of the First Amendment—closer analysis demonstrates that the courts' commitment to rigid separation is not so well fixed. The tension found among the leaders of the founding generation continues to haunt those who formulate public policy, be they judges, legislators, executives, or administrators.

EARLY CONSTITUTIONAL DEVELOPMENTS

The struggle for religious freedom and tolerance in colonial America was by and large an intra-Protestant affair. There was little sympathy for Catholics, Jews, or nonbelievers. Not surprisingly, the maintenance of a Protestant culture lasted well into the twentieth century. The influx of Catholic and Jewish immigrants created a more robust diversity that would eventually lead to greater tolerance, but for many decades the instruments of government—most notably public education—were used to foster the virtues of the dominant religious culture, Protestantism. One significant consequence of Protestant influence in public education was the development of an extensive system of Catholic schools, which in cities with large Catholic populations rivaled public schools in size and stature.

The era of Protestant hegemony produced few opportunities for courts to explore the significance of the religion clauses. For one thing, the First Amendment, as well as the other guarantees of the Bill of Rights, addressed only the federal government.[18] A minimalist interpretation of the First Amendment's religion clauses, therefore, would be that it simply prevented the federal government from intruding in an area reserved to the states. Several states, after all, did have established religions when the amendment was enacted and for some time thereafter.[19] One interpretation of the establishment clause, paradoxically, posits both a disestablishment and an antidisestablishment goal in the constitutional proscription.[20] Under this theory, the federal government could neither establish a religion nor disestablish whatever forms of religious establishment the states had chosen. In any case, the federal government never attempted to establish a federal religion, and accordingly the courts had little reason or opportunity to develop a body of law regarding religious liberty.

When the federal government was challenged during the nineteenth century for allegedly interfering with the rights of citizens who were seeking to exercise their religious beliefs freely, the courts were not protective of religious liberty. Members of the Church of Jesus Christ of Latter-day Saints (Mormons), for example, driven by persecution from several states, moved to what would become the federal territory of Utah. In response to anti-Mormon public opinion, the federal government made polygamy, which was then practiced by members of that faith, a crime. Distinguishing between beliefs, which could not be regulated under the First Amendment, and actions, which could, the Supreme Court upheld the federal criminal statute as applied to a Mormon who asserted that his religious beliefs obliged him to take several wives.[21] Exercise of the franchise in Utah was also limited to prospective voters who would swear they were not members of an organization that advocated polygamy. Ultimately, the federal government dissolved the Mormon Church and confiscated its property. The Supreme Court affirmed all of these actions.[22] The church eventually relented and changed its doctrine regarding polygamy. The Court's decisions were openly protective of the prevailing religious culture, that of Christianity as the Court viewed it.[23]

The Civil War amendments, particularly the Fourteenth Amendment, altered the relationship between the citizens and the states. It provides that

> no State shall make or enforce any law which shall abridge the privileges or immunities of citizens of the United States; nor shall any State deprive any person of life, liberty, or property, without due process of law; nor deny to any person within its jurisdiction the equal protection of the laws.[24]

The U.S. Supreme Court, in the *Slaughter-House Cases*,[25] adopted a restrictive interpretation of the amendment and particularly the privileges and immunities clause. Subsequent decisions began to protect "fundamental" rights as part of the "liberty" protected by the due process clause.[26] The Court gradually "incorporated" and applied to the states most of the protections of the Bill of Rights, including those contained in the First Amendment.[27] The states, therefore, became subject to the same prohibitions as the federal government with regard to the establishment and free exercise of religion.

Prior to the 1940s, there was one area where the Court did protect the rights of non-Protestant Christians. A wave of anti-immigrant, and largely anti-Catholic, feelings following World War I produced several state laws affecting education. A Nebraska law prohibited teaching in any language but English. Oregon prohibited parents from sending their children to nonpublic schools, a regulation that posed a particular dilemma for Catholic parents; Catholic schools, after all, were intended to protect the Catholic children from assimilation into the Protestant culture. The U.S. Supreme Court, in strikingly libertarian decisions, rejected the notion that the state could use public education to create a homogeneous people, at least during peacetime. Addressing the issue directly, the Court held in *Meyers v. Nebraska*[28] that the states' interest in fostering "a homogeneous people with American ideals" had been understandable in the context of the war that had just ended. During times of "peace and domestic tranquility," however, interference with the liberty interests of parents, as well as teachers, would not be countenanced. In *Pierce v. Society of Sisters*,[29] the Court invalidated the Oregon law, rejecting the notion once again that the state had a right to "standardize" its children. The right of parents to control the education their children received was fundamental.

Meyers and *Pierce* did not apply First Amendment standards. They were clearly within the fundamental-rights strain of substantive due process, and the rights involved were, to the Court's thinking, part of the liberty interests protected by the due process clause.[30] They did, however, foster a more pluralistic society, by rejecting what may be considered an extreme civic-republican view that the state may indoctrinate its children into the civic religion, which at that time was essentially a nondenominational Protestantism. The upbringing of children, including decisions about the religious values that a child would be taught, was a matter for parents and not the state.

As this brief overview demonstrates, in spite of the prominent role that the religion clauses have always held rhetorically in the hierarchy of protected rights, the United States has been content for much of its history with a loose, de facto Protestant primacy. Those most concerned about the unity of civic and Protestant values—the mass of Catholic immigrants—created their own schools to indoctrinate their children in the Catholic faith.[31] The Supreme Court in *Pierce* secured their right to do so. Religions that differed more radically, such as the Latter-day Saints, were strong-armed into submission, and the courts found this tolerable. There was simply little reason to question the assumption that the United States was a Christian nation, committed to the value system of its Protestant founders.

THE MODERN CONSTITUTIONAL ERA

Several factors converged in the latter half of the twentieth century and prompted a more active development of constitutional principles regarding religion. Governments at both the state and federal levels became more active regulators—these decades saw the establishment of the modern regulatory or administrative state. There was, accordingly, more opportunity for conflicts to arise between religious beliefs and government decision making. The practices of some minority religions, such as the Jehovah's Witnesses, Seventh-Day Adventists, and the Amish, did in fact conflict with policies regarding proselytizing in public places, employment practices, and education. Catholics and Jews seemed, by and large, to have reached an accommodation with the prevailing order, and traditional Protestant evangelicals would remain largely out of the political fray until the 1970s, but religious groups that did not fit in the religious mainstream sought protection from majoritarian impositions on the exercise of their religions. Members of these churches, for example, were expected to proselytize in places and in ways that offended many who were exposed to their messages (like those of the Jehovah's Witnesses), kept a nontraditional Christian Sabbath (Seventh-Day Adventists), or simply wanted to be left out of the secular mainstream (the Amish).

The growth of Islam, changes in secular society, waves of immigrants bringing non-Western religions, and other factors ultimately created in American society a level of diversity that could not support the old Protestant-based social orthodoxy. Adherents of minority religions sought protection under the free exercise clause with increasing frequency and success. At the same time, a significant coalition of religious and secular groups agitated against the presence of religion in public life. The establishment clause was used to challenge any "entanglement" between church and state, be it Protestant prayers and Bibles in public schools, financial aid to parochial schools, or religious symbols in the public square.

THE ESTABLISHMENT CLAUSE: A BRIEF OVERVIEW

The principal focus of this chapter is the free exercise clause. It is important, however, to note that establishment clause jurisprudence was developing at the same time, in many similar ways, and occasionally in cases that did not recognize a clear distinction between the two provisions. Moreover, judicial decisions developing and applying the principles underlying the modern establishment clause have, like free exercise cases, often met with strong public and congressional opposition. The American public remains divided, at least at the margins, about the role that religion may and should play in the life of society. Prayer in public schools and support for private religious education, for example, remain divisive issues among members of the public and politicians in the United States.

The standard that probably best exemplifies the process used to determine whether or not a particular state action violates the establishment clause was announced in *Lemon v. Kurtzman*.[32] A statute must meet the following three criteria to survive an establishment clause challenge: "First, the statute must have a secular legislative purpose; second, its principal or primary effect must be one that neither advances nor inhibits religion; finally, the statute must not foster an excessive government entanglement with religion."[33]

The so-called *Lemon* test has been widely criticized, both on and off the Supreme Court, and courts do not rigidly adhere to it.[34] It does, however, provide a good sense of the way the Court has approached establishment clause cases.

The application of whichever test the Court may be applying in establishment clause cases—*Lemon* or some variant—has produced a complex and inconsistent body of law.[35] Some justices have been concerned about a state practice appearing to *endorse* religion, others about whether or not the practice *coerces* individuals into supporting religion.[36] The ability of the state to provide financial support to religiously affiliated schools, for example, depends on the nature of the aid, how it will be employed, and even the level of sophistication of the students. Government may display religious symbols, such as a crèche or menorah, if they have attained secular significance and are presented in a context that conveys no endorsement of religion.[37] The nation may declare itself to be "one nation under God," and its currency may state "In God We Trust." Congress and the military services have always had chaplains to invoke God's guidance. Yet the Ten Commandments may not be taught in public schools or displayed in courts. The examples are numerous, and essentially they reflect a balancing of competing interests. Some observers believe that the courts are too tolerant of practices that touch on religion, while others suggest that the judiciary has been hostile to religion. The balance is not easily struck.

This very brief introduction to the establishment clause is adequate for the purposes of this chapter. Judicial interpretations of the establishment clause, like those we will consider involving the free exercise clause, change with time, circumstances, and judges.

The Free Exercise Clause: Modern Developments

Prof. Michael McConnell, a prominent expert on the religion clauses of the First Amendment, has captured well in the following passage the essence of the historical tension in the interpretation and application of the free exercise clause:

> Some 206 years after ratification of the First Amendment, the meaning of the free exercise clause remains in doubt. Under one view, the clause, like that governing free speech, protects a specified freedom: presumptively, all people may worship God in accordance with the dictates of their own conscience, subject only to governmental interference necessary to protect the public good. Under a second view, the free exercise clause, like the equal protection clause, protects against a particular kind of governmental classification or discrimination: the government may not "single out" religion (or any particular religion) for unfavorable treatment.[38]

McConnell identifies these two competing interpretive models as the "freedom-protective interpretation" and the "nondiscrimination interpretation." They help, I believe, to understand the ebb and flow of decisions involving the free exercise clause. At times the Supreme Court and other state and federal courts seem to be fostering religious liberty. At other times, they seem to focus on neutrality—that is, nondiscrimination.

Prior to the middle of the nineteenth century, *Reynolds v. United States*[39]— the Mormon polygamy case—best reflected the Supreme Court's judgment about the protection provided by the free exercise clause. The Court distinguished between beliefs and opinions, which were protected, and acts and practices, which were not. In response to the defendant's claim that his faith required him to take more than one wife when circumstances permitted, the Court raised the specter of human sacrifices and wives throwing themselves on funeral pyres. If citizens could set their religious beliefs against the laws, the Court held, every citizen would "become a law unto himself. Government could exist only in name under such circumstances."[40] *Reynolds* seems to have fostered neither freedom nor nondiscrimination. Congress specifically targeted the members of the Mormon faith for their practice of polygamy. The First Amendment protected their right to believe that refusing to practice polygamy was a damnable offense, but they were not free to act on that belief.

The modern era of free exercise cases begins in 1940. In *Cantwell v. Connecticut*[41] the Supreme Court heard the appeal of Jesse Cantwell, a member of the Jehovah's Witnesses who was convicted of inciting others to breach the peace by distributing religious literature and playing a phonograph record on the streets of New Haven, Connecticut. The neighborhood he was canvassing was predominately Catholic, and the recording and literature attacked the Catholic Church. Cantwell played the recording for two Catholic men who later testified that they had been incensed by the message and tempted to strike Cantwell, although in fact they merely asked him to leave, and he complied. There was no evidence that Cantwell's behavior was itself disruptive in any way, but he was convicted of inciting others—the two listeners—to a breach of the peace. The Supreme Court overturned the conviction.

The Court in *Cantwell* applied the First Amendment's religion clauses to the states by incorporating them into the Fourteenth Amendment's due process clause. Rather than drawing a bright line between beliefs and actions, however, as had been done in *Reynolds*, the Court held that the Constitution protects the freedoms to believe *and to act*. The right to believe is protected absolutely, but the freedom to act is subject to appropriate regulation. Borrowing from free speech precedents, the Court upheld the power of states to regulate the time, place, and manner of religious solicitations in a reasonable and nondiscriminatory way. Continuing to apply free speech principles, the Court found that the restriction of religious speech would not be permitted "in the absence of a statute narrowly drawn to define and punish specific conduct as constituting a clear and present danger to a substantial interest of the State."[42] Clearly the Court had abandoned the notion that government could freely regulate the actions of individuals exercising their religious beliefs. At least in the context of proselytizing activities, state-imposed restraints had to be justified by a fairly exacting standard—the proscribed activities had to present a clear and present danger to a substantial state interest. *Cantwell* may in part be understood as a free speech case, but the Supreme Court also clearly opted for a freedom-promoting interpretation of the free exercise clause.

In 1963, the Supreme Court applied strict scrutiny to a South Carolina law that, as applied, denied unemployment benefits to a member of the Seventh-Day Adventist Church.[43] Mrs. Sherbert, a Seventh-Day Adventist, was discharged because she would not work on Saturdays because of her religious beliefs. She was unable to locate another job, again in part because her religion forbade her to work on Saturdays. The state refused to pay unemployment benefits, because Mrs. Sherbert had failed to accept "suitable work when offered." Her religious scruples did not exempt her from the requirement that she accept suitable work. The denial of benefits was confirmed through the state court system. The Supreme Court reversed it.

The Court in *Sherbert* applied the freedom-protective interpretation of the free exercise clause. It adopted a two-pronged test: (1) Did the regulation impose a burden on the free exercise of a claimant's religion? and (2), if it did, could the state demonstrate some compelling justification for upholding the law as applied? A facially neutral law of general application, such as South Carolina's unemployment compensation scheme, would have to withstand exacting judicial scrutiny when applied in a manner that burdened an individual's free exercise of religion. In other words, Sabbatarians would have to be accommodated by employment laws unless the state could demonstrate some compelling reason not to grant the believer relief from the general operation of the law.

Wisconsin v. Yoder[44] applied the *Sherbert* standard to Wisconsin's mandatory-school-attendance law. The state required all children to attend school until they reached the age of sixteen. Mr. Yoder, a member of the Old Order Amish, refused to send his fifteen-year-old daughter to school. Members of his religion believe that public high school education introduces children to "worldly influences" that are inconsistent with the Amish lifestyle. Without questioning the sincerity of his beliefs, a state court convicted Yoder of violating the law and fined him five dollars. The Wisconsin Supreme Court overturned the conviction, and the U.S. Supreme Court affirmed the state high court.

Wisconsin maintained that its interest in universal education was compelling. The Court, rejecting once again the state's effort to rely on a belief-action distinction, and relying on S*herbert*, held that the state's interest would prevail against a free exercise claim only if it was of the "highest order" and could not be achieved in a less intrusive way. *Sherbert and Yoder* established that governments must consider the likely impact of generally applicable laws on the rights of individuals to exercise their religious beliefs freely. If religious exercise is likely to be burdened, the law as written or applied must accommodate the exercise of religion unless the state meets the compelling interest standard. That heightened level of review—generally characterized as "strict scrutiny"—requires the state to demonstrate that its interest is compelling and that there are no less restrictive ways to achieve its goals. This standard, at least in theory, is most difficult for the state to satisfy.

The application of strict judicial scrutiny to a law under constitutional review is, in many contexts, invariably fatal to the law. The standard has been characterized as "'strict' in theory and fatal in fact."[45] In the context of the free exercise clause, however, the test has proven to be less exacting. Cases factually similar to *Sherbert* have produced similar results. Unemployment benefits cannot be denied to individuals who cannot work without violating the tenets of their faith.[46] In most other contexts, however, the Court has been less protective of free exercise rights. The Old Order Amish could not refuse to pay Social Security taxes for employees even though their faith required them to take care of their own elderly and needy community members.[47] The military could prohibit Orthodox Jews from wearing yarmulkes[48]—that is, impose uniform dress rules without accommodating religious dress requirements—and prisons did not have to stretch general rules to accommodate inmates.[49] Also, the federal government could build roads and harvest timber on federally owned lands although the activities violated areas that were sacred to Native Americans.[50]

Sherbert and *Yoder* adopted a standard of review that was highly protective of free exercise rights. Applications of the standard, however, have demonstrated a less protective reality. The need for uniformity in the tax and social welfare systems has satisfied the supposedly heavy burden; military and prison regulations have been subjected to something far less exacting than strict scrutiny; and the Court has refused to permit litigants to require government agencies to conform their internal processes to private religious beliefs. The apparent inconsistency in the application of the standard established in *Sherbert* led the Court ultimately to reverse course quite radically. The freedom-protective interpretive model had proven unmanageable, and the Court shifted to the nondiscrimination model.

Employment Division v. Smith: A New Test or a Clarification?

Alfred Smith and Galen Black were terminated from their positions at a drug rehabilitation center for using peyote. The hallucinogenic drug is an illegal, controlled substance under Oregon law. Since the parties had been fired for activities that violated state law, they were considered to have been terminated for "misconduct," which rendered them ineligible for unemployment compensation. Smith and Black were members of the Native American Church, which uses peyote for sacramental purposes. Relying on the prevailing interpretation of the free exercise clause, particularly the employment-related decisions in *Sherbert, Thomas v. Review Board,* and *Hobbie v. Unemployment Appeals Commission,* the plaintiffs convinced the Oregon Supreme Court that the application of state drug laws to them under the circumstances violated their rights. The U.S. Supreme Court reversed the state court, in *Employment Division, Department of Human Resources v. Smith.*[51]

The Court's opinion, written by Justice Antonin Scalia, stated that the free exercise clause had never, by itself, been held to invalidate a neutral, generally applicable law.[52] *Cantwell* involved freedom of speech as well as religion. *Yoder* recognized the fundamental right of parents to raise their children, a right identified in *Pierce* many years earlier. In short, these cases involved "hybrid" situations, where the level of scrutiny was heightened because several constitutional rights were implicated.

The rationale of *Sherbert*, Justice Scalia stated, had in application been limited to unemployment compensation cases. *Sherbert*'s heightened standard of review had never been applied successfully outside of that context, the Court noted, and was generally being ignored by courts in contemporary free exercise cases. The application of the "compelling state interest" standard in employment cases was justified because individualized assessments were made by administrative agencies in such cases. Justice Scalia concluded that the "decisions in the unemployment cases stand for the proposition that where the state has in place a system of individual exemptions, it may not refuse to extend that system to cases of 'religious hardship' without compelling reason."[53]

Reverting to the principles announced in *Reynolds v. United States*, the Court found that the general rule to be applied in free exercise cases is that neutral, generally applicable laws do not violate the free exercise clause even when applied in ways that burden an individual's practice of his or her religion. In the absence of evidence of discrimination, additional constitutional concerns ("hybrid" cases), or individualized applications of the law, a state is under no constitutional obligation to accommodate individual religious practices. To allow individuals to oppose an otherwise neutral and valid law based on conscientious beliefs would, as the Court had earlier opined in *Reynolds*, set each person above the law and shake the foundations of organized society. To borrow Professor McConnell's terminology once again, the Court had clearly rejected the freedom-protective rationale of the free exercise clause, in favor of the "nondiscrimination" model.

The Court in *Smith* did not find that legislative efforts to accommodate religious practices were forbidden by the Constitution. The weighing and balancing necessary to determine when a religious exemption or accommodation is justified, however, is a task better suited to legislative processes, the Court found. It is beyond judicial competence.

The majority opinion in *Smith* provoked a strong reaction from four justices. Justice Sandra Day O'Connor concurred in the result but sharply differed with Justice Scalia regarding the standard. The freedom-protective interpretation of *Sherbert* and *Yoder,* she argued, should be retained. They ask the judiciary to do no more than is typical in constitutional litigation involving individual liberties—that is, to make specific determinations in concrete cases about the nature and extent of any constitutionally cognizable burden imposed on a litigant, and to weigh that against the state's justification for the imposition.[54] Justice O'Connor concluded that

the compelling interest test effectuates the First Amendment's command that religious liberty is an independent liberty, that it occupies a preferred position,
and that the Court will not permit encroachments upon this liberty, whether direct or indirect, unless required by clear and compelling governmental interests
"of the highest order" [citing *Yoder*].[55]

The *Smith* Court's majority found that the "compelling interest" standard
had generally been avoided and ignored outside of unemployment compensation cases. Justice O'Connor concluded that the cases following and
applying *Sherbert* and *Yoder* had appropriately concluded that the states or
federal government had met the burden. The law, in her judgment, was in-
ternally consistent and rational. If applied in this case, as Justice O'Connor
believed it should have been, the state would have prevailed, because its interest in controlling the use of peyote, as well as the decision not to provide
an exemption for religious purposes, met the compelling interest standard.

Justices Harry Blackmun, William Brennan, and Thurgood Marshall agreed
with Justice O'Connor's view that the "compelling interest" standard should
continue to be applied in free exercise cases. They concluded, however, that
the state had not satisfied its burden and that the law violated the free exercise
clause as applied to religious uses by members of the Native American Church.

The Religious Freedom Restoration Act: A Legislative Response to *Smith*

The reaction to the *Smith* decision was striking. Diverse groups—religious
and secular, liberal and conservative—believed that the decision represented
a significant threat to the free exercise of religion in the United States, particularly by minority religions. Congress joined the struggle and passed by
overwhelming majorities in both houses the Religious Freedom Restoration
Act of 1993 [RFRA].[56] Congress found that the free exercise of religion is an
"unalienable right" protected by the First Amendment, that neutral laws
could inhibit the exercise of this right as well as overtly discriminatory laws,
and that the compelling interest test applied by the courts prior to *Smith* was
a workable standard that struck a reasonable balance between individual
rights and governmental interests.[57] The stated purpose of the law was "to restore the compelling interest test as set forth in *Sherbert v. Verner* and *Wisconsin v. Yoder* and to guarantee its application in all cases where free exercise of religion is substantially burdened."[58]

The substantive provisions of RFRA provide that

government shall not substantially burden a person's exercise of religion even
if the burden results from a rule of general applicability, except [when] it
demonstrates that application of the burden to the person—
   (1) is in furtherance of a compelling governmental interest; and
   (2) is the least restrictive means of furthering that compelling governmental
interest.[59]

RFRA clearly represented Congress's considered judgment that the pre-*Smith* free exercise standard was workable, appropriate, and necessary to protect a fundamental liberty interest recognized and embodied in the First Amendment. The law, however, seems to have been viewed as a challenge to and by the Court. It was invalidated, at least as applied to the states.

City of Boerne v. Flores.[60] The Saga Continues

When a Catholic parish in Boerne, Texas, was denied a building permit to expand its church, the archbishop of San Antonio brought suit on behalf of the parish. The suit alleged that the denial of the permit represented to the church a substantial burden that was not necessary to effectuate a compelling municipal interest. The plaintiff alleged that it therefore violated RFRA. The district court found RFRA to be unconstitutional but was reversed by the court of appeals. The Supreme Court agreed with the district court; RFRA, the Supreme Court held, violated principles of federalism and separation of powers.

Unlike the states, which in the American constitutional order are sovereign entities with general "police power," the federal government is one of enumerated powers.[61] Its enactments must be founded on a granted power. In the case of RFRA, Congress purported to be exercising authority granted by section 5 of the Fourteenth Amendment, which gives Congress the power to enact laws "enforcing" the provisions of the amendment. Since the free exercise clause had been incorporated into the rights protected by the Fourteenth Amendment, Congress believed it could enforce these rights by reestablishing the compelling state interest test that had existed prior to *Smith.*

The Supreme Court held that Congress exceeded its authority by attempting to define the substantive scope of the Fourteenth Amendment rather than providing a remedy for violations of the amendment's provisions. The power to enforce the amendment granted Congress remedial authority, and remedies had to meet the standards of congruence and proportionality. "There must be a congruence and proportionality between the injury to be prevented or remedied and the means adopted to that end."[62] RFRA failed in both respects.

The Court was perhaps most concerned that Congress was encroaching on the authority of a coordinate branch of the federal government, the Court itself.

> When the Court has interpreted the Constitution, it has acted within the province of the Judicial Branch, which embraces the duty to say what the law is. When the political branches of the Government act against the background of a judicial interpretation of the Constitution already issued, it must be under-

stood that in later cases and controversies the Court will treat its precedents with the respect due them under settled principles, including *stare decisis,* and contrary expectations must be disappointed.[63]

The authority and duty of the nonjudicial branches of government to interpret the constitution within their own spheres of responsibility, as well as the respect due that interpretation in judicial proceedings, have been a source of some controversy.[64] The Court in *Boerne,* however, asserted a particularly pointed claim to supremacy as the Constitution's interpreter and in essence rebuffed Congress for attempting to enact through legislation a differing view. The Court, having at least for the moment adopted the nondiscrimination interpretation of the free exercise clause, would not permit Congress to reinstate the freedom-protective interpretation.

Legislative Response to *Boerne*

For some time following the Supreme Court's decision in *Boerne,* the legislative will and broad-based political support to recapture the substance of the Religious Freedom Restoration Act remained intact. Experience under RFRA, however, caused a rift to develop between congressional liberals and conservatives. A bill entitled the "Religious Liberty Protection Act of 1999" was intended to reinstate most of the RFRA requirements, only to do so under powers that could be more readily justified in any subsequent judicial challenge. The proposed law, therefore, purported to be based on Congress's power to regulate interstate commerce[65] and its spending powers. The bill's general proscriptions applied only to governmental activities that were funded by the federal government or that affected interstate commerce. The bill also singled out zoning authorities for specific restriction.[66] Relying on cases upholding civil rights laws, as well as dicta in *Boerne,* the majority of the members of the Judiciary Committee found that there was a pattern of discrimination by zoning authorities against minority religions.[67] This pattern and the individualized determinations producing them justified, the majority of the committee believed, the exercise of the remedial powers granted by section 5 of the Fourteenth Amendment.

The House report[68] demonstrated the ideological divisions that had developed since RFRA was enacted. Many of the Democratic members of the House Judiciary Committee filed dissenting views, based largely on their concerns that the proposed law, like RFRA before it, could be used to limit the reach of antidiscrimination laws. The additional dissenting views of Representatives Berman, Nadler, Lee, and Hunt expressed this concern very directly: "The legislation, as drafted, would not simply act as a shield to protect religious liberty, but could also be used by some as a sword to attack the rights of many Americans, including unmarried couples, single parents, lesbians and gays."[69] While there remained a uniform belief that religious free exercise rights should receive greater protection than the Court-adopted standard of *Smith* and *Boerne*, liberal organizations and politicians feared the application of the new legislation in situations that would diminish the rights of nonreligious minorities. As a result of these concerns, the 1999 Religious Liberty Protection Act, though it passed the House, was not adopted by the Senate.

On July 13, 2000, a bill for a "Religious Land Use and Institutionalized Persons" act was introduced in the Senate. This narrow law, which appeared to have broad bipartisan support, was quickly enacted by both the Senate and the House of Representatives, and was signed into law by President Bill Clinton on September 22, 2000.[70] This law proscribes any level of government in the United States from adopting or implementing any land-use regulation that imposes a substantial burden on the free religious exercise of any persons or that discriminates against religious institutions or the rights of religious assembly.[71] It also specifically protects the religious exercise rights of individuals who reside in or are confined to institutions.[72] In both instances, the law requires a government that adopts a regulation having the proscribed effect to demonstrate that the action is the "least restrictive means" to meet a "compelling governmental interest."

CURRENT LAW: A CRITIQUE

There is much to criticize in both the Court's current approach to the free exercise clause and the congressional effort to remedy the situation. Leaving the protection of minority religious interests in the hands of legislatures, as the *Smith* and *Boerne* decisions do, denies members of small, unusual, or unpopular religions access to the only forum likely to be sympathetic to antimajoritarian pleas. The courts remain available to remedy blatant statutory discrimination against a particular sect,[73] but intentional discrimination can be subtle and difficult to prove. Moreover, legislative bodies may well simply be unaware of or unconcerned about the effects of laws on small religious sects. Statutory accommodations, therefore, are most likely to be accorded to large and politically well-organized religions. The Court in *Smith* acknowledged that small religions would be at a disadvantage in the political arena but concluded that the judicial balancing of religious and state interests would present a more serious constitutional dilemma.

The Court's concern about the dangers inherent in judicial balancing is justified, particularly when the interests being weighed cannot be quantified or otherwise objectively measured. Determining when activities proscribed by law are required by bona fide religious doctrine or scruple will be challenging in many situations. Having to decide when a state's interest justifies an imposition on, or prohibition of, the exercise of religious duties exacerbates the judicial task. The judiciary, however, has a special obligation to be accessible to those who lack the influence to sway majoritarian governmental bodies. One of the most influential judicial passages in constitutional law is Justice Harlan Stone's famed footnote 4 in *United States v. Carolene Products Co.*[74] The Court in *Carolene Products* applied the most deferential of judicial standards—the "rational basis" test—and upheld a federal law prohibiting the interstate shipment of "filled milk." Stone's footnote, however, provided the rationale that future Courts would use to review certain governmental actions under a more exacting standard. In addition to laws that appear to violate explicit constitutional provisions, Justice Stone marked for stricter judicial scrutiny those laws that either impede the political processes—for example, restrict voting rights—or adversely affect groups, "discrete and insular minorities," that cannot rely on the political processes to protect them.[75] Laws that burden the exercise of religion, even if neutral and of general applicability, do intrude on rights explicitly protected by the Constitution; the Court's decision to leave relief in the hands of legislatures may abandon discrete and insular religious minorities to an unresponsive and indifferent forum.

Religious minorities, to be sure, should not win every case. A judiciary that is unduly solicitous of minority religious rights cannot always frustrate democratic majorities. In a highly pluralistic society like the United States, however, adherents of small, obscure, and even unpopular religions must have some meaningful way to assert their free exercise rights. Their participation in the processes of governmental decision making is important in a nation that has identified the free exercise of religion as being among its most significant constitutional values. Imperfect as may be the judicial processes that mediate disputes involving religion and conscience, the judicial branch has a structurally and historically based duty to enforce constitutional rights, a duty that is heightened when the right ranks high in the constitutional hierarchy and the parties seeking judicial relief cannot rely on the political branches. If the balance has tipped too far in favor of those asserting a right to disregard on the basis of personal scruples otherwise valid regulations, the Court should perhaps readjust the scales. This chapter proposes an intermediate standard of review.

Professor McConnell makes a compelling argument that the Court in *Boerne* was too quick to dismiss an appropriate congressional role in the processes of constitutional interpretation.[76] Particularly in an area where the Supreme Court has left the authority to exempt or accommodate religious exercise solely in the hands of the legislature, it is remarkable for the Court to be so dismissive of a congressional judgment that the judiciary has the ability, and should have the authority, to resolve individual cases and controversies challenging laws that allegedly burden unduly the free exercise of religion. The Court may not totally defer to Congress on a matter of constitutional interpretation, but in an instance such as this—when the Court shifted constitutional gears by a bare majority, its judgment was widely criticized by constitutional scholars, and Congress evinced its belief that a more protective standard of judicial review is both manageable and necessary— the assertion of the judiciary's ultimate interpretive authority could have demonstrated greater respect for the congressional action. To use a popular phrase, *Boerne* was a lost opportunity for the Court to engage in a meaningful dialogue—the only appropriate way in which the two branches can interact—with a coordinate branch of government by seriously reconsidering its decision in *Smith* in light of the very deliberate action of Congress.

If the Court's actions left members of minority religions with little opportunity to seek judicial relief from burdens on the exercise of their faiths, and asserted a hubristic judicial supremacy in the realm of constitutional interpretation, the congressional response was also flawed. The problem, I believe, is that both the pre-*Smith* cases and RFRA imposed a burden on government that can seldom be satisfied. The compelling interest standard, whether established by the Court or Congress, has been met with such widespread resistance in application that it should be reconsidered.[77]

The solution, I suggest, is for the Court and Congress to recognize that the standard, as applied, has always been less than strict scrutiny, at least as that standard has been employed in equal protection cases involving racial discrimination. Justice Scalia was right in *Smith* when he suggested that the high court had itself been avoiding strict application of the *Sherbert* compelling state interest standard. Government actions were upheld that could never survive strict scrutiny in its most exacting form. Justice O'Connor, however, was also correct, when she concluded that the Court had reached the right outcomes in the cases that applied *Sherbert* and *Yoder.* The government interests at issue were arguably sufficient to overcome the individual's claim to exemption for religious reasons, even if those interests were less than compelling.

The Supreme Court majorities that decided *Smith* and *Boerne* would hardly be satisfied with the "sliding scale" standard associated with Justice Marshall's decisions in equal protection cases. Marshall's critique of a rigid two-tiered system, however, both accurately captured the Court's processes and called the Court to engage in reasoned judgment when individual rights are threatened. His dissenting opinion in *San Antonio Independent School District v. Rodriguez,* which dealt with educational rights for children in poor school districts, states,

[The] Court apparently seeks to establish today that equal protection cases fall into one of two neat categories which dictate the appropriate standard of review—strict scrutiny or mere rationality. But this Court's [decisions] defy such easy categorization. A principled reading of what this Court has done reveals that it has applied a spectrum of standards in reviewing discrimination allegedly violative of [equal protection]. This spectrum clearly comprehends variations in the degree of care with which the Court will scrutinize particular classifications, depending, I believe, on the constitutional and societal importance of the interest adversely affected and the recognized invidiousness of the basis upon which the particular classification is drawn.[78]

Marshall's formula, at least implicitly, attracted a majority of the Court several years later in *Plyler v. Doe*,[79] which invalidated a Texas law denying the children of undocumented aliens access to the state's free public schools.

Rodriguez and *Plyler* deal, of course, with a different constitutional provision (equal protection) and different issues (education, alienage, and poverty), but they do provide some guidance for a Court seeking to determine how best to resolve disputes involving deeply held and constitutionally based rights. The "sliding scale" approach is surely too amorphous for justices that are seeking to limit judicial discretion. The majority of the current Court, however, is willing to apply "reasoned judgment" under substantive due process, a constitutional doctrine that is far less fixed and far more controversial than the explicit constitutional guarantee of the free exercise of religion.[80] The Court should arguably be able to apply the same level of reasoned judgment to resolve free exercise cases.

Since neither the "sliding scale" nor "reasoned judgment" standard lends itself to precise statutory articulation, and since both invite open-ended ad hoc judicial balancing, language traditionally associated with an intermediate level of scrutiny could help to ensure a proper protective role for the courts. The standard used in cases involving gender-based discrimination—the means must be "*substantially related* to an *important* governmental objective"[81]—could ameliorate the problems of an excessively rigid standard of judicial review, while avoiding the appearance of excessive judicial discretion.

CONCLUSION

The current state of the law related to the constitutional right of individuals to exercise their religion freely is unsettled and unsettling. The Supreme Court has opted for a standard that promotes neutrality at the price of protection. Its rulings leave claims for accommodation to the legislative branch, which diminishes governmental responsiveness to the claims and needs of minority religions. The congressional attempt to remedy this situation, the Religious Freedom Restoration Act, imposed a standard of judicial review that is too extreme in application. The remedy, I believe, whether accomplished through judicial or legislative means, is to create a more realistic standard, one that recognizes that majoritarian policies cannot be held hostage to every personal claim to conscience-based freedom from the constraints of law, while still valuing highly the rights of citizens to practice their faiths freely. The intermediate standard of review, one that upholds laws that are reasonably related to important governmental interests, strikes a sound balance.

An intermediate level of scrutiny would leave the judiciary open to those seeking relief from government regulations that substantially burden their religious practices. It would also induce legislative bodies to consider seriously the implications of their actions for religions and their members, while providing room for the adoption of reasonable regulations. Finally, given the recent struggle between the branches, it would demonstrate a healthy and dynamic approach to separation of powers. Giving up the compelling interest standard may be a rhetorical defeat for those seeking to maximize the rights of individuals wishing to exercise their religious beliefs free of government interference. It would, however, I believe, return the law to the level of protection that existed prior to the *Smith* decision and achieve what RFRA was intended to accomplish, with less interbranch tension.

NOTES

1. U.S. Const., Amend. I.

2. Thomas Jefferson, letter to the Danbury, Connecticut, Baptist Association (1 January 1802). Jefferson's metaphor was adopted by the Supreme Court in *Everson v. Board of Education*, 330 U.S. 1, 16 (1947), with the admonition that the wall must remain "high and impregnable." Jefferson was not the originator of the notion or the particular phrase, but his stature as a "founding father" gave it constitutional credibility.

3. Thomas C. Berg, *The State and Religion* (St. Paul, Minn.: West Group, 1998), 13–25.

4. As noted in the text, it is difficult to discuss either one of the religion clauses without the other. Protecting free exercise rights, certainly if done in a discriminatory way, implicates the establishment prohibition. While acknowledging the presence and significance of this tension, the chapter focuses on the free exercise clause because it is the principal focus of the modern debate about accommodation and neutrality.

5. *Employment Division v. Smith*, 494 U.S. 872 (1990).

6. *Religious Freedom Restoration Act of 1993*, 107 Stat. 1488 [hereafter RFRA], 42 U.S.C. § 2000bb et seq.

7. *City of Boerne v. Flores*, 521 U.S. 507 (1997).

8. *Employment Division v. Smith*, 494 U.S. 872 (1990).

9. The RFRA standard, "compelling state interest," is one part of the two-pronged, means-ends analysis known as "strict scrutiny."

10. Identifying the "original intent" of the Framers of the U.S. Constitution is always fraught with difficulty. The amendments in particular were drafted by many

individuals, subject to debates and amendments before being adopted by Congress, and were then ratified in state proceedings that themselves generated declarations about the perceived "intent" of those voting for or against ratification.

11. John Witte Jr., *Religion and the American Constitutional Experiment* (Boulder, Colo.: Westview, 2000).

12. Witte, *Religion,* 25–28.

13. Witte, *Religion,* 28–31.

14. Witte, *Religion,* 25–26.

15. Witte, *Religion,* 31–34.

16. Witte, *Religion,* 34–36.

17. Witte, *Religion,* 34.

18. *Barron v. Mayor and City Council of Baltimore,* 32 U.S. (7 Pet.) 243 (1833).

19. See Berg, *The State and Religion,* 46.

20. Jed Rubenfeld, "Antidisestablishmentarianism: Why RFRA Really Was Unconstitutional," 95 *Michigan Law Review* 2347, 2350 (1997).

21. *Reynolds v. United States,* 98 U.S. 145 (1878).

22. *Late Corporation of Church of Jesus Christ of Latter-Day Saints v. United States,* 136 U.S. 1 (1890), and *Davis v. Beason* 133 U.S. 333 (1890).

23. The Court held that polygamy threatened "the spirit of Christianity and of the civilization which Christianity has produced in the western world." *Church of Jesus Christ of Latter-Day Saints,* 136 U.S. at 49.

24. U.S. Const., Amend. XIV.

25. *Slaughter-House Cases,* 83 U.S. (16 Wall.) 36 (1872).

26. For a short time, the Court struggled with the notion that the Fourteenth Amendment merely incorporated and imposed upon the states all of the rights and limitations contained in the Bill of Rights. Eventually, the Court accepted the concept of selective incorporation, which has applied most, but not all, of the first eight amendments to the states. The debate over incorporation is exemplified by the decision of Justice Black (dissenting) in *Adamson v. California,* 332 U.S. 46 (1947), and Justices Black (concurring) and Harlan (dissenting) in *Duncan v. Louisiana,* 391 U.S. 145 (1968). The strongest case for incorporation relies on the privileges and immunities clause rather than due process. See Michael W. McConnell, "Institutions and Interpretations: A Critique of *City of Boerne v. Flores,*" 111 *Harvard Law Review* 153, 170 (1997).

27. Full incorporation of the religion clauses did not actually occur until the 1940s. See *Cantwell v. Connecticut,* 310 U.S. 296 (1940) (incorporating the free exercise clause) and *Everson v. Board of Education of Ewing Township,* 330 U.S. 1 (1947) (incorporating the establishment clause).

28. *Meyers v. Nebraska,* 262 U.S. 390 (1923).

29. *Pierce v. Society of Sisters,* 268 U.S. 510 (1925).

30. The notion of "substantive due process"—that is, that the due process clause protected substantive rights as well as procedural interests—was ultimately repudiated by the Court in the context of economic interests, but it was resurrected in *Griswold v. Connecticut,* 381 U.S. 479 (1965), for noneconomic interest. Incorporation of the free exercise and establishment clauses into the Fourteenth Amendment has put religious rights on a more solid footing, I believe, than has relying on the liberty interests embodied in the due process clause.

31. On matters of so-called civic virtues, there seems to have been little difference between Protestant and Catholic citizens. The Catholic hierarchy worked hard to establish that its congregants were loyal, patriotic, hardworking citizens, just like their Protestant neighbors. The anti-Catholic animus following World War I is particularly puzzling given the significant effort by the Catholic hierarchy to support the war effort.

32. *Lemon v. Kurtzman*, 403 U.S. 602 (1971).

33. *Lemon v. Kurtzman*, 403 U.S. 602 (1971) at 612–13.

34. See Kathleen M. Sullivan and Gerald Gunther, *First Amendment Law* (New York: Foundation, 1999), 500.

35. The Court's most recent establishment clause decision, *Mitchell v. Helms,* 120 S.Ct. 2530, 68 U.S.L.W. 4468 (U.S. June 28, 2000), continues to demonstrate the sharp divisions on the Court regarding the proper standard in establishment clause cases.

36. See *Allegheny County v. American Civil Liberties Union*, 492 U.S. 573 (1989). In this case, Justices O'Connor, Brennan, and Stevens opt for the "endorsement" test, while Justices Kennedy, Rehnquist, White, and Scalia adopt the "coercion" standard.

37. *Lynch v. Donnelly*, 465 U.S. 668 (1984); *Allegheny County v. American Civil Liberties Union*, 492 U.S. 573 (1989).

38. Michael W. McConnell, "Institutions and Interpretations: A Critique of *City of Boerne v. Flores,*" 111 *Harvard Law Review* 153, 156 (1997).

39. *Reynolds v. United States*, 98 U.S. 145 (1878).

40. *Reynolds v. United States*, 98 U.S. 145 (1878) at 166–67.

41. *Cantwell v. Connecticut*, 310 U.S. 296 (1940).

42. *Cantwell v. Connecticut*, 310 U.S. at 311.

43. *Sherbert v. Verner*, 374 U.S. 398 (1963).

44. *Wisconsin v. Yoder*, 406 U.S. 205 (1972).

45. Gerald Gunther, "Forward: In Search of Evolving Doctrine on a Changing Court: A Model for a Newer Equal Protection," 86 *Harvard Law Review* 1, 8 (1972).

46. *Thomas v. Review Board*, 450 U.S. 707 (1981); *Hobbie v. Unemployment Appeals Commission*, 480 U.S. 136 (1987); *Frazee v. Illinois Employment Security Department*, 489 U.S. 829 (1989). The petitioner in *Frazee* did not even belong to a specific religion—he refused to work on Sundays because he was a Christian. His personal religious beliefs were protected although they did not reflect the doctrine of any particular denomination.

47. *United States v. Lee*, 455 U.S. 252 (1982).

48. *Goldman v. Weinberger*, 475 U.S. 503 (1986).

49. *O'Lone v. Estate of Shabazz*, 482 U.S. 342 (1987). Both the *Goldman* and *O'Lone* cases reflect a generally heightened deference to the judgments of the other branches by the judiciary in the contexts of military and prison regulation.

50. *Lyng v. Northwest Indian Cemetery Protective Association*, 485 U.S. 439 (1988).

51. *Employment Division, Department of Human Resources v. Smith*, 494 U.S. 872 (1990).

52. *Employment Division, Department of Human Resources v. Smith*, 494 U.S. at 878–80.

53. *Employment Division, Department of Human Resources v. Smith*, 494 U.S. at 884.

54. *Employment Division, Department of Human Resources v. Smith*, 494 U.S. at 899.

55. *Employment Division, Department of Human Resources v. Smith*, 494 U.S. at 895.

56. PL 103-141, November 16, 1993; 107 Stat 1488.

57. RFRA, 42 U.S.C., § 2000bb.

58. RFRA, 42 U.S.C., § 2000bb(b)(1).

59. RFRA, 42 U.S.C., § 2000bb-1.

60. *City of Boerne v. Flores*, 521 U.S. 507 (1997).

61. *McCulloch v. Maryland*, 17 U.S. (4 Wheat.) 316 (1819).

62. *City of Boerne v. Flores*, 521 U.S. at 520.

63. *City of Boerne v. Flores*, 521 U.S. at 536.

64. See, for example, Louis Fisher, *American Constitutional Law,* 2d ed. (New York: McGraw-Hill, 1995), 69–82.

65. The federal Civil Rights Act of 1964, the nation's first comprehensive civil rights law, was enacted as a regulation of interstate commerce rather than as a remedial provision authorized by the Fourteenth Amendment. John Marshall's expansive reading of the federal powers under the commerce clause, which were reinvigorated in the New Deal era, provided an apparent safe haven for congressional action.

66. *Religious Liberty Protection Act of 1999,* H.R. 1691, 106th Cong., 1st sess., sec. 3(b).

67. H.R. Rep. No. 219, 106th Cong., 1st Sess., 1 July 1999 at 14.

68. H.R. Rep. No. 219, 106th Cong., 1st Sess., 1 July 1999.

69. H.R. Rep. No. 219, 106th Cong., 1st Sess., 1 July 1999 at 32.

70. Religious Land Use and Institutionalized Persons Act of 2000, Public Law 106-274, 114 Stat 803 (codified as 42 U.S.C. § 2000cc).

71. Religious Land Use and Institutionalized Persons Act, PL 106-274, sec. 2.

72. Religious Land Use and Institutionalized Persons Act, PL 106-274, sec. 3.

73. *Church of the Lukumi Babalu Aye v. City of Hialeah*, 508 U.S. 520 (1993). This case invalidated a law that clearly targeted the animal sacrifices practiced by members of the Santeria religion.

74. *United States v. Carolene Products Co.*, 304 U.S. 144 (1938). The footnote states:

> There may be a narrower scope for operation of the presumption of constitutionality when legislation appears on its face to be within a specific prohibition of the Constitution, such as those of the first ten amendments, which are deemed equally specific when held to be embraced within the Fourteenth.
>
> It is unnecessary to consider now whether legislation which restricts those political processes which can obviously be expected to bring about repeal of undesirable legislation, is to be subjected to more exacting judicial scrutiny under the general prohibitions of the Fourteenth than are most other types of legislation [related to voting rights, freedom of expression, political organization, and peaceable association].
>
> Nor need we enquire whether similar considerations enter into the review of statutes directed at particular religions or national or racial minorities; whether prejudice against discrete and insular minorities may be a special condition, which tends seriously to curtail the operation of those political processes ordinarily to be relied upon to protect minorities. [Cases and citations omitted].

75. *United States v. Carolene Products Co.*, 304 U.S. 144 (1938).

76. McConnell, "Institutions and Interpretations."

77. The evidence is overwhelming that courts, including the Supreme Court even prior to *Smith*, and others applying the compelling interest standard have avoided the rigidity that generally attaches to strict scrutiny. See, generally, Ira C. Lupu, "The Failure of RFRA," 20 *University of Arkansas Little Rock Law Journal* 575 (1998) (this article contains detailed data demonstrating that the compelling interest standard of RFRA was being avoided by courts and states' attorneys general during the years that the statute was being enforced); McConnell, "Institutions and Interpretations"; Eugene Gressman and Angela C. Carmella, "The RFRA Revision of the Free Exercise Clause," 57 *Ohio State Law Journal* 65 (1996).

78. *San Antonio Independent School District v. Rodriguez*, 411 U.S. 1, 98–99 (J. Marshall dissenting, 1973).

79. 457 U.S. 202 (1982).

80. See *Planned Parenthood of Southeastern Pennsylvania v. Casey*, 505 U.S. 833, 849 (1992).

81. *United States v. Virginia*, 518 U.S. 515, 570–71 [emphasis added].

9

The Constitutional Context of Religious Liberty in the United States

Bette Novit Evans

Religious liberty, although imperfect, is surely one of the most impressive achievements of the United States. The First Amendment religious liberty guarantees create legally enforceable religious rights and symbolize our nation's commitment to protecting them. These "parchment guarantees" have proven far more powerful than some of their authors might have expected, but words alone do not create practices. I am convinced that religious liberty has succeeded because it is consistent with the pluralism of our major institutions.[1] Americans' memberships, identities, and authority patterns tend to be plural and crosscutting rather than monolithic or segmented, and the fragmentation of power in American government reinforces and sustains social pluralism. This chapter explores the ways in which fragmented governmental institutions provide the constitutional context within which the religious freedom guarantees are embedded. Governmental pluralism not only helps sustain religious liberty; it actually helps define our very understanding of its meaning. Of course, the Constitution is only one among many contexts that support and reinforce American religious freedom. A thorough account of the contexts would surely include the particular patterns of religious experience, as well as the broader patterns of ethnicity, economics, and social mobility.[2] Thus my focus on the governmental pluralism created by the U.S. Constitution is only a partial description of the broader pluralist context.

The way Americans experience religion is pluralistic. We go church shopping, selecting doctrines from a cafeteria of options, without much regard to denomination; we intermarry and give our children mixed religious heritages; we change affiliations easily; and we consider our religious identities as one of a package of many crosscutting identities. In short, we have come to think of religion as one of many voluntary associations to which we belong. Thus, religious pluralism is part of a more general social pluralism characterized by a multiplicity of "mediating institutions" such as families, voluntary associations, religious, educational, and economic institutions, the composite of which defines our individual values, meanings, and identities.

That description should not be taken to trivialize the importance of religion or diminish its distinguishing characteristics. Religions can be distinguished from other sources of meaning by the fact that they offer *comprehensive answers to "ultimate questions."* For many people, religion provides comprehensive systems of meaning that address the ultimate question of human life—the human place in the cosmos—and help organize other kinds of meaning.[3] This insight is captured in theologian Franklin Gamwell's definition of religion as the "primary form of culture in terms of which the comprehensive question is asked and answered."[4] In Peter Berger's words, religion "posits a cosmos that locates life in an ultimately meaningful order."[5]

Precisely because religious meanings are so powerful, many people look to them to provide a unifying vision to bind the society together. Robert Bellah long ago argued that a broadly defined civil religion constitutes the American unifying consensus.[6] James Davison Hunter describes a "culture war" between two contending factions for domination of the shared culture.[7] Fundamentalists of all faiths seem to share an insistence that a culture embody consistent values.[8] Philosophers from Plato to contemporary communitarians argue that a society cannot function harmoniously with a multiplicity of comprehensive meanings. Those who value the seamless lives of a unified system of beliefs find a multiplicity of meanings both disturbing and dangerous. I would not attempt to convince these believers that a religiously pluralistic society is any *better* than one that shares a religious heritage. I am convinced, however, that only a religiously plural system is compatible with American religious and cultural reality, and with its system of government. In an earlier argument, I phrased the point thus: "[The] vision of a unified life is surely an attractive one, perhaps ultimately preferable to the plural one. However, such a vision is ultimately not consistent with the American cultural and political heritage. Whether one thinks it is better or not, it is simply not *ours.*"[9]

The remainder of this chapter attempts to elaborate one part of that claim—the role of our constitutional structure of government. I begin with the religious guarantees of the First Amendment and proceed to the broader constitutional structure in order to demonstrate how our fragmented institutional structure contributes to the way we understand and practice religious liberty.

THE RELIGIOUS CLAUSES OF THE FIRST AMENDMENT

The very first words of our Bill of Rights provide that "Congress shall make no law respecting an establishment of religion or prohibiting the free exercise thereof." Somewhat inaccurately, these words are traditionally divided into the "establishment clause" and the "free exercise clause." The establishment clause offers protection against state-sponsored or imposed religious obligations, and the free exercise clause protects religious expression from state penalties. Establishment clause problems usually arise when a religiously dominant group seeks to use public resources for religious purposes or to carry on religious acts in the "public square." Free exercise problems usually arise when individuals or groups believe that their liberties have been burdened by laws or administrative decisions and seek judicial orders nullifying the offending policies or exempting them from them. Religious interest groups with sufficient political power may be accommodated administratively or legislatively; hence, free exercise cases are more often brought by less powerful religious groups.

The sixteen words of the religion clauses do not stand alone. Their immediate context is the whole of the First Amendment. The First Amendment links freedom of religion, speech, press, and assembly, all of which are ways of ensuring that government does not monopolize the role of definer of meanings and values.[10] What religion, speech, press, and what we have come to call "association" have in common is that they are ways people acquire not only information but also meanings and communicate them to other people. Taken together, the guarantees of the First Amendment provide for the acquiring and communicating of a variety of meanings. Nothing in its words forbids government itself from being a source of meaning—indeed, doing so is one of its most important functions.[11] But the First Amendment forbids government from acquiring a monopoly on meanings. Thus, the First Amendment symbolizes and legitimates for Americans the expectation that meanings are gained from multiple sources in which no source has a natural preeminence. Perhaps one reason that Hunter's anticipated culture war has not occurred is that there is no institutional framework for a system of meanings to dominate; also, neither our constitutional nor our religious structures condition us to expect systematic and comprehensive meanings.

Besides protecting religious minorities and individual conscience, the religion clauses perform two other important functions for a pluralist society. The establishment clause in particular helps depoliticize religious controversies. John Locke's *Letter on Toleration*, written in response to centuries of European religious wars, appreciated the importance of separating sectarian and political controversies.[12] In the American colonies, the virtue of toleration arose of necessity; the colonies quickly became so religiously heterogeneous that few were able to support a single religious establishment without conflict.[13] By separating religious and governmental institutional powers, the establishment clause helped prevent sectarian conflicts from becoming civic ones.[14] Government benefits to religions, especially those that confer finan-

cial advantages, risk creating just the kind of political conflict the establishment clause was intended to avoid.[15]

Moreover, independent religious institutions, like other voluntary associations, help counter government's policy monopoly by providing sources of
independent policy initiatives.[16] They offer alternative ways for groups of
people to achieve their ends and pursue alternative policies; they perform
community functions analogous to those performed by governments. Private
religious education is a classic example. Stephen Carter has emphasized the
importance of religions as counterweights to the state:

> Religions are in effect independent centers of power, with bona fide claims on
> the allegiance of their members, claims that exist alongside, are not identical to,
> and will sometimes trump the claims to obedience that the state makes. A reli-
> gion speaks to its members in a voice different from that of the state, and when
> the voice moves the faithful to action, a religion may act as a counterweight to
> the authority of the state. . . .
>
> First, [religions] can serve as the sources of moral understanding without
> which any majoritarian system can deteriorate into simple tyranny, and, second,
> they can mediate between the citizen and the apparatus of government, pro-
> viding an independent moral voice. Indeed, from [Alexis de] Tocqueville's day
> to contemporary theories of pluralism, the need for independent mediating in-
> stitutions has been a staple of political science.[17]

Voluntary associations not only provide private alternatives to governmental functions but offer competing conceptions of public policy, which
challenge the government's agenda.[18] The religious pacifist and civil rights
movements, the Catholic bishops' letter on the economy, the sanctuary
movement, and religious activists on both sides of the abortion controversy
illustrate some ways in which independent religious institutions foster alternative conceptions of public policy and attempt to influence public policy
toward those ends. Robert Cover terms these efforts "redemptive constitutionalism" and waxes almost poetic in defending the autonomy of religious
groups who seek to change the world.[19] These movements illustrate a sharp
tension between the advantages of institutional challenges to governmental
power and the danger that these institutions will substitute their own religious agendas for those of the rest of the polity.

THE MADISONIAN CONSTITUTION: FRAGMENTED POWER

Given the strength and divisiveness of religious and other commitments, a
religiously plural society is always in danger of "culture wars." Reflecting
on his new constitution, James Madison worried that the causes of faction
"are sown into the nature of man," and he knew that religious conflicts were

especially dangerous. "A religious sect may degenerate into a political faction in a part of the Confederacy, but the variety of sects dispersed over the entire face of it must secure the national Councils against any danger from that source."[20] He placed his faith in the multiplicity of religious factions to prevent tyranny by any one of them. In his famous *Federalist* 51, he looks to protection "by comprehending in the society so many separate descriptions of citizens, as will render an unjust combination of a majority of the whole, very improbable if not impractical. . . . [T]he society itself will be broken into so many parts, interests, and classes of citizens that the rights of individuals or of the minority, will be in little danger from interested combinations of the majority."[21]

Madison's solution is perhaps the outstanding American contribution to political philosophy. The dangers of faction are minimized by both the size of the republic and the heterogeneity of its parts: "Either the existence of the same passion or interest in a majority at the same time must be prevented, or the majority, having such co-existent passion or interest, must be rendered, by their number and local situation, unable to concert and carry into effect schemes of oppression."[22]

In short, the fragmented power structures created by the U.S. Constitution deprive the partisans in the "culture war" of a comprehensive battlefield. The Constitution creates a jurisdictional fragmentation almost unparalleled in institutional design. Hence, no single governmental body is capable of enforcing any dominant meaning. Federalism fragments power geographically, and the separation of powers reinforces this fragmentation at every level. Madison's justly famous *Federalist* 51 describes this insight.

> In the compound republic of America, the power surrendered by the people is first divided between two distinct governments, and then the portion allotted to each, subdivided among distinct and separate departments. Hence, a double security arises to the rights of the people. The different governments will controul each other, at the same time that each will be controuled by itself.
>
> Second, it is of great importance in a republic, not only to guard the society against the oppression of its rulers, but also to guard one part of the society against the injustice of the other part.[23]

The Constitution's framers struggled with a conflict between representative government and their fear of majority tyranny. Their solution was both to prevent the creation of permanent majorities and to prevent the accumulation of power in any governmental institution. Thus the Constitution created not only an extended and federal republic, with its numerous separate and independent governments, but also the separation and "blending" of powers among the three branches of the national government, so that no single one could act without the consent of the others. The fragmentation of political power and redundancy of functions within government multiply the points of access for groups attempting to influence public policy, thus enhancing citizen impact on government. Even the representative institutions are designed to hamper each other, and these are themselves balanced against nonrepresentative institutions, such as the judiciary.

Even more than the magnificent Bill of Rights, this structure makes possible the protection of individual liberties. Words on paper—Madison's "parchment guarantees"—may create rights, but the structure of government turns the words into a political practice. The effective enforcement of a right—especially a right against government—requires a source of power independent of the offending institution. Whether or not the practice of judicial review was intended by the Constitution's framers, this power in the hands of a more or less independent judiciary has proven crucial to the American understanding of rights. This reflects Madison's belief that the fragmented structure of government was a better protection for individual rights than was any single document.

Typically, the protection of liberties is described as a conflict between majority rule and minority rights. In this interpretation, the acts of the elected branches of government or the agencies under their control represent majoritarian interests, while judicial intervention is inherently antimajoritarian. When religious minorities whose interests are not protected in the legislative process demand judicial enforcement of their constitutional rights, this process is seen as counter-majoritarian, even "undemocratic."

My pluralist argument rejects the foregoing description, and along with it the very distinction between political majorities and minorities. Most government enactments are the result of temporary coalitions of interests representing not a majority but those groups whose interests are at stake. Public decision making is almost always a minority phenomenon; what makes the situation democratic is that the coalition of minorities is fluid.[24] The distribution of power within government helps provide access to many different groups; those who may be disadvantaged in dealing with one institution may find more favorable access in another. Congress may be attentive to certain kinds of interests and courts to others; federal agencies have particular constituencies, while state agencies, city councils, and other institutions are receptive to others. In this view, there is no sharp distinction between elective and nonelective branches of government. Every branch is constituted to provide access to some different combination of interests, and the judiciary is simply another policy-making branch of government, with its own constituencies and procedures. Democracy results from the multiplicity of access points for different interest groups.

I must emphasize that this is an ideal, not an empirical description of American politics. In practice, political and economic inequalities skew the public agenda and seriously challenge these optimistic assumptions. Some groups are more politically favored as coalition partners and hence more successful than others. Some groups are so disfavored that they are never wanted as coalition partners, and some may be excluded entirely from effective participation, so that their interests are never represented. The resulting distortion of equal representation provides one of the best justifications for the role of the courts in protecting minorities who are systematically excluded from the effective electoral representation.[25] This approach abandons the "majority rule/minority rights" dichotomy inherent in so much of the literature of constitutional jurisprudence; instead it views legislators, administrators, judges, and all other officials as legitimate actors in this system of fragmented power and multiple access points.[26]

All of this is a very general and probably familiar statement of constitutional pluralism. Now let me focus more specifically on how this constitutional context shapes two very thorny religious clause problems—the accommodation of religion, and the balancing of religious rights against other interests.

ACCOMMODATION OF RELIGION

The standard language for describing arguments about religious liberty contrasts advocates of *accommodation of religion* with advocates of *separation of church and state*. Those favoring separation take their metaphor from Thomas Jefferson's call for a "wall of separation between church and state." They argue that government must be neutral not only among religions but also between religion and nonreligion; their goal is a religion-blind constitution.[27] This view would mandate vigorous enforcement of the establishment clause and minimize governmental accommodations to religion. Those favoring accommodation, on the other hand, begin with the premise that the Constitution singles out religion for special protection, intending to foster it, in all of its diversity. Accommodating religion is entirely constitutional as long as doing so does not favor one sect over another or disadvantage any. Advocates of this view tend to take a weaker view of the establishment clause and a stronger one of the free exercise clause.

The distinction between accommodation and separation conveys the broad outlines of the controversy but masks much of its subtlety— particularly, *which institutions*, if any, should accommodate religion. Should legislatures be responsive to the demands of politically dominant or sensitive groups? Should administrators have discretion to accommodate individual or group needs as they arise? Or should both be religion blind and "neutral"? Should courts require the accommodation of religion as a right under the free exercise clause, by exempting religiously motivated people from laws that inadvertently burden their religious obligations?

When religious groups desire public support for religious activities, to engage in religious activities "in the public square," or to create legislative exemptions from general obligations, they may be successful in achieving these accommodations through the political process. For example, a public school authorizes prayers at school events,[28] or a state legislature authorizes the expenditure of public funds for religious purposes,[29] or local officials use public spaces for religious displays,[30] or persons with religious motivations receive benefits denied to people with nonreligious motivations.[31] Any of these accommodations may persist unchallenged; constitutional controversies arise only when someone perceives a violation of establishment clause and seeks a judicial remedy.

Free exercise jurisprudence most often arises at the margins of law. Although some laws are challenged as intentional discrimination against particular religious practices, most contemporary challenges arise because some seemingly "neutral" law inadvertently burdens a religious exercise. In those cases, the burdened individuals or groups assert a right to be exempt under the free exercise clause in order to "accommodate" the religious practice.

In short, religious interest groups with sufficient political power can often rely on *legislative accommodation* of their interests, while less successful ones are likely to seek *judicial accommodation*. Yet even that distinction is misleading. Any simple distinction between "legislative" and "judicial" accommodation misses the fact that a great deal of ordinary religious accommodation is in fact administrative. Many, if not most, are matters of simple selective enforcement by law enforcement agencies. It is almost inconceivable, for example, that a local prosecutor would choose to bring charges of serving alcohol to a minor to a Jewish family celebrating a Passover seder.

Debates about religious accommodation have almost ignored the role administrative discretion plays in these situations. When an administrative agency has discretionary authority, granting religious exemptions is simple, and failure to accommodate raises the inference of discrimination against religion. The case of *Sherbert v. Verner* is illustrative. South Carolina's unemployment compensation agency was specifically empowered to make individualized judgments about whether a person's unavailability for work was legitimate or not but refused to consider Mrs. Sherbert's religious excuse. Hence, the Supreme Court majority concluded that "a state that puts in place a discretionary process to assess reasons for quitting work, and then turns a deaf ear to adherence to religious commandments as good cause, opens itself to the conclusion that it is not giving equal regard to the deep religious commitments of non-mainstream believers."[32]

In contrast, when rules make no provisions for administrative discretion, exemptions allow the inference of special favors to religion. Justice Antonin Scalia made much of this distinction in *Employment Division v. Smith*. The criminal law, he argued, is not supposed to be enforced with discretionary authority; hence, decision makers lack the authority to exempt religious believers from its commands. Yet even this distinction blurs in practice, as we shall see in *Goldman v. Weinberger,* below.

The following two cases illustrate the complex interplay of governmental institutions involved in controversies over religious accommodation. They have been selected both because they are relatively recent and well-known, and because they illustrate the multiple institutions involved in free exercise and establishment clause controversies.

Goldman v. Weinberger

Consider the 1986 case of *Goldman v. Weinberger.*[33] Capt. Simcha Goldman, an air force officer and an Orthodox Jew, was required by his faith to keep his head covered at all times. Air force regulations, on the other hand, prohibit wearing "headgear" indoors. In spite of this regulation, Captain Goldman had been unofficially accommodated for some time and permitted to wear his yarmulke with his uniform indoors. When another office complained,[34] this accommodation ended. Ultimately, Goldman sought a federal court order for religious accommodation under the free exercise clause. In defending its refusal to accommodate Goldman's yarmulke, the air force expressed the need for discipline and uniformity. Furthermore, it saw the case as placing the service in a dilemma between the two religion clauses. Accommodating an innocuous yarmulke would be relative simple, but to avoid religious discrimination, it would then be necessary to accommodate dreadlocks, saffron robes, and turbans, which the air force was not prepared to permit. The Supreme Court upheld the air force's refusal, relying on a special deference for military judgments. But the issue did not end there. Subsequently, Congress enacted a law that created the exemption legislatively, requiring the military to permit conservative religious articles worn with military uniforms.[35]

Notice the multiple loci of decision making: military regulations, commanding officers, courts, and ultimately, the U.S. Congress. In the first instance, there is an interesting interplay between the uniform code, which stated no exceptions and had no mechanisms for administrative discretion, and the fact of informal discretion that had operated for some time. In the second instance, the air force hierarchy both enforced and defended its regulation. The next players were several levels of federal courts, ending with the U.S. Supreme Court, which in turn based its ruling on a stronger deference for military judgment than would have been appropriate in civilian institutions. But in the final instance, a coalition of interest groups brought the issue to the attention of Congress, which overrode the military judgment by enacting a revised uniform standard.

Kiryas Joel School District v. Grumet

The second example is the 1994 *Kiryas Joel*[36] case—a virtual "poster child" for jurisdictional pluralism. The events surrounding this case illustrate the frustrating but ultimately beneficial interplay of legislative and judicial approaches to religious interests. The village of Kiryas Joel consisted almost entirely of members of the very insular Satmar Hasidic sect of Judaism. The villagers educated most of their children in private religious schools, but they were unwilling or unable to provide the full range of rehabilitative services in private schools for their disabled children. Before 1985, disabled children had been receiving state services on the grounds of private religious schools—a legislative accommodation. In 1985, the Supreme Court ruled that this kind of accommodation violated the establishment clause.[37] Therefore, the villagers chose to exercise their right to publicly funded special education classes in public schools. However, attending public schools with children of surrounding communities created hardships ranging from unfamiliar language (the Satmar predominantly speak Yiddish), to taunts about their strange clothing, to the religiously objectionable mixed sex education. So the villagers reached an agreement with the surrounding school district to secede and create a new one consisting almost exclusively of members of the Satmar sect. The New York legislature accordingly accommodated the village by creating its own public school district.

From a pluralist perspective, the village of Kiryas Joel was acting entirely appropriately in exercising its political power to persuade the legislature to grant this unusual accommodation. Likewise, the state legislature was responding appropriately to constituent interests in granting it. Constitutional doctrine is not the highest priority of either interest groups or legislative bodies. When the accommodation was challenged, the dispute passed out of the legislative process and into the judicial system, where other priorities became dominant. Both New York courts and the U.S. Supreme Court ruled the plan unconstitutional, ruling that the establishment clause forbids religious gerrymandering. Interestingly, Justice David Souter's majority opinion itself suggested some administrative solutions to the problems his ruling created. Ultimately the New York legislature followed the suggestion and passed a new statute, creating a general right for communities to create smaller school districts out of larger ones under certain conditions. The New York Supreme Court struck down this law.[38] But the story did not end there. In 1997, the Supreme Court overturned its 1985 decision regarding special education facilities in private schools, which had made the Kiryas Joel district seem necessary in the first place.[39]

The Kiryas Joel narrative illustrates how religious establishment controversies are interwoven with the complicated relationship among governmental institutions. Important participants in this controversy included the governing bodies of Kiryas Joel and the surrounding town of Woodbury, religious and secular interest groups, state educational agencies, the New York state legislature, New York State courts at various levels, and the U.S. Supreme Court. In the long run, such conflicting legislative and judicial solutions reflect the numerous opportunities for formulating and reformulating policy.

The two foregoing examples should lay to rest any simple distinction between majority and minority interests as reflected in legislative and judicial functions. Certainly, when legislatures adopt accommodation for religious interests, they may reflect majoritarian sentiments and dominant religions. But this is not always true. Sometimes the interests accommodated are not majority ones at all—as both of the above cases illustrate. Furthermore, both cases illustrate the important role of administrative officials in accommodation controversies.

Arguments about constitutionally required accommodation ultimately demand that we explore the meaning and value of governmental neutrality, the nature of discrimination, and the position of religious groups in American life. We shall examine both legislative and judicial accommodation, noting the establishment and free exercise problems they raise but focusing more on their implications for religious and constitutional pluralism.

LEGISLATIVE ACCOMMODATION AND THE VALUE OF DEMOCRACY

Legislative accommodations—those achieved through the political process—are not strictly required by the free exercise clause, and may or may not be permitted by the establishment clause. They occupy the "disputed border" between the two religion clauses. The first judicial reference to this kind of accommodation was Justice William O. Douglas's description of the released-time program the court upheld in *Zorach v. Clauson*: "When the state encourages religious instruction or cooperates with religious authorities by adjusting the schedule of public events to sectarian needs, it follows the best of our traditions. For it then respects the religious nature of our people and accommodates the public service to their spiritual needs."[40]

Some legislative accommodation consists of legislatively granted exemptions to general laws, aimed at accommodating religious interests. Typical state exemptions include the Texas law exempting religious publications from sales taxes, policies accommodating the schedules of religious minorities in school calendars, and state exemptions from criminal prosecution for sacramental peyote use. Congressional accommodations include provisions for religious conscientious objection to military service, exemptions from Social Security self-employment taxation for persons with religious objections to receiving Social Security benefits, excusing people with religious objections to labor unions from paying union dues, and exempting religious institutions from some of the requirements of Title VII of the Civil Rights Act.[41] All of these policies raise establishment clause questions. To grant exemptions from valid, neutral laws for persons whose motivations are religious and to deny the same consideration to persons with equally pressing nonreligious motivations appears to be the kind of special religious privilege that the establishment clause forbids.[42]

Various members of the current Supreme Court support wide legislative latitude in granting accommodation. Justice Sandra Day O'Connor supports such accommodations so long as they do not "endorse" religion. Chief Justice William Rehnquist does so on originalist grounds. Justice Anthony M. Kennedy argues that accommodation is permissible so long as it does not coerce unwilling participation. Justice Scalia does so on majoritarian grounds, as suggested in his dissents in *Edwards v. Aguilard,*[43] in *Texas Monthly v. Bullock,*[44] and his majority opinion in *Smith.*[45] In that opinion, Scalia denied any free exercise *right* to religious exemptions but insisted that legislatures are free to grant them as part of the normal political process. Scalia recognized that the majority approach leaves religious liberty within the political process: "Values that are protected against government interferences through enshrinement in the Bill of Rights are not thereby banished from the political process." He readily admits that "leaving accommodation to the political process will place at a relative disadvantage those religious practices that are not widely engaged in; but that unavoidable consequences of democratic government must be preferred to a system in which each conscience is a law unto itself."

Legislative accommodations have also attracted some serious critics, because they risk sacrificing religious equality, thereby enabling religiously dominant groups to use the political process to gain unequal advantages.[46] Constitutional scholar Ira Lupu reads the establishment clause as prohibiting legislative accommodations of religion because these decisions are likely to be divisive and to favor politically successful religious groups rather than marginal ones. He supports, however, the power of courts to order accommodation under the free exercise clause. Lupu's concern is a serious one; legislative accommodations are often inconsistent, unprincipled, and sometimes divisive. Nevertheless, they are so much a part of our ordinary practice that it is difficult to imagine their absence. We take for granted such simple accommodation as religious excuses for school absences or exempting Catholic sacraments from laws forbidding serving alcohol to minors. Imagine how contentious life would be if every one of these simple accommodations required a court case. Moreover, our constitutional tradition holds all government authorities to constitutional standards; it seems almost perverse to deny legislators the opportunity to exercise their own constitutional judgment about religious freedom.

Free Exercise Accommodation and the Values of Neutrality and Equality

When religious interest groups fail to receive accommodation in the legislative or administrative process, they may go to the courts and demand accommodation as a matter of constitutional right. Typically, they seek judicial orders exempting them from religiously burdensome aspects of the law. Beginning with *Sherbert v. Verner*,[47] the Supreme Court has considered at least some degree of accommodation to be required by the free exercise clause. Arguments about constitutionally required accommodation demand that we explore the meaning and value of governmental neutrality, the nature of discrimination, and the position of religious groups in American life.

A substantial tradition of constitutional scholarship considers this kind of accommodation as preference for religion and hence a violation of governmental neutrality. A generation ago, Philip Kurland argued that neutrality was the heart of the religion clauses: religion should not be used to confer either a benefit or a disability. The exemptions granted to persons with religious motivations are like subsidies that are not available to persons with other kinds of motivations, in his view, and should be constitutionally prohibited.[48] He saw court-ordered exemptions as privileging religious over nonreligious motivations and inevitably preferring some religions over others. In a society as religiously heterogeneous as ours, it is impossible that every religious motivation could be accommodated; that is precisely the kind of "anarchy" that Justice Scalia evoked in *Smith*. In short, in Kurland's view, court-ordered religious accommodation implicitly violates the values of neutrality and equality.[49]

In light of this argument, any justification for judicial accommodation must come to terms with the value of neutrality. Several powerful arguments take on that challenge. Most reject the premise of neutrality itself. The simplest arguments note that if neutrality ever made sense, it is a concept appropriate to a much simpler form of government. Neutrality might have been appropriate in an era of limited government, when most governmental regulations took the form of prohibitions, such as criminal penalties. But the regulatory state has so multiplied the interactions among governmental institutions, religious institutions, and individuals that simply avoiding penalties no longer ensures freedom of religious practice. The multiplicity of regulations almost guarantees that one of them will conflict with someone's religious convictions. For example, the requirement to have a photograph on a drivers license will impact on those who believe that such photographs are "graven images" prohibited in the Bible;[50] regulations about the equipment worn by high school athletes will affect people who believe either that the clothing is immodest or who are religiously required to cover their heads at all times.[51] Hence, without accommodation, persons will inadvertently and constantly be deprived of their ability to practice their religion while participating as full members of the larger society. To refuse accommodation will deprive them of the benefits of full citizenship, causing harm not only to the individuals but also to the society, by fragmenting identities and making people choose between civic and religious commitments.

A deeper probe challenges our ordinary understanding of religious preferences, and hence of equality itself. Many ordinary regulations already accommodate widely practiced religions; they are simply so much a part of our lives that we fail to see them. School and government office closings on Sundays and on Christmas and Easter reflect the needs of the Christian majority. But when Jews ask for excused absences from work or school for the Jewish high holidays, we *notice* the accommodation request. Religious majorities protect themselves legislatively; the very point of making religious freedom a constitutional *right* is to protect those whose interests will not be reflected in majority decisions.[52] The *Sherbert* case itself reaffirms this point. South Carolina law had already accommodated Sunday sabbath observers by providing that no employee was to be required to work on that day in violation of religious conscience.

Pursuing this point leads us to question whether the very notion of neutrality even makes sense. A purely formal neutrality may mask significant substantive disabilities, when background conditions are unequal. We are familiar with this idea in the jurisprudence of the equal protection clause. Some of the lessons learned in combating race and gender discrimination are relevant to the religion clauses. Religious minorities are not really in an equal position with members of mainstream groups with respect to the burdensome laws: "The person whose religious life is invaded by a legal provision is not similarly situated to the person for whom the provision has no such effect. The impact of the legal provision on those differently situated persons is not equal."[53]

The most cursory knowledge of religious group conflict in American history reminds us that religious minorities have long suffered both overt and purposeful discrimination, and "selective indifference" to the burdens of laws that seem to be religiously neutral. This is all the more true when the religious beliefs and practices in question are so incomprehensible to the majority that the members of the majority cannot really appreciate the religious impact. In these instances, exemptions are necessary to create a substantive equality that mere formal equality fails to achieve. For Christopher Eisgruber and Lawrence Sager,[54] the "selective insensitivity" to religious minorities suggests the key to understanding the free exercise clause. They argue that the distinguishing characteristic of religion in the United States is not its singular value but its singular vulnerability. Religious accommodation is not to be justified because religion merits special privileges but because doing so is necessary to achieve *equal respect*. Discrimination against religious groups, often in the form of insensitivity, is the real threat that the free exercise clause confronts; hence, the model of equal protection provides appropriate analogies and guidance. Religious discrimination takes several forms and has several explanations:

> Religious commandments are not necessarily founded on or limited by reasons accessible to nonbelievers; often they are understood to depend on fiat or covenant and to implicate forces or beings beyond human challenge or comprehension. Religion is often the hub of tightly knit communities, whose habits, rituals, and values are deeply alien to outsiders. At best, this is likely to produce a chronic interfaith "tone deafness," in which the persons of one faith do not easily empathize with the concerns or persons of other faiths. At worst, it may produce hostility, even murderous hatred, among different religious groups.
> . . . From the perspective of some faiths, it is desirable to convert nonbelievers rather than to injure them. . . . [T]hey may even have the welfare of the unbelievers fully in mind as they seek to shape the legal regime to discourage or prevent the nonbelievers from pursuing their own faiths. Even when conversion is not their aim, dominant faiths (or clusters of faiths) that recognize the value and concerns of others may nevertheless use political power to favor themselves. . . .
> . . . These nonantagonisitic variations may be "kinder, gentler" forms of discrimination, but they remain stark failures of equal regard.[55]

Ultimately, the argument about religious exemptions has led us to consider the concept of equal citizenship. If we are persuaded that more than formal neutrality is necessary to achieve equal citizenship, we must consider subtler problems. The question then becomes not *whether* religious practices must be *ever* accommodated but under what conditions and with what limitations. Do legislatures have the discretion to accommodate religious interests, and if so, under what conditions? When should courts require such accommodations as a matter of constitutional right? How deferent should courts be to legislative judgments when religious exercises are burdened?

The pluralist is likely to accept *both* legislative accommodations *and* a vigorous enforcement of establishment clause limits on them. The free exercise clause mandates judicial accommodation for those persons and practices not protected in the political process, and the establishment clause prevents public policy from being captured by a dominant religious interest. Moreover, legislative and administrative accommodations are often the simplest and most humane ways of protecting religious freedom. After all, the judicial process is an adversarial one—a crucial last resort, but surely not to be preferred to consensual or negotiated ones. From a pluralist perspective, the patchwork administrative, legislative, and judicial solutions protect the strength and resiliency of the system. The more institutions involved in a decision, the more persons and interests have access to the entire process. Congressional action reversing *Goldman* and *Smith* illustrates the strength of the

Madisonian system of divided and overlapping power. The results are seldom elegantly principled, but the porousness of the processes is itself advantageous.

PLURALIST GOVERNMENT AND THE
COMPELLING-STATE-INTEREST CONTROVERSY

The religion clauses create constitutional *rights*. To identify something as a right is to recognize, prima facie at least, a valid claim to its protection, even in the face of strong conflicting values. Sometimes the cost of these values is substantial indeed—sometimes large enough to outweigh the rights claim. When a right is constitutionalized, it is protected from change through the ordinary political process. Under the American constitutional system, one of the most important duties of the judiciary has been to reconcile conflicts between rights and the countervailing values that emanate from the political process.

When rights claims reach the courts, judges are asked to weigh the relative importance of an individual claim against the state's interest in its limitation. Ordinary balancing often places the individual claimant at a disadvantage, because more widely shared interests can easily outweigh the interests of dissenting individuals or groups. In fact, the very notion of balancing reduces *rights* to *interests* and weights them along with all other social interests; hence, this kind of balancing essentially replicates the legislative process.[56]

The compelling-state-interest approach is aimed at redressing this imbalance by adding extra weight to the individual's claims. Ordinarily, the person challenging the constitutionality of a law bears the burden of proof; failing to overcome this burden leaves the law intact. But in cases involving fundamental rights,[57] the courts have reversed this burden of proof, tasking the law's defenders with the burden of establishing its constitutionality. Such laws are subjected to "strict scrutiny," requiring their defenders to show (1) that the challenged law served not just an important public purpose but a genuinely *compelling* one, (2) that the law was well tailored to achieve that purpose, and (3) that the purpose could not be achieved by some less burdensome legislative method. Thus, the compelling-state-interest test requires defenders of a challenged law to persuade a court that its burdens are justified by extremely important state interests that could not be achieved in any less objectionable way. This process removes final determination from the legislature and enables courts to weigh the balance by a different standard—again, another example of jurisdictional pluralism.[58] This fact is at the heart of the most tangled free exercise controversy of the generation, one that began with the case of *Employment Division, Department of Human Resources of Oregon v. Smith.*[59] No constitutional controversy in this generation illustrates as sharply the immensely complex relation among institutions of government as does the series of events that began with this case.

The narrative of the *Smith* case is well-known; I give only the barest outlines here. Alfred Smith and Galen Black were fired from their jobs in a private drug rehabilitation program when it was discovered that they used peyote as part of a religious ritual of the Native American Church, of which they were members. They applied for unemployment compensation, but their application was denied. They appealed the denial of benefits, and both the Oregon appellate and state supreme court ruled in their favor, on the grounds that religious exercises could not be considered misconduct. In 1986 Oregon's appeal reached the U.S. Supreme Court, which vacated the state judgment and remanded the case to the Oregon Supreme Court to determine whether state law prohibited sacramental use of peyote and whether the Oregon constitution protected sacramental peyote use. On remand, the Oregon Supreme Court concluded that Oregon law "makes no exception for the sacramental use" of peyote, but it noted that if the state should ever attempt to enforce the law against this religious practice, that prosecution would violate the free exercise clause of the U.S. Constitution. In 1990 the Supreme Court granted certiorari for the second time and overturned Oregon's decision by a six-to-three majority.[60]

Justice Scalia's majority opinion held that the free exercise clause is directly breached only by laws that specifically target religious practice for unfavorable treatment, not by generally applicable, religiously neutral laws. Consequently, laws such as Oregon's antidrug law, which only inadvertently burdened a religious practice, need not be justified by a compelling state interest. Justice Scalia's much-criticized majority opinion is, at its heart, an argument about the relative authority of courts and legislatures.

Recall that the compelling-state-interest standard places the burden on the state to defend any policy that (even inadvertently) burdens someone's religious interests. It begins by assuming any law burdening religion unconstitutional, leaving the state with the burden of showing a state interest in retaining it. Justice Scalia invokes an image of anarchy that this doctrine would create. Especially in a religiously plural society, virtually every ordinary policy, from labor to health policy, from foreign policy to education, could potentially burden the religious interests of some faith. In Scalia's words, "To make an individual's obligation to obey such a law contingent upon the law's coincidence with his religious beliefs, except where the state's interest is 'compelling'—[would permit] him, by virtue of his beliefs, 'to become a law unto himself.'"[61] This danger is all the more troubling, he argues, because "we are a cosmopolitan nation made up of people of almost every conceivable religious preference." Hence, "we cannot afford the luxury of deeming *presumptively invalid*, as applied to the religious objector, every

regulation of conduct that does not protect an interest of the highest order."
He then recounts what critics term a "parade of horribles" to illustrate the dis-
array of governmental policy that would result from such a doctrine.

Justice Scalia and the other members of the *Smith* majority found the
compelling-state-interest standard inconsistent with judicial restraint
and thus a misuse of judicial power. The presumption of unconstitutional-
ity is a presumption against the judgment of representative institutions.
Scalia forcefully identifies the counter-majoritarian implications of the
compelling-state-interest approach, as well as the fact that it enables a dissenting minority's interest to outweigh determinations made in the political process, thus disrupting the normal course of public policy. Furthermore, by removing the balancing from the legislative process and placing
it in the hands of unelected judges, this process enhances the power of
courts to substitute their judgment for those of elected officials. Justice
Scalia's majoritarianism, therefore, moves him to reject judicially mandated
exemptions but to take a very permissive attitude toward legislative ones.

Although Justice Scalia wrote for a six-justice majority, his rejection of
the compelling-state-interest test did not win majority support. Justice
O'Connor's concurring opinion and the vigorous dissent authored by Justice
Harry A. Blackmun provide strong defenses of compelling state interest. To
O'Connor, the test is not an anomaly but "a fundamental part of our First
Amendment doctrine." Without serious judicial scrutiny, the fate of minority
religions would indeed be left up to the political process, which is precisely
what the Bill of Rights was intended to prevent. "The very purpose of a Bill
of Rights was to withdraw certain subjects from the vicissitudes of political
controversy, to place them beyond the reach of majorities and officials and
to establish them as legal principles to be applied by the courts."

> The compelling interest test effectuates the First Amendment's command that
> religious liberty is an independent liberty, that it occupies a preferred position,
> and that the Court will not permit encroachments upon this liberty, whether di-
> rect or indirect, unless required by clear and compelling governmental interests
> "of the highest order." "Only an especially important government interest pur-
> sued by narrowly tailored means can justify exacting a sacrifice of First Amend-
> ment freedoms as the price for an equal share of the rights, benefits, and privi-
> leges enjoyed by other citizens."

Like the dissenters, she would maintain the compelling-state-interest test;
unlike them, she believed that Oregon had shown a compelling state interest in maintaining the consistency of its antidrug policy. Justices Harry Blackmun, William Brennan, and Thurgood Marshall joined Justice O'Connor in
this part of her concurring opinion. They departed from her judgment that
the state had shown a compelling interest in refusing to exempt sacramental
peyote use.

Had the controversy over *Smith* ended here, it would have constituted one of the most sharply contested disputes about the relative value of religious rights and state interests—and the concomitant issue of who should decide them. For here the Supreme Court majority took a position professing judicial restraint, limiting its own power and leaving more authority in the hands of legislative bodies. But subsequent chapters of the *Smith* case brought new twists: the U.S. Congress demanded that the courts use the more activist standard, and the Supreme Court refused Congress the power to make that demand. The whole narrative illustrates Madisonian pluralism in all its frustration and all its complexity.

Almost before the ink had dried on the *Smith* opinion, constitutional scholars and religious advocates assailed its devastating implications for the rights of religious minorities. An unusually broad coalition of religious interest groups formed the Coalition for the Free Exercise of Religion to petition Congress to reverse the effects of decision legislatively. In November 1993 Congress adopted the Religious Freedom Restoration Act, which legislatively restored the standard for constitutional review in cases where federally supported programs were involved.[62] Its first-stated purpose was the following: "To restore the compelling interest test as set forth in *Sherbert v. Verner* and *Wisconsin v. Yoder*, and to guarantee its application in all cases where free exercise of religion is substantially burdened."

The key section of the bill stated that government may restrict a person's free exercise of religion only if government can show that such a restriction "(1) is essential to further a compelling governmental interest; and (2) is the least restrictive means of furthering that compelling governmental interest" standard.

Under the traditional understanding of the separation of powers, Congress has no authority to reverse a Supreme Court decision by ordinary legislation. But Congress believed it was on safe grounds in adopting the RFRA under its Fourteenth Amendment authority to "enforce [constitutional guarantees] by appropriate legislation." Detractors, however, argued that this law was invalid on two grounds—first, that it went beyond enforcing a constitutional amendment by actively changing its interpretation, and that it usurped state authority by extending the requirement to many issues under state jurisdiction.

A constitutional challenge to this law reached the Supreme Court in June 1997, in the case of *City of Boerne v. Flores*.[63] That case introduced a new set of actors and institutions into the narrative. Its issue began as a local one. P. F. Flores, the archbishop of San Antonio, applied for a building permit to expand a Catholic church located in Boerne, Texas, but the local zoning board denied the permit because the church was located in a historic preservation district. Archbishop Flores then brought suit in federal district court under the new Religious Freedom Restoration Act, which would have required a permit unless the city could show a compelling state interest in refusing it. A U.S. district court upheld the city, holding the law unconstitutional; the federal appeals court reversed and upheld the law.

When the case reached the Supreme Court, a divided Court took the opportunity to strike down the Religious Freedom Restoration Act, as violating the separation of powers by infringing on the judicial power. The majority ruled that while the Fourteenth Amendment grants Congress the power to enforce a constitutional right, the RFRA went beyond enforcement and, in fact, altered the meaning of the right, thus infringing upon the power of the judiciary and upon the traditional prerogatives of states. As Justice Kennedy wrote, "Legislation which alters the free exercise clause's meaning cannot be said to be enforcing the clause. Congress does not enforce a constitutional right by changing what the right is."

Yet the story still did not end. Since the demise of the RFRA, a number of state legislatures have adopted their own versions of the statute, making many state courts friendlier to religious claims than are the federal courts. Thus, when litigants can choose between federal and state venues for hearing religious freedom cases, they sometimes choose state courts over federal ones. At the same time, Congress is again considering a variation of the RFRA that supporters hope will pass constitutional muster.

These cases demonstrate how religious freedom controversies fold into a debate about the nature of American constitutionalism. Before Congress passed the Religious Freedom Restoration Act, the lines seemed more clearly drawn. Those who understand our institutions as essentially majoritarian tended to find Justice Scalia's argument persuasive. Those who emphasize constitutional limitations as hedges against majoritarianism countered that the very point of having a constitution is to remove certain protections from the ordinary political process—to give them, if not absolute status, at least the kind of special weight that the compelling interest standard offers. But the adoption of the RFRA placed the popularly elected branch of government squarely on the side previously identified with antimajoritarian arguments. This complication seems to reinforce my own rejection of any simple majority/minority distinction.

What these cases illustrate most of all is the very wide variety of governmental institutions involved in the interpreting of religious freedom. Notice the variety of actors in this continuing controversy: an Oregon private employer, an Oregon state agency, two levels of Oregon courts, the U.S. Supreme Court (twice), an extraordinarily diverse religious coalition, the U.S. Congress, the Catholic Church, a local zoning board and landmarks commission, two levels of federal courts, the U.S. Supreme Court again, and then various state legislatures and courts, and again the U.S. Congress.

The absence of any definitive principle for reconciling religious claims against competing interests may appear to be a weakness in the American protection of religious rights. However, this absence seems not so much a failure of principle as evidence of the nonessentialist, pluralist nature of this constitutional problem. Considered from the perspective of institutional structure, this apparent muddle illustrates the strength of our fragmented and even illogical system of overlapping governmental powers. The compelling state interest standard is "counter-majoritarian," in that it empowers courts to consider balances in different ways than legislative or administrative procedures. I would prefer the term "counter-mainstream," in view of my argument that policy making is a matter of minority coalitions rather than majorities. In the first instance, policies are made by legislative or administrative bodies, which can be presumed to be responsible to mainstream interests or to politically favored minorities. When these policies are challenged in court, an alternative institution is invoked; when courts use the compelling-state-interest standard, they weigh the balance with different criteria. The different institutions and different measuring devices contribute a crucial redundancy to the system of constitutional protections. They do not literally guarantee anything, but they increase the likelihood that religious interests will be given a serious hearing.

This is essentially the same situation we discovered in the accommodation controversy. Legislative (or administrative) accommodation of religion provides a first-instance opportunity for religious interests to be taken into account in the decision-making structure. Often accommodation is simple and relatively noncontroversial. Sometimes, of course, it may be unfair, biased toward favored religions, contentious, or unprincipled. For that very reason, the establishment clause provides a method for removing the issue to a different venue, where the accommodation may be challenged. In these cases, the courts provide a place for conflicting interests to be heard and to be weighed on a different scale than those used in the original instance. None of this guarantees that the judicial decision will be different from the legislative one, but the redundancy both improves opportunities for a good decision and helps legitimate any decision rendered. Judicial enforcement of the religion clauses provides "a second opinion" for religious interests not accommodated in the first instance. Perhaps the real genius of fragmented government is to increase the access points for these interests to influence government. While this is far from a "guarantee" in the literal sense, it adds a crucial redundancy in the protection of religious liberty.

The constitutional context of religious freedom is thus consistent with the patterns of religious meanings in American society. Thus, plural religions and plural decision-making structures are all part of the same whole—a part of the constitutional pluralism that sustains our tradition of religious liberty.

NOTES

1. This chapter is adapted from a more sustained argument on the same subject. See Bette Novit Evans, *Interpreting the Free Exercise of Religion* (Chapel Hill: University of North Carolina Press, 1998).

2. See, for example, Richard E. Wentz, *The Culture of Religious Pluralism* (Boulder, Colo.: Westview, 1998).

3. Sociologist Milton Yinger, for example, defines religion as a system of beliefs and practices by which a group of people struggles with the ultimate problems of human life. See Milton Yinger, *The Scientific Study of Religion* (New York: Macmillan, 1970). Anthropologist Clifford Geertz emphasizes religious symbols that help one interpret the meaning of life itself within a cosmology. Clifford Geertz, "Religion as a Cultural System," in *Anthropological Approach to the Study of Religion,* ed. Michael Banton (London: Tavistock, 1966), 1–46.

4. Franklin Gamwell, *The Meaning of Religious Freedom* (Albany: State University of New York Press, 1995), 30.

5. Peter Berger, *Sacred Canopy* (Garden City, N.Y.: Doubleday, 1967), 26 and 28.

6. Robert Bellah, "Civil Religion in America," in *Beyond Belief: Essays on Religion in a Post Industrial World* (New York: Harper and Row, 1970), 168–215.

7. James Davison Hunter, *Culture Wars: The Struggle to Define America* (New York: Basic, 1991).

8. Frank Lechner, "Fundamentalism Revisited," in *In Gods We Trust,* ed. Thomas Robbins and Dick Anthony, 2d ed. (New Brunswick, N.J.: Transaction, 1990), 77, 80.

9. Evans, *Interpreting the Free Exercise of Religion,* 245.

10. Not being an advocate of constitutional originalism, I do not suggest that the framers of the Constitution intended this conjoining of guarantees to make that point. Rather, the conjoining of guarantees has created a meaning beyond and separate from the intention or understanding of any of their authors.

11. Thus I do not adopt Robert Cover's controversial "nonstatist premise"—the position that the interpretations offered by judges are "not superior" to those of a community, with its own "normative boundaries" and "sacred narratives that ground the understanding of law they offer." See Robert Cover, "The Supreme Court 1982 Term: Forward: Nomos and Narrative," *Harvard Law Review* 97 (1983).

12. John Locke, *A Letter Concerning Toleration,* ed. John Horton and Susan Mendus (London: Routledge, 1991).

13. Leonard Levy, *The Establishment Clause: Religion and the First Amendment* (New York: Macmillan, 1986).

14. When the majority approved state funding for transportation to parochial as well as public schools in *Everson v. Board of Education,* 330 U.S. 1 (1947), Justice John Rutledge dissented, fearing that any financial benefits to religions would initiate an unseemly competition among sects for state monies. In *Meek v. Pittinger,* 421 U.S. 349 (1975), the majority rejected a Pennsylvania plan to loan textbooks and teaching materials, and to provide ancillary services to private schools, in part because of the program's potential to foment political divisiveness. One of the strongest statements of this concern is Justice Hugo Black's dissenting opinion on the potential divisiveness of state aid to education in *Board of Education v. Allen,* 392 U.S. 236 (1968): "state aid to religion . . . generates discord, harmony, hatred, and strife among our people."

15. The Supreme Court has often recognized this danger, as Chief Justice Warren Burger's word in *Lemon v. Kurtzman* illustrates: "Political division along religious lines was one of the principal evils against which the First Amendment was intended to protect. . . . The political divisiveness of such conflict is a threat to the normal political process. *Lemon v. Kurtzman*, 402 U.S. 602 (1971). The fear of sectarian conflict has been a frequent theme in Supreme Court opinions. In *Grand Rapids School District v. Ball*, 473 U.S. 373 (1985), for example, the Court noted that religion "can serve powerfully to divide societies."

16. Alexis de Tocqueville very early in our history appreciated the importance of private associations in American life. Alexis de Tocqueville, *Democracy in America*, ed. Phillips Bradley (New York: Vintage), 1945.

17. Stephen Carter, *The Culture of Disbelief* (New York: Basic, 1993), 36–37.

18. See Dean Kelley, "Confronting the Danger," in *Church, State, and Public Policy*, ed. A. Melching (Washington D.C.: American Enterprise Institute, 1978), 15.

19. Cover, "Nomos and Narrative," 33–34.

20. James Madison, *Federalist 10*, in James Madison, Alexander Hamilton, and John Jay, *The Federalist Papers* (orig. pub. 1787–1788; repr. New York: Bantam, 1982), 46.

21. James Madison, *Federalist 51*, in *Federalist Papers*, 264.

22. Madison, *Federalist 10*, in *Federalist Papers*, 46.

23. Madison, *Federalist 51*, in *Federalist Papers*, 261.

24. The classic description of this process is still Robert Dahl's *Who Governs* (New Haven: Yale University Press, 1961).

25. The most articulate spokesman for the representation enhancing view of judicial review is John Hart Ely, *Democracy and Distrust* (Cambridge, Mass.: Harvard University Press, 1980).

26. My interpretation is consistent with, and much influenced by, such works as Robert Cover, "The Uses of Jurisdictional Redundancy: Interests, Ideology, and Innovation," 22 *William and Mary Law Review* 639 (1981), and Martha Minow, "Pluralisms," 21 *Connecticut Law Review* 965 (1989).

27. The most famous advocate of this view is Philip Kurland, *Religion and the Law* (Chicago: Aldine, 1961).

28. *Lee v. Weisman*, 505 U.S. 577 (1992).

29. This has been a special concern in the perpetual controversies over state aid to parochial schools. See, for example, *Everson v. Board of Education*, 330 U.S. 1 (1947); *Board of Education v. Allen*, 392 U.S. 236 (1968); and *Grand Rapids School District v. Ball*, 473 U.S. 373 (1985).

30. *Lynch v. Donnelly*, 465 U.S. 668 (1984), and *County of Allegheny v. ACLU*, 492 U.S. 573 (1989).

31. Congress has engaged in legislative accommodation by providing for religious conscientious objection to military service, exempting persons with religious objections to receiving Social Security benefits from paying Social Security self-employment taxes, exempting those with religious objections to labor unions from paying union dues, and exempting religious institutions from some of the requirements of Title VII of the Civil Rights Act. All of these policies raise establishment clause questions. To grant exemptions from valid, neutral laws for persons whose motivations are religious and to deny the same consideration to persons with equally

pressing nonreligious motivations appears to be the kind of special privilege for religion that the establishment clause forbids. See, for example, *Estate of Thornton v. Caldor,* 472 U.S. 703 (1985).

32. Christopher Eisgruber and Lawrence Sager, "The Vulnerability of Conscience: The Constitutional Basis for Protecting Religious Conduct," 61 *University of Chicago Law Review* 1245, 1280 (1994).

33. *Goldman v. Weinberger,* 475 U.S. 503 (1986). See the excellent analysis of this case in Michael Sandel, "Religious Liberty: Freedom of Conscience or Freedom of Choice?" *Utah Law Review* 597 (1989).

34. Captain Goldman, an Air Force psychologist, was testifying as a defense witness in a court-martial when the opposing counsel complained about his violation of uniform regulations.

35. P.L. 100-180, 101 Stat. 1086–1087, sec. 508 (1987).

36. *Kiryas Joel School District v. Grumet,* 512 U.S. 687 (1994).

37. See *Aguilar v. Felton,* 473 U.S. 402 (1985), and *Grand Rapids v. Ball,* 473 U.S. 373 (1985).

38. *Grumet v. Cuomo* (900 N.Y.2d 57 (1997); 681 N.E.2d 340 (1997).

39. *Agostini v. Felton,* 521 U.S. 203 (1997).

40. *Zorach v. Clauson,* 343 U.S. 306 at 313–14 (1952).

41. See *Corporation of the Presiding Bishop of the Church of Jesus Christ of Latter Day Saints v. Amos,* 483 U.S. 327 (1987).

42. See, for example, *Estate of Thornton v. Caldor,* 472 U.S. 703 (1985). Among the arguments of this sort, see Jesse Choper, "The Free Exercise Clause: A Structural Overview and an Appraisal of Recent Developments," 27 *William and Mary Law Review* 943 (1985–86).

43. *Edwards v. Aguilard,* 482 U.S. 578 (1987).

44. *Texas Monthly v. Bullock,* 489 U.S. 1 (1989).

45. *Employment Division v. Smith,* 494 U.S. 872 (1990).

46. Ira Lupu, "Reconstructing the Religion Clauses," 140 *University of Pennsylvania Law Review* 555 (1991).

47. *Sherbert v. Verner,* 374 U.S. 398 (1963).

48. Kurland, *Religion and the Law,* and "The Irrelevance of the Constitution: The Religion Clauses of the First Amendment and the Supreme Court," 24 *Villanova Law Review* 3, 24 (1978).

49. Numerous Supreme Court opinions invoke the value of government neutrality, equal treatment, and nonpreference between citizens regardless of religious belief. See, for example, Justice Black's classic statement in *Everson v. Board of Education*: "[The First] Amendment requires the state to be neutral in its relations with groups of religious believers and nonbelievers; . . . State power is no more to be used so as to handicap religions, than it is to favor them." 330 U.S. 1, 18 (1947).

50. *Jensen v. Quaring,* 472 U.S. 478 (1985).

51. *Menorah v. Illinois High School Athletic Association,* 683 F.2d 1030 (7th Cir. Ill. 1982).

52. This was the underlying logic of the Jewish merchant's arguments in *Braunfeld v. Brown,* 366 U.S. 420 (1961). Notice the sharp contrast with Justice Scalia's approach to minority religions in *Smith.*

53. Stephen Pepper, "Conflicting Paradigms of Religious Freedom: Liberty versus Equality," *Brigham Young University Law Review*, 7, 41 (1993).

54. "The Vulnerability of Conscience: The Constitutional Basis for Protecting Religious Conduct," 61 *University of Chicago Law Review* 1245 (1994).

55. Eisgruber and Sager, "The Vulnerability of Conscience," 1283–84.

56. Ronald Dworkin, *Taking Rights Seriously* (Cambridge, Mass.: Harvard University Press, 1977).

57. See Justice Stone's famous Footnote Four in *U.S. v. Carolene Products*, 304 U.S. 144 (1938). The most thorough and persuasive argument on this approach is found in John Hart Ely, *Democracy and Distrust* (Cambridge, Mass.: Harvard University Press, 1980). Particularly during the Warren Court years, this standard was used when laws were challenged as burdening "fundamental freedoms" or "discrete and insular minorities."

58. The application of the compelling-state-interest standard to free exercise cases was made explicit in *Sherbert v. Verner*: "The compelling state interest standard requires that when religious practices are burdened by acts of government, the government must demonstrate that the burden is necessary to achieve a compelling state interest which can be achieved in no less burdensome way." 347 U.S. 398 (1963). Perhaps the single clearest statement of this doctrine is in *Wisconsin v. Yoder*: "Only those interests of the highest order and those not otherwise served can overbalance legitimate claims to the free exercise of religion." 406 U.S. 205 (1972). After *Yoder*, compelling state interest was widely understood to be the prevailing method of constitutional analysis in free exercise cases. While the standard gives special weight to religious freedom claims, that extra weight has not often been sufficient to outweigh state claims. In spite of the standard, government claims have prevailed against free exercise challenges before the Supreme Court only in *Yoder* and four unemployment compensation cases.

59. *Employment Division v. Smith*, 494 U.S. 872 (1990).

60. There is an enormous literature on this case. The present summary is taken from Bette Novit Evans, *"Employment Division, Oregon Department of Human Resources of Oregon v. Smith,"* in *Encyclopedia of Religion and American Law*, ed. Paul Finkelman (New York: Garland, 2000), 147–51.

61. 494 U.S. 872 (1990), quoting *Reynolds v. U.S.*, 98 U.S. 145 (1878).

62. Pub. L. No. 103–144; 107 Stat. 1480.

63. *Agostini v. Felton*, 521 U.S. 507 (1997).

10

Political Culture, Political Structure, and Political Conflict: The Persistence of Church-State Conflict in the United States

Ted G. Jelen

In the final half of the twentieth century, conflict over relations between church and state has animated politics in the United States. Based in part on the increased religious diversity of the United States, the "incorporation" of the Bill of Rights to apply to the actions of state and local governments, and increases in the political activism of religiously motivated citizens at all points along the political spectrum, the extent and manner of controversy concerning the proper relationship between the sacred and the secular have rarely been more intense than is the question of church-state relations at the outset of the twenty-first century.

As this is being written, the Supreme Court of the United States has recently ruled that organized prayer at high school football games violates the establishment clause of the First Amendment. In response, many high school districts have found both legal and extralegal ways to circumvent this ruling. The high court has also been charged with the task of resolving conflicting court decisions over the constitutionality of tax vouchers for tuition at private (usually religious) elementary and secondary schools. In defiance of several court orders, school districts around the country are posting copies of the Ten Commandments in an effort to reduce the incidence of violence in public schools, and the state of Alabama has just elected to its state supreme court a candidate who has openly defied the federal courts on this issue.[1] Indeed, it is difficult to pick up a daily newspaper in the United States without seeing evidence of the persistent conflict over the proper relationship between religion and government.

The purpose of this chapter is to explain why it has been so difficult to resolve issues of church-state relations in American politics. Such conflicts appear to have been managed quite successfully in other democracies,[2] and the apparent inability of the American political system to settle this issue poses an interesting puzzle for analysts of American and comparative politics alike.

My argument here is that the persistence of church-state conflict in U.S. politics has multiple sources. For purposes of this chapter, I single out three: the importance of liberal individualism, with its emphasis on unalienable "rights"; the specific constitutional provisions governing church-state relations; and the decentralized structure of political authority in the United States. Some aspects of church-state conflict in the United States have deep historical roots, while others are as ephemeral as the day-to-day operation of electoral politics at the subnational level. It is to the former set of considerations that attention is first turned.

CULTURAL CONDITIONS

Many observers have suggested that an important source of the unique U.S. political culture is general agreement on the public philosophy of liberal individualism.[3] The American political tradition is replete with references to John Locke and Thomas Jefferson (the latter being the author of the U.S. Declaration of Independence) in which humans are characterized as possessing "natural," "God-given," and "unalienable" rights that exist prior to membership in society and can only be relinquished voluntarily. Rights, in this conception, are essentially nonnegotiable limitations on the power and prerogatives of government. The successful assertion of a "right" means that within a particular area of individual sovereignty, the exercise of government power is, a priori, illegitimate.[4] Thus, the very notion of a "right" entails placing certain citizen prerogatives outside the reach of government intervention—and by extension, beyond the reach of popular majorities.

As will be shown in the following section, church-state issues in the United States are framed by two distinct (and perhaps competing) rights listed in the First Amendment to the Constitution. As such, church-state relations essentially involve the gray area in which the very right of government to make policy is regarded as controversial. Public policy in this area involves much more than the simple implementation of the will of a popular or a legislative majority. The fact that such questions necessarily involve the assertion of different and competing rights exacerbates the problem considerably. Issues of rights involve the question of what governments *can* do within the limits of their legitimate authority.

The interplay between politics and rights, which are presumed to transcend politics, suggests that the courts, which are the least "democratic" branch of the federal government, have a great deal of authority in making policy in the area of church-state relations. Issues in this area are often debated in contexts in which the demands of democracy and personal freedom are in conflict, which in turn provides much of the passion with which church-state relations are contested.[5]

To illustrate, one area of virtually constant conflict in American politics is the question of organized prayer in public schools. The customary practice of beginning each school day with an organized (usually Christian) prayer was declared unconstitutional by the U.S. Supreme Court in the case of *Engel v. Vitale* in 1962. Consistently, public opinion surveys taken in the United States since the *Engel* decision have shown that large majorities of Americans approve of the idea of school prayer. If government decisions in this area were made democratically, in accordance with the will of the majority, it might be expected that public school prayer would be mandatory within most jurisdictions in the United States. However, in *Engel*, and in subsequent decisions, an unelected U.S. Supreme Court ruled that such prayers violate the establishment clause of the First Amendment (to be discussed in the next section) and thus constitute illegitimate government endorsement of religion. In this case, the Court decided that the "rights" of a small minority of nonreligious students and parents trumped the right of the majority to enact its preferences into law. While this issue continues to be contested in U.S. politics, the Court in this instance took a clearly antimajoritarian stance. Such a position is controversial but seems to reinforce the intrinsic nature of a constitutional "right."

Thus, the centrality of "rights talk" in the area of church-state relations has made any resolution of controversies in this area extremely difficult, by rendering the very process of conflict resolution problematic. Indeed, the subsuming of religious politics under the rubric of rights has had an important consequence for U.S. politics—it has made acts of defiance against court decisions limiting the exercise of religious rights extremely common. As will be seen in the final section of this chapter, elected officials are continually challenging apparent limits to religious liberty, by enacting laws that appear to violate the Supreme Court's understanding of the religion clauses of the First Amendment. Moreover, individual citizens in school districts, local governments, and other settings in American politics routinely defy church-state law in the United States. Such defiance is generally characterized as the exercise of a right against unwarranted government intrusion, or as obedience to a "higher law" from a divine source. Resistance to illegitimate government authority is an important component of America's mythological political history, and active dissenters from contemporary church-state jurisprudence can draw on a rich U.S. tradition of opposition to "unjust" laws.

CONSTITUTIONAL ISSUES

The general characteristic of religious politics to be cast in terms of "rights" is further complicated by the nature of the specific rights in question. In the

United States, many observers have noted that "freedom of religion," as defined by the religion clauses of the First Amendment to the U.S. Constitution, is the first right listed in the Bill of Rights.[6] The specific language of the religion clauses is as follows: "Congress shall make no law respecting an establishment of religion, or prohibiting the free exercise thereof."

These two parts of this sentence, respectively termed the "establishment clause" and the "free exercise clause," provide the legal setting for church-state relations in American politics. At a minimum, the establishment clause appears to guarantee freedom *from* religion, while the free exercise clause seems to guarantee freedom *of* religion.[7] Scholars, judges, and other public officials find what often appears conflicting guidance in the spare language of the religion clauses of the First Amendment.

At some risk of oversimplification, there are two general interpretations of the establishment clause, often termed "accommodationism" and "separationism."[8] Accommodationists hold that the establishment clause simply prohibits government from designating a *particular* religion as an "official" state-sponsored religion, or that governments are proscribed under the establishment clause from conferring benefits on particular religions. However, accommodationism also entails the belief that the proper relationship between church and state is one of "benevolent neutrality,"[9] in which general government assistance to religion is considered permissible. This stance, also termed "nonpreferentialism,"[10] does not require government to be neutral between religion and irreligion.

By contrast, "separationists" tend to view the establishment clause quite broadly and argue that this clause of the First Amendment proscribes government assistance to religion in any form.[11] This view of the First Amendment was put most clearly in Supreme Court Justice Hugo Black's opinion in the 1947 case of *Everson v. Board of Education:* "The 'establishment of religion' clause of the First Amendment means at least this: Neither a state nor the Federal government can set up a church. Neither can pass laws which aid one religion, *aid all religions,* or prefer one religion over another."[12]

The difference between accommodationists and separationists can perhaps be reduced to differences over the italicized portion of the above quote. A proscription against neutral, nonpreferential government assistance to religion may be the defining characteristic of a separationist position on the establishment clause.

At this writing, the prevailing Supreme Court doctrine on the establishment clause is *Lemon v. Kurtzman* (1972), a generally separationist ruling. However, the Court in recent years has relaxed the separationist tendencies of *Lemon,* without explicitly overruling the earlier precedent.[13]

Similarly, there are two general schools of interpretation of the free exercise clause, "libertarianism" and "communalism."[14] A "libertarian" reading of the free exercise clause would entail the belief that freedom of religion and conscience is a fundamental human right, with which government can rarely, if ever, interfere. Libertarians would argue that religious practices that violate otherwise valid laws are generally entitled to exemptions from such laws. Thus, adherents of unconventional or unpopular religious beliefs would be granted broad latitude in the practice of their beliefs.

To illustrate, until the 1990s the U.S. Supreme Court took a generally libertarian view of religious free exercise[15] and generally applied the "*Sherbert-Yoder*" test to questions of religious freedom.[16] The *Sherbert-Yoder* test involved a three-step process, in which government was required to meet a very high burden to justify legal interference with religious free exercise.[17] Under *Sherbert-Yoder,* government was first required to show that it had a "compelling interest which justifies the abridgement of the . . . right of free exercise of religion."[18] This has typically proven to be a rather formidable hurdle, in that, historically, the compelling-state-interest standard has required government to demonstrate that a particular regulation is practically *essential* to government if it is to perform its necessary functions.[19] Second, the *Sherbert-Yoder* test required that petitioners arguing for religiously based exemptions from legal regulation demonstrate that the religious practice in question was central to the religion in question and that the pertinent government regulation would result in a "substantial infringement" on religious practice. Finally, government was required to demonstrate that the proposed regulation was the least restrictive alternative available, that government could not achieve its ends by less intrusive means.

During the 1990s, the U.S. Supreme Court moved from a libertarian to a more communalist understanding of religious free exercise.[20] A communalist would argue that the free exercise clause prohibits government only from specifically proscribing religiously motivated conduct and that religious bodies are entitled to no special exemptions from otherwise valid laws. The Court took this position in the case of *Employment Division v. Smith* (1990) and reaffirmed this more communalist reading of the free exercise clause in *Boerne v. City of Flores* (1997). Under the *Smith* ruling, religiously based exceptions to a state's criminal code can only be granted if such exemptions are specifically granted by the legislature.[21]

This pair of court decisions has occasioned a great deal of opposition from a variety of religious groups, which have sought to restore the *Sherbert-Yoder* test by means of several acts of Congress. The first of these, the 1993 Religious Freedom Restoration Act, was struck down by the Court in *Boerne.* The second, the Religious Liberty Protection Act, was considered by Congress in 2000. After a good deal of controversy over the question of whether such a measure would provide legal protection for religiously motivated discrimination on the basis of race, gender, or sexual orientation, Congress passed a substantially limited version of the measure, renamed the Religious Land Use and Institutionalized Persons Act. This bill, which was signed by

President Bill Clinton in September of 2000, would provide a great deal of legal protection for the religious liberty of persons under the control of others (such as prison inmates) and would enhance the religious freedom of religious organizations with respect to regulations concerning zoning, parking, or new construction.[22] Such public and congressional reaction is not surprising, since the Court's recent communalist turn would seem to qualify substantially the characterization of religious freedom as an unalienable "right."

Taken individually, the establishment and free exercise clauses would seem to provide ample material for continued conflict over church-state issues. However, church-state conflict in the United States is often exacerbated by the fact that many issues appear to involve questions of religious establishment *and* free exercise. Such issues typically arise because modern governments often provide services not contemplated by the Framers of the Constitution. When government becomes an affirmative provider of certain services or resources, it is not often clear whether granting such prerogatives to religious organization amounts to an unconstitutional "establishment" of religion, or whether withholding such services is a proscribed infringement on religious free exercise.

For example, an important contemporary church-state issue in U.S. politics revolves around the question of tuition tax credits for private schools. Many religious and secular citizens are alarmed by the state of public education in America and seek to provide alternatives to public schools. Some states have begun issuing vouchers, or tuition tax credits, to offset the costs of tuition at private schools at the elementary and secondary levels (a large majority of which in the United States are religious), and a number of proposals for revising the federal tax code in this manner have been introduced in Congress. Most separationists have regarded the enactment of such tax credits as a violation of the establishment clause, since religious schools would receive the undeniable benefit of a tax exemption or credit. Conversely, accommodationists have tended to regard the denial of such tax credits as an infringement on the free exercise rights of the parents of parochial school children, since such parents are often considered the victims of "double taxation." That is, the parents of children enrolled in religious institutions must pay taxes to support public schools and also tuition at the private schools their children actually attend. The possible violation of the free exercise clause occurs because the combination of taxation *plus* tuition makes sending children to religious schools (a practice clearly protected under the free exercise clause) more costly. Of course, such tension between the religion clauses of the First Amendment would not occur if government did not provide public schools in the first place.

Similarly, certain libertarian views of the free exercise clause can be viewed as violating the establishment clause. For example, consider the issue of military conscription. For several periods in the history of the United States, the federal government drafted young men into the armed services. During most periods in which a military draft was in operation, Congress granted exemptions or opportunities for substitute service for people who are proscribed for reasons of conscience from participating in armed conflict.[23] Jesse Choper has suggested that such provision for conscientious objectors may well violate the establishment clause. If religious denominations vary in the extent and severity of their condemnation of warfare (as they clearly do), and if exemption from compulsory military service is a valuable privilege (as it clearly is), government may be discriminating in favor of traditional "peace churches" (such as Quakers and Mennonites). Enhanced access to the status of conscientious objector might be regarded as a governmentally induced incentive to join particular churches. Such a policy, so described, would violate even a very narrow reading of the establishment clause.[24]

Examples of this type could be multiplied for pages.[25] The general point is that there is often a very real tension between the establishment and free exercise clauses. In an era of activist government, simple governmental "neutrality" between religions, or between religion and irreligion, is often elusive. Restricting the scope of religious activity to a "private sphere" would seem to violate the free exercise clause. The concept of religious freedom would seem plausibly to include attempts to promote one's religious values in the making of public policy. However, such efforts, if successful, would likely entail establishment clause violations. Government adoption and enforcement of religiously based policies could, in some instances, involve direct government endorsement of religious beliefs and values.

Of course, many analysts have attempted to escape this dilemma by suggesting that there is no inherent tension between the religion clauses of the First Amendment. Such integration of the establishment and free exercise clauses typically involves asserting that for some (usually historical) reason, one or the other clause "trumps" the other. For example, some accommodationists have argued that the overall purpose of the religion clauses is to ensure religious liberty and on that basis would question interpretations of the establishment clause that would limit the prerogatives of religious individuals or organizations.[26] Conversely, others, such as Levy,[27] have argued that the purpose of the religion clauses was to reduce the potential for religious conflict by limiting the public presence of religion. Such a viewpoint is generally associated with a separationist reading of the establishment clause, and it would limit the application of the free exercise clause to instances in which no issue of religious establishment could plausibly be raised.

In both cases, the tension between the religion clauses of the First Amendment is "resolved" by declaring one or another of the clauses to be dominant. Unfortunately, the Constitution of the United States does not come equipped with a user's manual, and academic and legal controversies of this type seem destined to continue.[28]

STRUCTURAL SOURCES OF CHURCH-STATE CONFLICT

A final source of continued conflict over church-state issues in American politics consists of structural constraints on final resolution of the relationship
between God and Caesar. In many ways, political institutions in the United
States are unique, as if designed to prevent coherence in the making of public policy. In particular, the American constitutional features of federalism
and the separation of powers provide incentives for self-interested political
activists to keep the issue alive.

These institutional incentives are, in turn, activated by the nature of public opinion in the United States concerning religious politics. In a word, public attitudes in the United States can be characterized as coherent yet conflicted. The beliefs of ordinary Americans about the nature of church-state
relations are structured by two competing cultural forces. First, relative to the
citizens of other industrialized nations, Americans are highly religious.[29] This
means that for at least some U.S. citizens, there often exists a strong tempta-
tion to translate their religious values into public policy. Second, the concept
of a constitutional "separation of church and state" is a powerful symbol in
U.S. political rhetoric. Although, as this chapter will attest, there is little
agreement on the application of the principle of church-state separation, the
value itself is not seriously contested in American politics.

With respect to issues of religious establishment, Americans can be characterized as "abstract separationists" and "concrete accommodationists."[30]
That is, large majorities of respondents in opinion surveys in the United
States endorse such concepts as a "high wall" of separation between church
and state; however, many Americans are also supportive of particular public
support for religion, such as organized school prayer, public displays of religious symbols (especially during the Christmas season), and the posting of
the Ten Commandments in public schools. Many citizens of the United States
appear to perceive little tension between these attitudes. Similarly, U.S. attitudes toward issues involving religious free exercise can be described as "abstract libertarian" and "concrete communalist." Again, there is widespread
public support for the *idea* of religious freedom as a symbol, but many
Americans are quite willing to restrict the actual religious liberty of specific
groups considered dangerous or strange. A great many Americans would
deny "Moonies" (adherents of Sun Myung Moon's Unification Church) or sa-
tanists the right to recruit among high school students, or deny native Americans the right to use hallucinogenic drugs as part of religious rituals.[31]

The key to these apparent paradoxes seems to lie in the fact that few
Americans have much experience with genuine religious diversity. In focus groups we conducted in 1994, we found that many respondents favored various accommodationist practices, such as organized school
prayer. However, we also found that it was quite easy to persuade these

respondents to switch to more separationist responses when we raised the issue of accommodating the religious beliefs of non-Christians, such as Muslims or Hindus. For example, the apparently simple idea of rotating the daily organized prayer among members of different religious groups was rejected with virtual unanimity when it was made explicit that Muslims or Buddhists might have turns.[32] More important for present purposes is the fact that the experience of religious diversity is not uniformly distributed throughout the United States. In certain coastal cities, such as New York, Washington, or San Francisco, exposure to neighbors from outside the Judeo-Christian tradition is rather common. However, in rural areas and in parts of the South or Middle West, such social interaction with people whose religious beliefs differ fundamentally from one's own is much less common. Thus, many Americans are capable of holding simultaneously apparently inconsistent beliefs about the appropriate relationships between religion and politics.

These characteristics of American public opinion create the public space in which issues of church-state relations continue to be conducted. Different, and perhaps inconsistent, values are available to candidates for some elective offices; the candidates can activate particular aspects of public opinion for personal or private advantage. At the national level, such strategic rhetoric is extremely problematic. Thus, American presidential candidates typically do not take strong positions on church-state issues, and they tend to confine themselves to pious generalities about the importance of religion in public life. Recent U.S. presidents who have been publicly associated with a particular religious tradition (Roman Catholicism in the case of John Kennedy, or evangelical Protestantism in the case of Jimmy Carter) have been especially scrupulous about maintaining separationist rhetoric when confronting issues involving questions of religious establishment. Even Ronald Reagan, who took public positions in favor of school prayer, the teaching of creationism, and tuition vouchers, did not use the full power of his office to turn these proposals into public policy.

However, apart from the offices of president and vice president, American elections are held in subnational constituencies, among candidates of very weak political parties. The feature of the American regime known as federalism creates, in effect, a system of multiple sovereignties, with policy being made at the national, state, and local levels. In the course of their ordinary lives, citizens of the United States may have more direct contact with local government bodies than with relatively remote federal agencies in Washington. "Retail" politics often involve questions of public aesthetics, zoning, local taxation, or public education, which has been the "stuff" of recent church-state issues. A very high percentage of church-state questions have dealt with elementary and secondary education, which is a policy area in which decentralized "local control" is a prized political value.

When local governments deal with such issues as Sabbath observances or school curricula, they are operating at an applied level, one at which many citizens (and some public officials) are unaware of the possible relevance of a more general constitutional principle. For example, a number of state and local governments have passed laws mandating the display of the Ten Commandments in public schools, in large part in response to highly visible acts of violence within American public high schools. The posting of the Ten Commandments is taken to be a reminder of a shared moral and ethical framework, and it is most common in jurisdictions characterized by low levels of religious diversity. The pressing goal of reducing violence in public schools may seem much more important than adherence to an abstract principle of constitutional law.

At the subnational level, public opinion is likely to be highly accommodationist. Not only are accommodationist positions quite popular at the level of application,[33] but a growing body of empirical research has shown that churches are important sources of political learning.[34] Moreover, church-based socialization is most effective in precisely the evangelical congregations in which accommodationist viewpoints are most popular.[35] By contrast, those who hold separationist viewpoints do not have comparable opportunities for social interaction and may come to believe that their views are not widely shared among their neighbors. Thus, Americans have more opportunities to learn accommodationist positions than separationist ones and are more likely to express viewpoints favorable to the public accommodation of religious beliefs.

If subnational governments are in fact responsive to public opinion, and if the publicly visible aspect of public opinion is likely to be strongly accommodationist, it follows that local officials in at least some jurisdictions will pass and enforce measures that may violate the establishment or free exercise clause. The electoral incentives to pass possibly unconstitutional measures on church-state issues may be quite strong, while there may exist only weak or nonexistent incentives to avoid passing legislation vulnerable to constitutional challenges.[36] On occasion, state and local officials have publicly emphasized their defiance of judicially imposed restrictions on public support for religion. In 1998, Fob James (a Republican candidate for governor of Alabama) made the assertion of Christian symbols in public life the centerpiece of his campaign. James argued that restrictions on such practices as organized prayer in public schools (at high school football games) or the display of the Ten Commandments in public schools were based on illegitimate decisions of an undemocratic, remote, federal Supreme Court.[37] More recently, an Alabama judge, Roy S. Moore, easily won the Republican nomination for the state supreme court after gaining notoriety by hanging the Ten Commandments in his courtroom and inviting pastors to open court sessions with prayers, in defiance of a court order.[38] Moore was subsequently elected to the Alabama Supreme Court in the general election of 2000.

Thus, the federal structure of American government suggests that there will exist jurisdictions in which it is rational (in the narrow, self-interested sense) for political candidates to take positions, and for elected candidates to enact policies, that are clearly unconstitutional and that would be very unlikely to withstand judicial scrutiny. A similar point can be made about the separation of powers at the national level. As a consequence of the fact that elections to the U.S. House of Representatives, Senate, and presidency are separate matters, American political parties are characterized by extremely low levels of party discipline. Thus, elections to seats in either house of the national legislature are primarily local affairs, and candidates are generally much more responsive to the demands of constituents than to the dictates of national party elites.

In such a decentralized electoral context, candidates from religiously homogenous states or districts have taken the lead in proposing legislation (including constitutional amendments) that would make federal policy concerning religious politics much more accommodationist. This tendency has been most pronounced in the House, in which legislators typically represent smaller, more homogenous constituencies.[39] In such congressional districts, or in comparable subnational jurisdictions, it may advantage candidates to have "fought the good fight" on behalf of religious accommodation, regardless of the ultimate outcome of such measures.

Moreover, it seems likely that the tendency of members of the House to raise issues of church and state will increase in the future. An important change in electoral politics in the United States over the final third of the twentieth century was the partisan "dealignment" of the mass electorate. In general, fewer and fewer Americans identified with one of the political parties. Consequently, an increasing number of American citizens came to exhibit low levels of political interest and activity.[40]

One important countertrend to the general pattern of electoral dealignment in the United States is the shift over the past generation or so of evangelical Christians toward the Republican Party.[41] Due in large part to the identification of the Democratic Party since 1972 with permissive positions on such lifestyle issues as abortion, gay rights, feminism, and drug use, many conservative evangelicals established psychological attachments to the Republicans.

Further, certain distinctive characteristics of the American political system seem certain to enhance the power of evangelical Protestants within the Republican Party. Most legislative elections in the United States, at all levels, are contested in single member districts. That is, a given jurisdiction, such as a state or municipality, is divided into districts, each of which typically elects one member to the legislative body in question. Following the national census taken at the beginning of each decade, legislatures in each state capitol draw maps of electoral districts for election to the state legislature, as well as for the U.S. House of Representatives. Clearly, members of state legislatures seek to draw maps that maximize the possibilities that certain candidates (or candidates of certain parties) will be elected.

In recent years, the strategy underlying partisan legislative redistricting appears to have changed, based on the aforementioned partisan characteristics of the electorate. A standard view of legislative "gerrymandering" is that the party empowered to draw a legislative map (typically the majority party) will isolate supporters of the opposition party into a very few highly homogenous districts. This tactic is thought to create a few safe districts for the minority, while allowing the majority power to be competitive in as many other legislative districts as possible. However, McDonald has suggested that the dominant strategy of redistricting might change as the electorate becomes less partisan and more independent. The creation of competitive, even if relatively safe, districts becomes risky to the extent that there are few highly reliable blocs of voters. In such periods of electoral volatility, the first order of business in legislative redistricting may well be the creation of a reliable base for the majority party, which in turn would suggest that the *majority* party might seek to create electorally homogenous districts for itself.[42]

If this argument adequately describes the behavior of contemporary state legislatures, and if white evangelical Christians indeed constitute an increasingly reliable bloc of Republican voters, we might anticipate that Republican-controlled legislatures will create districts for U.S. House elections, as well as for state legislative elections, that contain very high concentrations of religious conservatives. The representatives from such districts will have strong incentives to promote policies that provide for specific public accommodations of religious belief. This means that issues of church-state relations will be raised with increasing frequency in state legislatures, and in the lower house of the national legislature as well. Further, if it is assumed that seniority remains at least an informal source of political influence in legislative bodies, representatives from such "safe," religiously homogenous districts may come to wield political power disproportionate to their actual numbers. Over time, we might expect to see religious conservatives attain positions of legislative leadership within the Republican Party at an increasing rate—and it is well-known that a party's leadership in U.S. legislative bodies has an important effect on that party's legislative agenda.

Thus, political power within the American system, and within American political parties, is widely dispersed. This dispersion, and the possible strategic concentration of religiously conservative constituencies, suggests that candidates for some local, state, and federal offices will continue to have incentives to raise issues of church-state relations, even if such measures are of questionable constitutionality. In particular, I would offer the prediction that measures supporting school prayer, the teaching of "scientific" creationism, and tuition tax vouchers for private schools will increasingly occupy the agenda of the House of Representatives during the first decade of the twenty-first century.

CONCLUSION

It seems clear that conflict over the proper relationship between church and state remains a permanent feature of politics in the United States. Given that the population of the United States is both highly religious and highly religiously diverse, the vitality of religious politics is in some ways quite unsurprising. In religious matters, what is often considered personal is also ineluctably political.

In this chapter, I have attempted to show that the persistence of church-state conflict in the United States has multiple sources, ranging from broad-scale cultural facets of the United States, which have deep historical roots, through competing versions of the exegesis of specific constitutional texts, to the minutiae of electoral strategies for winning such "minor" offices as state legislator or local school board member. In perhaps no other political setting are the demands of "rendering unto Caesar that which is Caesar's, and unto God that which is God's" so frequently invoked or the possible conflicts between the requirements of citizenship and those of discipleship drawn so clearly. In perhaps no other setting are the potential electoral rewards for the defiance of civil authority so great or the political possibilities for the public mobilization of religious belief so infinitely varied. Both principled and practical considerations permit and encourage the continuation of church-state conflict in the United States, and such controversies show few signs of abating.

Why should any of this matter? It has, after all, been argued that religious liberty is perhaps best protected by legal and cultural tension between the religion clauses of the First Amendment. It is often argued that the inability of the American political and legal systems to settle definitively the relationship between the establishment and free exercise clauses creates an environment in which religious pluralism can be asserted most easily in the public sphere.[43] Indeed, I have argued elsewhere that Christian Right activity in U.S. politics provides to American political dialogue a prophetic voice that might otherwise be missing.[44]

However, given the larger question of church-state relations generally, the problem with the unsettled nature of the debate in U.S. politics is that such dynamic tension has a definite accommodationist bias. That is, those Americans who assert rights with respect to the establishment clause are forced by the permanent nature of the church-state debate to defend those rights over and over again. Such persons or groups are typically disadvantaged politically and perhaps legally as well. The fact that religious rights are continually renegotiated in American politics often means that the politically weaker side (typically separationists, given the analysis presented in this chapter) is forced to contest issues that religiously defined minorities would like to see settled.

An example may clarify this argument. The initial case in which organized prayer in public schools was declared unconstitutional *(Engel v. Vitale)* was decided in 1962. While school boards in many jurisdictions have complied with this ruling, many others have not but have instead sought legal and occasionally extralegal means to circumvent the Court's line in this area.[45] Thus, over a generation later, elected bodies such as Congress, state legislatures, and state and local school boards continue to enact measures mandating "moments of silence," organized prayer at extracurricular events, and the posting of the Ten Commandments in public schools. The free exercise clause provides the legal and rhetorical rationale for such actions ("voluntary" prayer, etc.). Further, given that non-Christians and nonbelievers remain minorities in U.S. politics, popularly elected bodies will have strong incentives to pass such regulations. Once such a measure is enacted, the mandated practice becomes the status quo unless and until someone wishes to object, which may require legal action. Even assuming that a willing plaintiff can be found with sufficient resources to raise the legal question of a violation of the establishment clause, the popularly and legislatively mandated accommodation of the majority religion is the prevailing practice and remains so until a judicial remedy is imposed.

The general point here is that given certain plausible empirical claims about American politics, the continuing cultural, legal, and political tensions involved in church-state relations advantage the accommodationist side of the debate. The fact that such issues are rarely "settled" in any definitive sense means that the rights of religiously defined minorities (which include nonbelievers) with respect to the unconstitutional establishment of religion are regularly and frequently contested in both political and legal arenas. The existence of such continual competition substantially qualifies the nature of First Amendment "rights" of citizens whose beliefs lie outside the prevailing range of acceptability. The fact that the American political system provides multiple access points for those who would accommodate the public expression of religious belief suggests that citizens whose beliefs fall within the political mainstream are advantaged in the continuing church-state debate. Absent some sort of resolution of these issues, the religious rights of some citizens will remain "more equal" than those of others.

NOTES

An earlier version of this chapter was presented at the International Congress of Americanists, Warsaw, July 10–14, 2000.

1. See Ted G. Jelen, *To Serve God and Mammon: Church-State Relations in the United States* (Boulder, Colo.: Westview, 2000); and Kevin Sack, "Ten Commandments' Defender Wins Vote," *New York Times,* 8 June 2000, A23.

2. Stephen V. Monsma and J. Christopher Soper, *The Challenge of Pluralism: Church and State in Five Democracies* (Lanham, Md.: Rowman & Littlefield, 1997).

3. Louis Hartz, *The Liberal Tradition in America* (New York: Harcourt, Brace, and World, 1955); and Garry Wills, *Under God: Religion and American Politics* (New York: Simon and Schuster, 1990).

4. See especially Mary Ann Glendon, *Rights Talk* (New York: Free Press, 1991).

5. See Jelen, *To Serve God and Mammon.*

6. James W. Wood, *The First Freedom: Religion and the Bill of Rights* (Waco, Tex.: J. M. Dawson Institute of Church-State Relations, Baylor University, 1990).

7. Derek H. Davis, "Resolving Not to Resolve the Tension between the Establishment and Free Exercise Clauses," *Journal of Church and State* 38 (1996): 245–59.

8. Ted G. Jelen and Clyde Wilcox, *Public Attitudes toward Church and State* (Armonk, N.Y.: Sharpe, 1995).

9. See Kenneth D. Wald, *Religion and Politics in the United States* (Washington, D.C.: Congressional Quarterly, 1997) and Stephen V. Monsma, *Positive Neutrality: Letting Religious Freedom Ring* (Westport, Conn.: Praeger, 1993).

10. Leonard W. Levy, *The Establishment Clause* (New York: Macmillan, 1986).

11. Leo Pfeffer, *Church, State, and Freedom* (Boston: Beacon, 1967). See also Leonard W. Levy, *Original Intent and the Framers' Constitution* (New York: Macmillan, 1988).

12. Robert Cord, *Separation of Church and State: Historical Fact and Current Fiction* (New York: Lambeth, 1982), p. 18 (emphasis added).

13. See Jelen, *To Serve God and Mammon.* See also John Witte, *Religion and the American Constitutional Experiment* (Boulder, Colo.: Westview, 1999).

14. A. James Reichely, *Religion in American Public Life* (Washington, D.C.: Brookings, 1985).

15. Frank Way and Barbara Burt, "Religious Marginality and the Free Exercise Clause," *American Political Science Review* 77 (1983): 654–65.

16. Derived from Supreme Court decisions in the cases of *Sherbert v. Verner* (1963) and *Wisconsin v. Yoder* (1972).

17. Jelen and Wilcox, *Public Attitudes toward Church and State.* See also Thomas Robbins, "The Intensification of Church-State Conflict in the United States," *Social Compass* 40 (1993): 505–27.

18. Leo Pfeffer, "The Current State of Law in the United States and the Separationist Agenda," *The Annals* 446 (December 1979): 1–9.

19. Wald, *Religion and Politics in the United States.*

20. Richard A. Brisbin, "The Rehnquist Court and the Free Exercise of Religion," *Journal of Church and State* 34 (1992): 57–76.

21. David G. Savage, *Turning Right: The Making of the Rehnquist Supreme Court* (New York: Wiley, 1993).

22. "U.S. Restores Special Protections for Religious Groups," *ACLU Newswire,* 2000, on the World Wide Web at www.aclu.org/news/2000/w092300a.html (23 September 2000).

23. It should be noted that the status of conscientious objector is created by Congress and would thus be sanctioned under *Smith*. At no point in American history has Congress or the Supreme Court asserted a constitutionally protected *right* to religiously based exemption from military service.

24. Jesse Choper, *Securing Religious Liberty* (Chicago: University of Chicago Press, 1995).

25. To illustrate, organized prayer in public schools (struck down by the Supreme Court as an unconstitutional "establishment" of religion) is often defended as involving the free exercise rights of students to engage in "voluntary" prayer. See especially John A. Murley, "School Prayer: Free Exercise of Religion or Establishment of Religion?" in *Social Regulatory Policy: Moral Controversies in American Politics,* ed. Raymond Tatalovich and Byron W. Daynes (Boulder, Colo.: Westview, 1988), 5–40.

26. Monsma, *Positive Neutrality.* See also Monsma and Soper, *The Challenge of Pluralism.*

27. See Levy, *The Establishment Clause,* and *Original Intent and the Framers' Constitution.*

28. See especially Laurence H. Tribe and Michael C. Dorf, *On Reading the Constitution* (Cambridge, Mass.: Harvard University Press, 1991).

29. Wald, *Religion and Politics in the United States.*

30. Jelen and Wilcox, *Public Attitudes toward Church and State;* and Jelen, *To Serve God and Mammon.*

31. Ted G. Jelen and Clyde Wilcox, "Conscientious Objectors in the Culture War? A Typology of Church-State Relations," *Sociology of Religion* 58 (1997): 277–88.

32. Jelen and Wilcox, *Public Attitudes toward Church and State.*

33. Jelen and Wilcox, *Public Attitudes toward Church and State;* Murley, "School Prayer"; and Kirk W. Elifson and C. Kirk Hadaway, "Prayer in Public Schools: When Church and State Collide," *Public Opinion Quarterly* 49 (1985): 317–29.

34. Kenneth D. Wald, Dennis Owen, and Samuel S. Hill, "Churches as Political Communities," *American Political Science Review* 82 (1988); and see Ted G. Jelen, *The Political Mobilization of Religious Beliefs* (Westport, Conn.: Praeger, 1991).

35. Wald et al., "Churches as Political Communities"; and see Jelen, *The Political Mobilization of Religious Beliefs.*

36. Christi Parsons, "Constitution, Shmonstitution," *Chicago Tribune,* 8 June 1997, sec. 2, 1, 7.

37. James won the Republican primary but was defeated in the general election.

38. Kevin Sack, "Ten Commandments' Defender Wins Vote," *New York Times,* 8 June 2000, A23.

39. Jelen, *To Serve God and Mammon.*

40. Herbert Asher, *Presidential Elections in American Politics: Candidates and Campaigns since 1952,* 5th ed. (Pacific Grove, Calif.: Brooks-Cole, 1992).

41. Wald, *Religion and Politics in the United States;* and Lyman A. Kellstedt, John C. Green, James L. Guth, and Corwin Smidt, "Religious Voting Blocs in the 1992 Election: The Year of the Evangelical?" *Sociology of Religion* 55 (1994): 307–26.

42. Michael McDonald, "Redistricting, Dealignment, and the Political Homogenization of the House of Representatives," paper presented at the annual meeting of the American Political Science Association, Boston, September 1998.

43. Davis, "Resolving Not to Resolve"; Witte, *Religion and the American Constitutional Experiment;* and Bette Novit Evans, *Interpreting the Free Exercise of Religion: The Constitution and American Pluralism* (Chapel Hill: University of North Carolina Press, 1997).

44. See Ted G. Jelen, "Citizenship, Discipleship, and Democracy: Evaluating the Impact of the Christian Right," in *Sojourners in the Wilderness: The Christian Right in Comparative Perspective,* ed. Corwin E. Smidt and James M. Penning (Lanham, Md.: Rowman & Littlefield, 1999), 249–68.

45. Murley, "School Prayer"; Jelen, *To Serve God and Mammon.*

11

Public Attitudes on Church and State: Coexistence or Conflict?

Clyde Wilcox, Rachel Goldberg, Ted G. Jelen

Americans in 2000 remain divided and often confused by issues of church and state. The First Amendment pronouncement that "Congress shall make no law respecting an establishment of religion or prohibiting the free exercise thereof" has inspired thousands of pages of heated and often tortured argument in law journals, political newsletters, and other publications. These debates are usually categorized as being over the establishment of dominant religions, or the free exercise of minority religions—two related but largely independent issues.[1]

In chapter 10 of this book, Ted G. Jelen suggests that church-state conflict is likely to be a permanent feature of politics in the United States. Jelen argues that there are three general aspects of U.S. politics that provide church-state issues with a continuing life.

First, the fact that the First Amendment to the Constitution contains two religion clauses creates a tension between questions of religious establishment and issues involving religious free exercise. The political conflict over church-state issues is fought in two very different arenas. Legal arguments rage about the meaning of both the establishment and free exercise clauses. These debates often center on the meaning of single words, such as *"an"* establishment of religion, on the limits of particular court-established criteria, such as "excessive entanglement" between government and religion, or on the "compelling state interest" to limit religious freedoms.

Many of the more complex issues are debated in the context of both establishment and free exercise: should schoolchildren be allowed to organize voluntarily a preschool prayer meeting, for example, or to vote to invite a student to offer a prayer at graduation ceremonies? The question is frequently raised as to whether permitting a particular practice (or granting a governmental benefit) constitutes an unlawful "establishment" of religion, or whether proscribing some practice (or withholding some benefit) constitutes an infringement on the religious free exercise of some person or group.

Second, church-state issues are also debated in the political arena. Most of this controversy has centered on limits on the ability of government to endorse majority religious symbols and rituals. Across the country, state governments have in recent years limited the teaching of evolution in public schools, sought to post the Ten Commandments in public places, and sought to expand public displays of Christian symbols during Christmas and other holidays. The U.S. Congress debated the usefulness of the Ten Commandments in limiting school violence; the House eventually passed a bill, which the Senate ignored.[2] The recent U.S. Supreme Court decision banning public prayer at football games in Texas has not ended the practice but made the public affirmation of religious sentiment more controversial, and perhaps more frequent as well.

Jelen suggests that the political resilience of such issues is in part a function of the structure of the American government. In particular, our system of divided governmental powers, which includes federalism and the separation of powers at both the federal and state levels, ensures that there will often be constituencies that favor pressing the limits of the establishment and free exercise clauses. In particular, the logic of legislative redistricting in recent years suggests that there will frequently exist electoral districts in state legislatures, and in the U.S. House of Representatives, in which majorities of voters will be religiously homogeneous and will favor government policies that benefit their particular traditions, or religion in general.

Finally, Jelen argues that the "rights" culture of the United States provides philosophical and rhetorical resources with which certain religious individuals and groups can justify resisting government authority. Rights (which clearly include religious rights) are thought to lie outside of the legitimate jurisdiction of government. Thus, many religiously motivated citizens will regard government policies that appear to limit religious freedom as inappropriate, and as policies that believers are permitted (or required by conscience) to resist.

Recent decisions that limit minority religious rights worry representatives even of majority religions, prompting ecumenical coalitions to push for greater protections for minority religions. A large and very diverse coalition persuaded Congress to pass the Religious Freedom Restoration Act, designed to invalidate certain U.S. Supreme Court decisions that appeared to limit religious freedom. The act was promptly overturned by the Court. The following year, Congress considered an alternative, dubbed the Religious Liberty Protection Act. The ecumenical coalition that supported RFRA fragmented during the debate over RLPA, since some believed that RLPA would provide a legal basis by which religiously motivated citizens could be exempted from laws prohibiting discrimination on the basis of race, gender, or sexual orientation.

Thus, Jelen suggests that there are several reasons why church-state conflict can be expected to persist in American politics. However, Jelen's analysis is intentionally static in suggesting that church-state conflict is a relatively permanent feature of politics in the United States. In this empirical study, we address the issue of the *dynamics* of religious politics in America. While church-state conflict *in some form* seems to be a constant element of the American political landscape, it seems likely that the extent, intensity, and direction of religious politics will change over time.[3] We locate a possible source of change in church-state issues—the changing nature of public opinion on these matters. In particular, we address in this chapter the effects of increasing exposure to religious diversity as a source of change in the attitudes of the mass publics.

PUBLIC ATTITUDES ON CHURCH-STATE ISSUES

Although the nuance in positions on church-state issues is infinite, it is helpful to think of both establishment and free exercise issues as being debated by two opposing sets of protagonists. On establishment issues, accommodationists argue that the Constitution mandates that the government be neutral among competing religions but not between religion and the lack of religion. Accommodationists would therefore generally oppose particularistic religious symbols of single Christian denominations but not the display of more general Christian symbols, such as the Nativity scene, on public property. Accommodationists believe that religion provides an underpinning to social and political life, and that the Judeo-Christian tradition serves to unify the United States.[4] Separationists, in contrast, believe that the government should be neutral between religion and irreligion. They see religion as a potentially divisive force, and government entanglement in religion as a potential threat to religion's power to critique the state.[5]

On free exercise issues, communitarians argue that certain religious traditions lie outside the moral consensus of society and that their rituals and practices may be accorded somewhat less protection than those of the majority. Elected officials might limit certain religious practices, so long as they do not prohibit worship. In contrast, libertarians argue that religious practice is constitutionally protected no matter how unpopular and that the government should limit religious freedom only in exceptional circumstances.[6]

In the first major study of public opinion on church-state issues, Jelen and Wilcox reported that the general public and elites alike support separation of church and state in the abstract but not in concrete applications of the principle.[7] Majorities simultaneously supported a "high wall" of separation of church and state, and extensive government endorsement and support of majority religions. Similarly, there was a consensus that minority religions have a right to their rituals and practices but also widespread support for limiting even the most symbolic public expression of minority religions.

The authors reported that respondents in focus groups sometimes changed their positions on issues involving questions of religious establishment as they confronted the true diversity of their communities. On school prayer, for example, some evangelical Protestants began with the position that all children should listen to a spoken prayer—one that might rotate among the religious traditions present in the classroom. They became less confident of this view when the religious rights of Catholics were included in the religious mix, and they abandoned it if Buddhists were mentioned. They objected to Christian children listening to Buddhist prayers; some reversed their support for spoken prayers in schools altogether.

The growing religious diversity in the United States confronts many Christians with new issues. Whereas once a public display of Christianity in their community might represent a consensual religious activity, today it may offend citizens with different faiths or seem to declare publicly that they are somehow not fully members of the community. Increasingly, new religious groups worship in different ways, wear special religious gear, and observe different religious holidays—raising issues for schools, governments, and business. How do attitudes on church and state change in the face of growing religious diversity?

Part of Jelen's and Wilcox's analysis was based on a phone survey of six hundred respondents conducted in the Washington, D.C., metropolitan area in 1993. The Washington "metro" area is one of great and growing religious diversity.

In this chapter, we update that analysis with data from a similar survey conducted in 2000. This latter survey used questions identical to those of the 1993 survey and produced 349 responses.[8] These data provide a glimpse into the stability and change of church-state issues in a geographic area of growing religious diversity.

CHURCH-STATE ATTITUDES AND RELIGIOUS DIVERSITY

The diversity of religious life in the Washington area can be seen in a ten-mile stretch along New Hampshire Avenue in Montgomery County, a suburb of Washington, D.C. In this small area are a synagogue, a mosque, a Cambodian Buddhist temple, a Hindu temple, a Unitarian church, and twenty-nine Christian churches, including three Catholic (one of which is Ukrainian), one Ukrainian Orthodox, two Seventh-Day Adventist, two Jehovah's Witness kingdom halls, and twenty-one Protestant churches. The Protestants range from Presbyterian, United Methodist, and Lutheran to a large and growing nondenominational Bible church. Some of the Protestant and Catholic churches serve particular immigrant communities—the Choong-Moo Evangelical Church of Washington, the Sung Hwa Presbyterian Church, the Our Lady of Vietnam Roman Catholic Church. Although the many religious citizens and residents worship different gods in different languages, they have joined together to lobby government about zoning and to remove graffiti from a mosque.[9] Yet the area's religious diversity would be significantly undercounted by a census of churches. One small Presbyterian church in Wheaton, Maryland (another Washington suburb), is home to four different congregations, speaking three different languages. After a worship service by a relatively sedate, older congregation of largely white Presbyterians, an affluent congregation of Taiwanese Presbyterians meets and worships in Chinese. Still later the New Baptist Creation Church, an African American congregation headed by a forceful woman pastor, meets for a lively service. In the late afternoon, the Iglesio Pentecostal Christo Rey (Christ the King Pentecostal Church) holds a Spanish-language service that attracts immigrants from El Salvador, Nicaragua, and Guatemala and that often lasts more than four hours.[10]

In the seven years since Jelen's and Wilcox's survey, this religious diversity has increased significantly. Across the region, schools face decisions about allowing Sikh headgear and Muslim veils in gym classes, while networks of cab drivers and day-care providers and hairdressers spring up along ethnic and religious lines, dramatically broadening metro area residents' exposure to diverse religious traditions.

How might growing religious diversity affect the substance of church-state attitudes in the Washington area? Clearly, overall attitudes are expected to change with the new mix of religious adherents, and although this in itself is interesting, it is also important to explore changes in attitudes among dominant religious groups, especially among orthodox Protestants, who might most resent the new immigrants.

A religious-conflict model might suggest that when the hegemony of majority religious groups is threatened by a rapid influx of people with sharply different beliefs and traditions, religious conflict would result. Orthodox Christians may see growing diversity as threatening their religious hegemony and undermining the nation's status as a "Christian nation." Within the context of evangelical doctrine, a growing non-Christian minority might be seen as threatening the nation's status as specially blessed by God.

On establishment issues, this backlash might show up as renewed support for more public displays of majority religious symbols—for example school prayer and Nativity displays. On free exercise issues, it might manifest itself as support for increased limitations on the displays of nonmajority religious symbols and practices.

A religious-exposure model might suggest that interactions with those of other faiths would lessen religious prejudice and increase support for free exercise. This might lead to increased support for displays of nonmajority religious symbols on establishment issues, and less support for limits on free exercise. When Christian mothers trust their children to Muslim day-care providers in Northern Virginia, it may become more difficult for either group to harbor narrow prejudices about the other. When Maryland residents ride in cabs driven by Sikhs wearing special religious attire, it may lessen objections to such attire in public schools. As District of Columbia residents come to know their Buddhist neighbors, they may be less willing to support school prayers that might isolate and stigmatize their neighbors' children.

CONTINUITY AND CHANGE IN CHURCH-STATE ATTITUDES

A comparison of the two samples supports the notion that religious diversity in the District of Columbia area has increased. Those who identified with a Christian denomination—mainline or evangelical Protestant, or Catholic—decreased from 72 percent in 1993 to 62 percent in 2000. There was an increase in those who identified as Jews, secular and eclectically religious, and people of faith outside the Judeo-Christian tradition. The small sample size in the 2000 survey makes comparisons among smaller religious groups problematic, but the decline in the number of Christians between the two surveys is statistically significant.

Table 11.1 shows the portion of metro area residents who took accommodationist positions on establishment issues in 1993 and 2000. Table 11.2 shows the percentage of respondents who took libertarian positions on free exercise issues. We begin our discussion with the substance of attitudes in 2000, and then we will focus on changes over time.

In 2000, minorities of metro area residents opposed a high wall of separation or supported government efforts to protect a Judeo-Christian heritage or to help religion. But majorities also supported Nativity scenes and menorahs on public property, and either Buddhist- or Christian-funded chaplains in the military. A substantial majority favored allowing religious student groups to meet on school property after hours, and a narrower minority would allow "moments of silence" in public schools, both issues that also involve free exercise of religion.

Minorities would require that schools teach Judeo-Christian values, teach creationism as an alternative to evolution, or allow public prayer in high school sporting events. A majority also opposed various provisions to provide public funding for religious education, whether through tax deductions, exemptions, or direct government vouchers.[11] These new items suggest at least initial resistance to school-choice plans that would channel tax funds into religious schools.

Table 11.1.   Establishment Attitudes in District of Columbia Metro Area, 1993–2000

(% accommodationist)	1993	2000
Oppose high wall of separation	19%	23%
Government protect Judeo-Christian heritage	54%	34%**
Government not help religion	24%	24%
Tax deductions for religious school tuition	na	44%
Parents of children in religious schools should subtract cost of tuition from tax bill	na	36%
If children go to religious schools, should not pay taxes to support public schools	na	21%
Government reimburse for costs of religious schools	na	14%
Nativity scene on government property	71%	55%*
Menorah on government property	58%	54%
Christian chaplains for military funded by gov't	78%	83%
Buddhist chaplains for military funded by gov't	60%	69%
Require schools teach Judeo-Christian values	36%	25%*
Teach creationism as an alternative to evolution	47%	34%*
Public prayer at high school sports events	48%	36%*
Moment of silence in schools	64%	56%*
Allow religious groups to hold meetings on school property	64%	70%

*difference significant at .05.
**difference significant at .01.

Table 11.2.   Free Exercise Attitudes, 1993–2000

(% Libertarian)	1993	2000
People have right to practice strange religion	96%	93%
Obey law even if it limits religious freedom	21%	27%
Immigrants should convert to Christianity	89%	85%
Permit religious headgear in schools	82%	90%*
Allow Jews to not work on high holy days	81%	84%
Allow religious leaders to picket porn shops	65%	75%*
Forbid fundamentalist preachers from evangelizing on college campuses	59%	58%
Allow conscientious objectors in wartime	55%	53%
Require Pledge of Allegiance of all children	44%	45%
FBI should not infiltrate Muslim groups	81%	86%
Allow Native Americans to take peyote in religious ceremonies	58%	57%
Ban satan worship	35%	46%*
Ban Hare Krishna solicitations in airports	40%	52%*
Allow animal sacrifice	28%	36%*
Ban unusual cults from converting teens	31%	34%
Christian Scientists can keep kids from medical care	15%	20%

*difference significant at .05.
**difference significant at .01.

Nearly all respondents in 2000 agreed that people have the right to practice their religions no matter how weird they may seem to other people, but many District of Columbia metropolitan area residents clearly have impoverished conceptions of weirdness. Among those who indicated that they believed that people had the right to practice strange religions, 6 percent would appear to be willing to ban a turban for a Sikh boy in public school, 30 percent would ban peyote use by Native Americans in their ceremonies, and more than half would apparently ban the sacrifice of a goat by Santerians.

Yet overall, D.C. metro residents are libertarian. Overwhelming majorities would allow religious headgear for public school children, allow Jews to be excused from work on religious holidays, permit religious leaders to picket pornographic shops, allow fundamentalist preachers to proselytize on college campuses, and oppose infiltration of Muslim groups by the Federal Bureau of Investigation. Majorities would allow conscientious objectors to avoid military conflict, Hare Krishnas to solicit in public airports, and Native Americans to take peyote in their ceremonies.

Large minorities would allow children to be exempted from the Pledge of Allegiance if their religion forbade it and would allow satan worship. Sizable majorities would ban animal sacrifice and proselytization of teens by cults, and would allow the state to provide medical care for children of Christian Scientists.

Between 1993 and 2000, aggregate attitudes on abstract and concrete issues were remarkably stable, despite changing political and religious contexts. This suggests that church-state attitudes are anchored in important orientations and values, primarily religion and support for civil liberties. Yet there was some attitude change in this period, and in each case where that change was statistically significant, attitudes changed in the same direction—toward more separatism on establishment issues, and more libertarian positions on free exercise.

Metro area citizens in 2000 were significantly less likely to believe that the government should protect a Judeo-Christian heritage or compel public schools to teach those values than were residents in 1993. Support also declined sharply for public displays of Nativity scenes, public prayers at high school sporting events, and moments of silence.

It seems reasonable to suppose that these changes might be related to the changing composition of the metro area population, especially the decline in the proportion of Christians. Yet when we compared the attitudes of Christians in the two surveys, the results were essentially identical—indeed, support for public prayers at high school sporting events declined more rapidly among Christians than among the overall population. On only one item, the teaching of Judeo-Christian values in public schools, did the increase among Christians fail (narrowly) to attain statistical significance.

Support for free exercise of religious minorities also increased. Metro residents in 2000 were significantly more supportive of the wearing by students of religious headgear, picketing by religious leaders of pornographic shops, and soliciting by Hare Krishna in airports, as well as of satan worship and animal sacrifice. Changing cultural contexts probably explain some of this change; in 1993 there had been a spate of news stories about satan worship among high school students, stories that were not repeated in 2000. Moreover, in 1993 many residents recalled the seemingly unavoidable blandishments of Hare Krishnas in public airports, but by 2000 these were at most a distant memory.[12] Once again, these changes cannot be attributed to the changing religious composition of the population, for the changes are evident also in the attitudes of Christians.

Taken together, these data provide some support for the notion that increased exposure to citizens with different religious faiths may foster greater tolerance for religious practices and a concomitant decrease in support for public displays of majority religious symbols. Yet once we begin to examine the underlying structure of attitudes, a more complex picture emerges.

CHANGING STRUCTURE OF CHURCH-STATE ATTITUDES

In their original study, Jelen and Wilcox reported that church-state attitudes were structured along substantive lines. Factor analysis of the 1993 data revealed that Washington metro area residents distinguished among concrete establishment issues that involved public funds, public schools, and public displays of religion. In 2000, residents drew similar distinctions. The data show that attitudes on public funds for religious schools are distinct from attitudes on teaching Judeo-Christian values and creationism. Attitudes on public funds for military chaplains (Buddhist or Christian) are distinct from those on public displays of religious symbols (a crèche or menorah). Attitudes on public prayer at high school sporting events are distinct from any of the other attitudes.

It is in concrete attitudes on free exercise issues that the 2000 results diverge from those of 1993. In 1993, free exercise attitudes were structured along a dimension that reflected perceived danger from nonmajority religious groups. Respondents appeared to distinguish between religions that might convert their children (cults, fundamentalist preachers), those that might pose a danger to society (Muslims, satan worshipers, Hare Krishnas soliciting at airports),[13] and less dangerous activity (religious headgear in classrooms, Jews missing work on high holy days, and Native Americans taking peyote in their ceremonies). In addition, a much less important dimension (accounting for only 7 percent of the common variance) focused on religion and immigration—the FBI infiltrating Muslim groups, and immigrants being encouraged to convert to Christianity.

In 2000, this final, smaller dimension had become paramount, accounting for 20 percent of the common variance and including a large number of items. The principal dimension in concrete church-state attitudes was one of majority versus minority religions. This dimension was defined by the belief that immigrants should convert to Christianity and by opposition to the view that everyone has a right to practice their religions freely even if they are strange to most Americans. Concrete issues that defined this dimension included attitudes toward the FBI infiltrating Muslim groups, Jews taking high holy days off, children wearing religious headgear to schools, forcing students to pledge allegiance to the flag, and allowing religious leaders to picket pornographic shops. A second dimension identified dangerous religious groups—in this case satan worshipers, cults that try to convert teens, and Hare Krishna solicitors in airports.

We should not read too much into these exploratory analyses, but the data do hint that at the same time that attitudes among some metro area residents are becoming more accommodating of religious minorities, a cultural conflict is brewing between orthodox Christian respondents and religious minorities.

One of the most interesting results from the factor analysis was a shift in the meaning attributed to the item about Jews missing work on high holy days. In 1993, this item was most strongly related to questions that identified minority religious practices thought to be largely benign (peyote among Native Americans, religious headgear in classrooms). In 2000, peyote remained as a separate item, not associated with other items on the survey, whereas Jewish religious holidays were related to questions that might be thought to define a "nativist" religious response. Indeed, the correlation between the question suggesting immigrants should convert to Christianity and the question on Jewish holy days was .11 in 1993 and .39 in 2000. Regression analysis suggests that two groups became less supportive between 1993 and 2000 of Jews' being excused from work for religious holidays—Catholics and African Americans.

The other interesting shift was on the "dangerous religion" dimension. In 2000, Muslims and fundamentalist campus evangelists were no longer parts of this dimension. This probably reflects the absence in the news of Islamic terrorist activity in the United States, and the decline in visibility of campuswide evangelists, whose activism used to be a common rite of spring at American colleges and universities. The attacks on the World Trade Center and the Pentagon in September 2001 are likely to have greatly increased support of FBI infiltration of Muslim groups. In addition, it seems likely that Muslims will be perceived by the public as a dangerous group.

DISCUSSION

It is important to note the limitations of this study. In particular, we would point out that the area surrounding the District of Columbia is not typical of the rest of the United States. We would expect that the D.C. sample is more religiously diverse, more highly educated, and more attentive to political and legal issues than the American population as a whole. Nevertheless, since we are unaware of studies of this type involving samples more representative of the U.S. population, we regard our findings as, if preliminary, suggestive of avenues for further inquiry.

These results appear to point in two distinct directions. Overall, D.C. metro area residents were less supportive in 2000 of the public displays of Christian symbols than they were seven years before, and more supportive of free exercise by minority religious groups. Moreover, these results hold when comparing only Christians in the two surveys. These data suggest that contact with non-Christians may be leading some District of Columbia area residents to be more tolerant of religious diversity.

Yet the changing structure of free exercise attitudes also suggests that many residents are beginning to think of church-state issues in terms of Christians versus non-Christians. Instead of drawing distinctions between groups they consider dangerous and others, some respondents are now primarily distinguishing between "us and (all of) them." This might hint at a future religious conflict. In other words, rather than making distinctions between different types of unconventional religious groups, D.C. residents appear to define the religious population in simpler terms, which may provide the basis for more frequent attempts to limit the religious freedom on non-Christians in the not-too-distant future.

The data do not provide a clear resolution between these conflicting possibilities, but our additional analysis does provide some support for the second (i.e., religious exposure) model. Most of the movement toward more religious tolerance appears to have happened among mainline Protestants, whereas white evangelicals, black Christians, and white Catholics have become slightly less supportive of free exercise of many groups, and in several cases more supportive of the accommodation of Christian symbols. The number of cases is small, and our results must be viewed as tentative, but they do suggest that at least some D.C. residents view the growing religious diversity with some alarm.

Yet we should interpret these results with caution. The increased support for free exercise among white mainline Protestants is statistically significant, but the decreased support among evangelicals, blacks, and Catholics is small and not significant. Overall, most District of Columbia metro area residents support free exercise of religion for religious minorities.

Further research is needed to help determine the impact of religious diversity on attitudes. Such studies could benefit from questions that ask respondents how often they see residents of different religious faiths, whether they know personally someone of another faith, and perhaps their knowledge about the worship styles and beliefs of other religions. In addition, contextual analysis could show whether citizens who live in the most rapidly diversifying parts of the metropolitan area are responding differently from those who live in homogenous neighborhoods and see diversity only in shopping malls or other public places.

NOTES

1. The connection between establishment and majority religion, and free exercise and minority religions, is cultural, not constitutional. In the United States, religious majorities do not seek to erect Buddhist statues on city property (although they do sometimes include the Jewish menorah with Christian crèches at Christmas), and laws limiting the free exercise of religion are not aimed at majority faiths.

2. Apparently the logic is that the two gunmen at Columbine High School simply had never heard that murder was wrong. Had they only seen on a school wall "Thou Shalt Not Kill," they might not have carried out their rampage.

3. For a general theory of changes in church-state politics, see Ted G. Jelen, *The Political Mobilization of Religious Beliefs* (New York: Praeger, 1991).

4. See A. James Reichley, *Religion in American Public Life* (Washington, D.C.: Brookings, 1985).

5. This argument is made in different forms in separate essays by Mary C. Segers and Ted G. Jelen in their recent book, *A Wall of Separation? Debating the Public Role of Religion* (Lanham, Md.: Rowman & Littlefield, 1998).

6. For discussions of this distinction, see Reichley, *Religion in American Public Life*. See also Ted G. Jelen and Clyde Wilcox, *Public Attitudes toward Church and State* (Armonk, N.Y.: Sharpe, 1995).

7. Jelen and Wilcox, *Public Attitudes toward Church and State*.

8. The survey was conducted by Georgetown University students, who were trained in the same manner as those who administered the earlier survey. Telephone exchanges were selected to represent the metro area, and random-digit dialing within those exchanges was used to reach unlisted numbers. The data in both years have been weighted to adjust for a bias toward residents with more education. The demographic profile of the sample closely resembles census data.

9. Susan Levine, "A Place for Those Who Pray: Along Montgomery's 'Highway to Heaven,' Diverse Acts of Faith," *Washington Post,* 3 August 1997, B1.

10. Michael Ruane, "A Church with Four Faces," *Washington Post,* 21 February 1999, A1.

11. It is interesting that vouchers are much less popular than direct tax rebates. Under a rebate plan, only those who paid sufficient taxes to qualify for the rebate would have government support for tuition; under a voucher plan, the poor could also use government money to pay for religious education. It is unclear whether this distinction was understood by respondents.

12. It might also be that the context of pornography changed with the Internet, which freed those who might wish to consume such materials from the annoyance of clerical picketers.

13. The inclusion of the Hare Krishnas on this factor might suggest a different interpretation—that these religions are seen as simply very different from Christianity. However, anyone who was ever accosted by Krishnas in the 1970s can attest that the danger of violence (by those solicited) was always present.

Bibliography

BOOKS AND ARTICLES

Abramowitz, Alan. "The Cultural Divide in American Politics: Moral Issues and Presidential Voting." In *Understanding Public Opinion*. Edited by Barbara Norrander and Clyde Wilcox. Washington, D.C.: Congressional Quarterly Press, 1997.

———. "It's Abortion, Stupid." *Journal of Politics* 57 (1995): 176–86.

Adams, Arlin M., and Charles J. Emmerech. *A Nation Dedicated to Religious Liberty*. Philadelphia: University of Pennsylvania Press, 1990.

Adams, Greg D. "Abortion: Evidence of an Issue Evolution." *American Journal of Political Science* 41, no. 3 (July 1997): 718–38.

American Jewish Committee. *The American Jewish Yearbook 1999*. New York: American Jewish Committee, 2000.

Aristotle. *The Politics of Aristotle*. Edited by Ernest Barker. New York: Oxford University Press, 1962.

Asher, Herbert. *Presidential Elections in American Politics: Candidates and Campaigns since 1952*. 5th ed. Pacific Grove, Calif.: Brooks-Cole, 1992.

Associated Press, "GOP Conservatives Give Bush the Edge." *Washington Times*, 8 March 2000, A12.

"Ballot Reform Imperative." *New York Times*, 17 December 2000, A1.

Bellah, Robert. "Civil Religion in America." In *Religion in America*. Edited by W. McLoughlin and Robert Bellah. Boston: Houghton Mifflin, 1968.

Benson, Mitchell. *2000 Catholic Almanac*. Huntington, Ind.: Our Sunday Visitor, 2000.

Berg, Thomas C. *The State and Religion*. St. Paul, Minn.: West Group, 1998.

Berger, Peter. *Sacred Canopy*. Garden City, N.Y.: Doubleday, 1967.

Berke, Richard L. "Stunned Decision." In *36 Days: The Complete Chronicle of the 2000 Presidential Election Crisis*. Edited by the *New York Times* Correspondents. New York: Henry Holt, 2001.

Bob Jones University Website, www.bju.edu (15 June 2000).

Brewer, Paul R. "Public Opinion, Economic Issues, and the Vote: Are Presidential Elections 'All about Benjamins'?" In *Understanding Public Opinion*, 2d ed. Edited by Barbara Norrander and Clyde Wilcox. Washington, D.C.: Congressional Quarterly Press, forthcoming.

Brisbin, Richard A. "The Rehnquist Court and the Free Exercise of Religion." *Journal of Church and State* 34 (1992): 57–76.

Burnham, Margaret A. "A Cynical Supreme Court." *New York Times*, 14 December 2000, A23.

Campbell, James E., and Thomas E. Mann. "Forecasting the Presidential Election: What Can We Learn from the Models?" *Brookings Review* 14, no. 4 (Fall 1996): 26–31.

"Camps Choose to Digest Supreme Court Ruling and Decline to End Their Struggles." *New York Times*, 13 December 2000, A1, A30.

Carter, Stephen L. *The Culture of Disbelief: How American Law and Politics Trivialize Religious Devotion*. New York: Basic, 1993.

Center for Applied Research in the Apostolate at Georgetown University. "Catholics in the Public Square." *Conscience* 21, no. 4 (Winter 2000–2001): 6.

Choper, Jesse. "The Free Exercise Clause: A Structural Overview and an Appraisal of Recent Developments." *William and Mary Law Review* 27 (1985–86): 943.

———. *Securing Religious Liberty*. Chicago: University of Chicago Press, 1995.

Complete Chronicle of the 2000 Presidential Election Crisis. Edited by the *New York Times* Correspondents. New York: Henry Holt, 2001.

Cook, Elizabeth Adell, Ted G. Jelen, and Clyde Wilcox. *Between Two Absolutes: Public Opinion and the Politics of Abortion*. Boulder, Colo.: Westview, 1992.

———. "Issue Voting in Gubernatorial Elections: Abortion and Post-*Webster* Politics." *Journal of Politics* 56 (1994): 187–99.

Cord, Robert. *Separation of Church and State: Historical Fact and Current Fiction*. New York: Lambeth, 1982.

Cover, Robert. "The Supreme Court 1982 Term: Forward: Nomos and Narrative." *Harvard Law Review* (1983): 97.

———. "The Uses of Jurisdictional Redundancy: Interests, Ideology, and Innovation." *William and Mary Law Review* 22 (1981): 639.

Curry, Tom. "Christian Coalition Rates McCain Highly," on the World Wide Web, www.msnbc.com/news/412356.asp?cp1+1.

D'Amico, Francine. "Sexuality and Military Service." In *The Politics of Gay Rights*. Edited by Craig A. Rimmerman, Kenneth J. Wald, and Clyde Wilcox. Chicago: University of Chicago Press, 2000.

Dahl, Robert. *Who Governs*. New Haven: Yale University Press, 1961.

Davis, Derek H. "Resolving Not to Resolve the Tension between the Establishment and Free Exercise Clauses." *Journal of Church and State* 38 (1996): 245–59.

"Daylight Magic and the Supreme Court." *The Economist*, 16 December 2000, 35.

De Tocqueville, Alexis. *Democracy in America*. 2 vols. Edited by Phillips Bradley. New York: Vintage, 1945.

"Democrats Say They Fear Time Is Running Out." *New York Times*, 10 December 2000, A1.

Diamant, Jeff. "Jackson, Invoking King, Says Black Voters Still Shorted." *Star-Ledger*, 14 December 2000, 32.

Dilulio, John Jr. "Supreme Court Action Run Amok." *Washington Post,* 25 December 2000.

Dionne, E. J. "Power, Not Authority." *Star-Ledger,* 14 December 2000, 39.

Dionne, E. J., and John J. DiIulio Jr. *What's God Got to Do with the American Experiment?* Washington, D.C.: Brookings, 2000.

Dworkin, Ronald. *Taking Rights Seriously.* Cambridge: Harvard University Press, 1977.

Edsall, Thomas B. "Powerful Antiabortion Lobby Targets McCain." *Washington Post,* 22 February 2000, A6.

———. "Senator Risking Key Constituency," *Washington Post,* 29 February 2000, A14.

Edsall, Thomas B., and Terry M. Neal, "Bush, Allies Hit McCain's Conservative Credentials." *Washington Post,* 15 February 2000, A1, A10.

Eisenberg, Avigail. *Reconstructing Political Pluralism.* Albany: State University of New York Press, 1995.

Eisengruber, Christopher. "Unthinking Religious Freedom." *Texas Law Review* 74 (1996): 577.

Eisgruber, Christopher, and Lawrence Sager. "The Vulnerability of Conscience: The Constitutional Basis for Protecting Religious Conduct." *University of Chicago Law Review* 61 (1994): 1245–80.

Elifson, Kirk W., and C. Kirk Hadaway. "Prayer in Public Schools: When Church and State Collide." *Public Opinion Quarterly* 49 (1985): 317–29.

Ely, John Hart. *Democracy and Distrust.* Cambridge: Harvard University Press, 1980.

Erikson, Robert S. "Economic Conditions and the Presidential Vote." *American Political Science Review* 83 (1989): 567–73.

Evans, Bette Novit. *"Employment Division, Oregon Department of Human Resources v. Smith." Encyclopedia of Religion and American Law.* Edited by Paul Finkelman. New York: Garland, 2000.

———. *Interpreting the Free Exercise of Religion: The Constitution and American Pluralism.* Chapel Hill: University of North Carolina Press, 1998.

Exit Poll data collected by the Voter News Service (available from several Websites, including CNN.com., www.cnn.com/ELECTION/2000/epolls/US/P000.html [7 February 2001]).

Fair, Ray C. "The Effects of Economic Events on Votes for President: A 1984 Update." *Political Behavior* 10 (1988): 168–79.

Farmer, John. "An 'Activist' Higher Court Conservatives Can Love." *Star-Ledger,* 18 December 2000.

Fessenden, Ford. "No-Vote Rates Higher in Punch-Card Counts." *New York Times,* 1 December 2000, A20.

Firestone, David. "Florida Supreme Court Moves Quickly to Hear Gore Contest of the Election." In *36 Days: The Complete Chronicle of the 2000 Presidential Election Crisis.* Edited by the *New York Times* Correspondents. New York: Henry Holt, 2001.

———. "Bush's Lead below 200 as Florida Supreme Court Orders Manual Recount." In *36 Days: The Complete Chronicle of the 2000 Presidential Election Crisis.* Edited by the *New York Times* Correspondents. New York: Henry Holt, 2000.

Fisher, Louis. *American Constitutional Law.* 2d ed. New York: McGraw-Hill, 1995.

"Florida Worms." *The Economist,* 6 December 2000, 33.

Foer, Franklin. "Spin Doctrine: The Catholic Teachings of George W." *Conscience* 21, no. 3 (Autumn 2000): 18–23.

Friedman, Richard D. "'Bush' v. 'Gore': What Was the Supreme Court Thinking?" *Commonweal,* 12 January 2001, 10–11.

Gamwell, Franklin. *The Meaning of Religious Freedom.* Albany: State University of New York Press, 1995.

Geertz, Clifford. "Religion as a Cultural System." In *Anthropological Approach to the Study of Religion.* Edited by Michael Banton. London: Tavistock, 1966.

Gibbs, Nancy. "Fire and Brimstone." *Time,* 13 March 2000, 33.

Glendon, Mary Ann. *Rights Talk.* New York: Free Press, 1991.

Glendon, Mary Ann, and Raul F. Yanes. "Structural Free Exercise." *Michigan Law Review* 90 (1991): 477.

"God Talk." *Commonweal,* 22 September 2000, 5.

Goodman, Ellen. "Very Human Beings under Those Robes." *Boston Globe,* 14 December 2000, A23.

Green, John C. "Religion and Voting in the 2000 Elections." Paper presented at the conference on Religion in the 2000 Elections, Rice University, New Orleans, Louisiana, February 2001.

Green, John C., Mark J. Rozell, and Clyde Wilcox, eds. *Prayers in the Precincts: The Christian Right in the 1998 Elections.* Washington, D.C.: Georgetown University Press, 2000.

Green, John C., Lyman Kellstedt, James Guth, and Corwin Smidt. "Who Elected Clinton: A Collision of Values." *First Things,* no. 75 (August–September 1997): 35–40.

Greenhouse, Linda. "Bitterly Divided High Court Suddenly Steps In." In *36 Days: The Complete Chronicle of the 2000 Presidential Election Crisis.* Edited by the *New York Times* Correspondents. New York: Henry Holt, 2000.

———. "*Bush v. Gore.*" In *36 Days: The Complete Chronicle of the 2000 Presidential Election Crisis.* Edited by the *New York Times* Correspondents. New York: Henry Holt, 2001.

———. "The Court's Credibility at Risk." In *36 Days: The Complete Chronicle of the 2000 Presidential Election Crisis.* Edited by the *New York Times* Correspondents. New York: Henry Holt, 2001.

———. "A Deeply Divided Court Ends the Struggle." In *36 Days: The Complete Chronicle of the 2000 Presidential Election Crisis.* Edited by the *New York Times* Correspondents. New York: Henry Holt, 2001.

Gressman, Eugene, and Angela C. Carmella. "The RFRA Revision of the Free Exercise Clause." 57 *Ohio State Law Journal* (1996): 65.

Gunther, Gerald. "Foreword: In Search of Evolving Doctrine on a Changing Court: A Model for a Newer Equal Protection." 86 *Harvard Law Review* (1972): 1–30.

Guth, James. "Congressional Elections of 1994 in South Carolina." In *God at the Grassroots: The Christian Right in the 1994 Elections.* Edited by Mark Rozell. Lanham, Md.: Rowman & Littlefield, 1995.

———. "Letter from Greenville: Living with Bob Jones." *The Christian Century,* 22–29 March 2000, 328–29.

Hallow, Ralph Z. "McCain's Religion Gambit Draws Quick Backlash in New York." *Washington Times,* 1 March 2000, A1.

Hartz, Louis. *The Liberal Tradition in America.* New York: Harcourt, Brace, and World, 1955.

Herbert, Bob. "Keep Them Out." *New York Times,* 7 December 2000, A39.

Hunter, James Davison. *Culture Wars: The Struggle to Define America.* New York: Basic, 1991.

Hunter, James Davison, and Os Guinnes, eds. *Articles of Faith, Articles of Peace: The Religious Liberty Clauses and the American Public Philosophy.* Washington, D.C.: Brookings, 1990.

Issacharoff, Samuel. "The Court's Legacy for Voting Rights." *New York Times,* 14 December 2000, A39.

Jefferson, Thomas. "Letter to the Danbury Baptist Association January 1, 1802." In *Religion and Constitutional Government in the United States: A Historical Overview with Sources.* Edited by John E. Semonche. Carrboro, N.C.: Signal, 1986.

Jelen, Ted G. "Citizenship, Discipleship, and Democracy: Evaluating the Impact of the Christian Right." In *Sojourners in the Wilderness: The Christian Right in Comparative Perspective.* Edited by Corwin E. Smidt and James M. Penning. Lanham, Md.: Rowman & Littlefield, 1999.

———. *The Political Mobilization of Religious Beliefs.* Westport, Conn.: Praeger, 1991.

———. *To Serve God and Mammon: Church-State Relations in the United States.* Boulder, Colo.: Westview, 2000.

Jelen, Ted G., and Clyde Wilcox. "Conscientious Objectors in the Culture War? A Typology of Church-State Relations." *Sociology of Religion* 58 (1997): 277–88.

———. *Public Attitudes toward Church and State.* Armonk, N.Y.: Sharpe, 1995.

Karlan, Pamela S. "Supreme Court's Incursion Was Not Needed." In *36 Days: The Complete Chronicle of the 2000 Presidential Election Crisis.* Edited by the *New York Times* Correspondents. New York: Henry Holt, 2000.

Kelley, Dean. "Confronting the Danger." In *Church, State, and Public Policy.* Edited by A. Melching. Washington, D.C.: American Enterprise Institute, 1978.

Kellstedt, Lyman A., John C. Green, James L. Guth, and Corwin Smidt. "Religious Voting Blocs in the 1992 Election: The Year of the Evangelical?" *Sociology of Religion* 55 (1994): 307–26.

Kohut, Andrew, John C. Green, Scott Keeter, and Robert Toth. *The Diminishing Divide: Religion's Changing Role in American Politics.* Washington, D.C.: Brookings, 2000.

Kramer, Larry. "No Surprise, It's an Activist Court." In *36 Days: The Complete Chronicle of the 2000 Presidential Election Crisis.* Edited by the *New York Times* Correspondents. New York: Henry Holt, 2000.

Kurland, Philip. "The Irrelevance of the Constitution: The Religion Clauses of the First Amendment and the Supreme Court." *Villanova Law Review* 24 (1978): 3–24.

———. *Religion and the Law.* Chicago: Aldine, 1961.

Langer, Gary. "Perception vs. Reality," on the World Wide Web, abcnews.go.com/onair/Nightline/poll0000225.html.

Lardner, George, Jr.. "Abortion Foes Spend $200,000 to Beat McCain." *Washington Post,* 7 March 2000, A8.

Larry King. "Interview with Dr. Bob Jones III." *Larry King Live.* March 3, 2000, on the World Wide Web, www.cnn.com/TRANSCRIPTS/0003/03/lkl.00.html (15 June 2000).

Laycock, Douglas, and Oliver S. Thomas, "Interpreting the Religious Freedom Restoration Act." *Texas Law Review* 73 (1994): 209.

Layman, Geoffrey C. "Culture Wars in the American Party System: Religious and Cultural Change among Partisan Activists since 1972." *American Politics Quarterly* 27 (1999): 89–121.

Lechner, Frank. "Fundamentalism Revisited." In *In Gods We Trust.* 2d ed. Edited by Thomas Robbins and Dick Anthony. New Brunswick, N.J.: Transaction, 1990.

Leege, David C. "The Catholic Vote in '96: Can It Be Found in Church?" *Commonweal,* 27 September 1996, 11–18.

———. "Divining the Electorate: Is There a Religious Vote?" *Commonweal,* 20 October 2000, 16–19.

Lemann, Nicholas. "The Redemption: Everything Went Wrong for George W. Bush, Until He Made It Go Right." *The New Yorker,* 31 January 2000, 48–63.

Levine, Susan. "A Place for Those Who Pray: Along Montgomery's 'Highway to Heaven,' Diverse Acts of Faith." *The Washington Post,* 3 August 1997, B1.

Levy, Leonard. *The Establishment Clause: Religion and the First Amendment.* Chapel Hill: University of North Carolina Press, 1994.

———. *Original Intent and the Framers' Constitution.* New York: Macmillan, 1988.

Lewis, Anthony. "Fair and Square." *New York Times,* 9 December 2000, A23.

Lewis-Beck, Michael S., and Thomas W. Rice. *Forecasting Elections.* Washington, D.C.: Congressional Quarterly Press, 1992.

Lieberman, Joseph I. *In Praise of Public Life.* New York: Simon and Schuster, 2000.

Locke, John. *A Letter Concerning Toleration.* Edited by John Horton and Susan Mendus. London: Routledge, 1991.

———. "The Second Treatise of Civil Government." In *Two Treatises of Government.* Edited by Peter Laslett. New York: Cambridge University Press, 1960.

Long, Carolyn N. *Religious Freedom and Indian Rights: The Case of* Oregon v. Smith. Lawrence: University Press of Kansas, 2000.

Lupu, Ira C. "The Failure of RFRA." *University of Arkansas Law Journal* 20 (1995): 575.

———. "Reconstructing the Religion Clauses." *University of Pennsylvania Law Review* 140 (1991): 555.

Madison, James. "A Memorial and Remonstrance on the Religious Rights of Man." In *Religion and Constitutional Government in the United States: A Historical Overview with Sources.* Edited by John E. Semonche. Carrboro, N.C.: Signal, 1986.

Madison, James. "Federalist Number 10 and Number 51." *The Federalist Papers.* 1787–88. Reprint New York: Bantam, 1982.

Madison, James, Alexander Hamilton, and John Jay. *The Federalist Papers.* 1787–88. Reprint New York: Bantam, 1982.

Markus, Gregory B. "The Impact of Personal and National Economic Conditions on the Presidential Vote: A Pooled-Cross-Sectional Analysis." *American Journal of Political Science* 32 (1988): 137–54.

Marty, Martin E., with Jonathan Moore. *Politics, Religion, and the Common Good.* San Francisco: Jossey-Bass, 2000.

McConnell, Michael W. "Accommodation of Religion: An Update and a Response to the Critics." *George Washington Law Review* 60 (1992): 685.

———. "Institutions and Interpretations: A Critique of *City of Boerne v. Flores.*" *Harvard Law Review* 111 (1997): 153–70.

———. "Religious Freedom at the Crossroads." *University of Chicago Law Review* 59 (1992): 115.

McDonald, Michael. "Redistricting, Dealignment, and the Political Homogenization of the House of Representatives." Paper presented at the annual meeting of the American Political Science Association, Boston, Massachusetts, September 1998.

Menendez, Albert. "Religion and the 107th Congress." *Conscience* 21, no. 4 (Winter 2000–2001): 7–9.

Miller, William Lee. *The First Liberty: Religion and the American Republic.* New York: Knopf, 1986.

Milligan, Susan. "In Long Run, Ruling May Aid Voters' Rights." *Boston Globe,* 14 December 2000, A1.

Minnow, Martha. "Pluralisms." *Connecticut Law Review* 21 (1989): 965.

Moen, Matthew. *The Transformation of the Christian Right.* Tuscaloosa: University of Alabama Press, 1992.

Monsma, Stephen V. *Positive Neutrality: Letting Religious Freedom Ring.* Westport, Conn.: Praeger, 1993.

Monsma, Stephen V., and J. Christopher Soper. *The Challenge of Pluralism: Church and State in Five Democracies.* Lanham, Md.: Rowman & Littlefield, 1997.

Monsma, Stephen V., and J. Christopher Sopher, eds. *Equal Treatment of Religion in a Pluralist Society.* Grand Rapids, Mich.: Eerdmans, 1998.

Moore, David. "Booming Economy No Advantage for Gore." Gallup Poll releases, 16 August 2000, on the World Wide Web, www.gallup.com/poll/releases/pr000816. asp (19 February 2001).

Murley, John A. "School Prayer: Free Exercise of Religion or Establishment of Religion?" In *Social Regulatory Policy: Moral Controversies in American Politics.* Edited by Raymond Tatalovich and Byron W. Daynes. Boulder, Colo.: Westview, 1988.

National Conference of Catholic Bishops/United States Catholic Conference. "Faithful Citizenship: Civic Responsibility for a New Millennium." Washington, D.C.: United States Catholic Conference, 1999.

Navarro, Mireya, and Somini Sengupta. "Arriving at Florida Voting Places, Some Blacks Found Frustration." *New York Times,* 30 November 2000, A1.

The *New York Times* Correspondents, eds. *36 Days: The Complete Chronicle of the 2000 Presidential Election Crisis.* New York: Henry Holt, 2001.

Nicholson, Joe. "Stop the Press." *Editor and Publisher,* 5 February 2001, 14–20.

Noonan, John T. *The Lustre of Our Country: The American Experience of Religious Freedom.* Berkeley: University of California Press, 1998.

Ogletree, Charles J., Jr. *Boston-Globe,* 27 December 2000, C7.

Oliphant, Thomas. "A Dishonest Rehnquist Five." *Boston Globe,* 17 December 2000, C8.

"Opening a Gavel of Worms." *The Economist,* 16 December 2000, 30.

Parsons, Christi. "Constitution, Shmonstitution." *Chicago Tribune,* 8 June 1997, sec. 2, 1 and 7.

Pepper, Stephen. "Conflicting Paradigms of Religious Freedom: Liberty versus Equality." *Brigham Young Law Review* 7 (1993): 41.

Perry, Michael. *Religion and Politics.* Oxford: Oxford University Press, 1997.

The Pew Research Center for the People and the Press. "Issues and Continuity Now Working for Gore." Washington, D.C.: Pew Reports, 14 September 2000.

————. "Presidential Debate Clouds Voters' Choice." Washington, D.C.: Pew Reports, 10 October 2000.

————. "Religion and Politics: The Ambivalent Majority." Washington, D.C.: Pew Reports, 20 September 2000.

Pfeffer, Leo. *Church, State, and Freedom*. Boston: Beacon, 1967.

————. "The Current State of Law in the United States and the Separationist Agenda." *The Annals* 446 (December 1979): 1–9.

Pomper, Gerald M. *The Election of 1996: Reports and Interpretations*. Chatham, N.J.: Chatham House, 1997.

Potter, Maximillian. "Life of Brian." *Philadelphia Magazine*, 2 February 2001, 88–97.

Prendergast, William B. *The Catholic Voter in American Politics: The Passing of the Democratic Monolith*. Washington, D.C.: Georgetown University Press, 1999.

"Race and the Florida Vote." *New York Times*, 26 December 2000, A30.

Rehnquist, William. *The Supreme Court*. New York: Knopf, 2000.

Reichley, A. James. "Democracy and Religion." *PS: Political Science and Politics* 19, no. 3 (Fall 1986): 805.

————. *Religion in American Public Life*. Washington, D.C.: Brookings, 1985.

"Republicans Scramble to Shore Up Pivotal Support among Catholics." *CQ Weekly*, 4 March 2000, 459–62.

Robbins, Thomas. "The Intensification of Church-State Conflict in the United States." *Social Compass* 40 (1993): 505–27.

Rosen, Jeffrey. "The Supreme Court Commits Suicide, Disgrace." *The New Republic*, 25 December 2001, 18–21.

Rosin, Hanna. "Christian Right's Fervor Has Fizzled." *Washington Post*, 16 February 2000, A1, A16.

Rozell, Mark J. "Growing Up Politically: The New Politics of the New Christian Right." In *Sojourners in the Wilderness: The Christian Right in Comparative Perspective*. Edited by Corwin Smidt and James Penning. Lanham, Md.: Rowman & Littlefield, 1997.

————. ". . . Or, Influential as Ever?" *Washington Post*, 1 March 2000, A17.

Rozell, Mark J., and Clyde Wilcox. *Second Coming: The New Christian Right in Virginia Politics*. Baltimore: Johns Hopkins University Press, 1996.

Ruane, Michael. "A Church with Four Faces." *Washington Post*, 21 February 1999, A1.

Rubenfeld, Jed. "Antidisestablishmentarianism: Why RFRA Really Was Unconstitutional." *Michigan Law Review* 95 (1997): 2347–60.

Russonello, John, and Katya Balasubramanian. "Winning the Catholic Vote." *Conscience* 21, no. 4 (Winter 2000–2001): 2–5.

Sack, Kevin, "Federal Court Rejects Bush Request to Bar Manual Recounts." In *36 Days: The Complete Chronicle of the 2000 Presidential Election Crisis*. Edited by the *New York Times* Correspondents. New York: Henry Holt, 2000.

Sarna, Jonathan D. "American Jews and Church-State Relations: The Search for 'Equal Footing.'" In *Religion and State in the American Jewish Experience*. Edited by Jonathan D. Sarna and David G. Dalin. Notre Dame, Ind: University of Notre Dame Press, 1997.

Savage, David G. *Turning Right: The Making of the Rehnquist Supreme Court*. New York: Wiley, 1993.

Schroth, Raymond A. "Stopping the Press." *National Catholic Reporter*, 2 March 2001, 10–11.

Segers, Mary C. "The Catholic Church as a Transnational Actor." Paper presented at the Annual Conference of the American Political Science Association, Boston, Massachusetts, September 1998.

———. "Sister Maureen Fiedler: A Nun for Gender Equality in Church and Society." In *Religious Leaders, and Faith-Based Politics.* Edited by Jo Renee Formicola and Hubert Morken. Lanham, Md.: Rowman & Littlefield, 2001.

Segers, Mary C., and Ted G. Jelen. *A Wall of Separation? Debating the Public Role of Religion.* Lanham, Md.: Rowman & Littlefield, 1998.

Shklar, Judith. "The Liberalism of Fear." In *Liberalism and the Moral Life.* Edited by Nancy L. Rosenblum. Cambridge: Harvard University Press, 1989.

Spiegel, Peter. "Candidates Put Their All into Battle for Catholic Hearts." *Financial Times,* 31 October 2000, 5.

Sullivan, Andrew. "Two Nations, Undivided." *New York Times Magazine,* 26 November 2000, 23–24.

Sullivan, Kathleen M., and Gerald Gunther. *First Amendment Law.* New York: Foundation, 1999.

Szabo, Liz. "Christian Coalition Losing Clout." *(Norfolk, Va.) Virginian Pilot,* 19 February 2000, on the World Wide Web, www.pilotonline.com/news/nw0219sou.html.

Tierney, John. "Bad Balloting. Poor Services. What's New?" *New York Times,* 12 December 2000, B1.

Tribe, Laurence H., and Michael C. Dorf. *On Reading the Constitution.* Cambridge: Harvard University Press, 1991.

"United States Probing Bias Claims in Florida Vote." *Star-Ledger,* December 4, 2000, 10.

U.S. Census Bureau. *Statistical Abstract of the United States.* Washington, D.C: U.S. Census Bureau, 1999.

"U.S. Restores Special Protections for Religious Groups." *ACLU Newswire.* 2000, on the World Wide Web, www.aclu.org/news/2000/w092300a.html (23 September 2000).

Verba, Sidney, Kay Lehman Schlozman, and Henry E. Brady. *Voice and Equality: Civic Voluntarism in American Politics.* Cambridge: Harvard University Press, 1995.

Wagner, Steven. "Catholics & Evangelicals: Can They Be Allies?" *Crisis,* January 2000, 12–17.

Wald, Kenneth D. *Religion and Politics in the United States.* Washington, D.C.: Congressional Quarterly Press, 1997.

Wald, Kenneth D., Dennis Owen, and Samuel S. Hill. "Churches as Political Communities." *American Political Science Review* 82 (1988): 531–49.

Walzer, Michael. *Spheres of Justice.* New York: Basic, 1983.

The *Washington Post* Political Staff, eds. *Deadlock: The Inside Story of America's Closest Election.* New York: Public Affairs, 2001.

Way, Frank, and Barbara Burt. "Religious Marginality and the Free Exercise Clause." *American Political Science Review* 77 (1983): 654–65.

Wayne, Stephen J. *The Road to the White House 2000: The Politics of Presidential Elections.* New York: Bedford/St. Martin's, 2000.

Weigel, George. "Analysis of Voting Pattern Shows Church Attendance Makes Difference." *The Catholic Advocate,* 28 February 2001, 11.

Wentz, Richard E. *The Culture of Religious Pluralism.* Boulder, Colo.: Westview, 1998.

Wilcox, Clyde. "The Christian Right in the 2000 Elections." Paper presented at the conference on Religion in the 2000 Elections, Rice University, New Orleans, Louisiana, February 2001.

Wilcox, Clyde, and Robin Wolpert. "Gay Rights in the Public Sphere: Public Opinion on Gay and Lesbian Equality." In *The Politics of Gay Rights.* Edited by Craig A. Rimmerman, Kenneth J. Wald, and Clyde Wilcox. Chicago: University of Chicago Press, 2000.

Williams, Roger. "Mr. Cotton's Letter Lately Printed, Examined and Answered." In *Roger Williams: His Contribution to the American Tradition.* Edited by Perry Miller. Indianapolis: Bobbs-Merrill, 1953.

Wills Garry. *Under God: Religion and American Politics.* New York: Simon and Schuster, 1990.

Witte, John. *Religion and the American Constitutional Experiment.* Boulder, Colo.: Westview, 2000.

Wittes, Benjamin. "Maybe the Court Got It Right." *Boston Globe,* 21 February 2001, A23.

Wood, James W. *The First Freedom: Religion and the Bill of Rights.* Waco, Tex.: J. M. Dawson Institute of Church-State Relations, Baylor University, 1990.

Wyman, David. *The Abandonment of the Jews: America and the Holocaust 1941–1945.* New York: New Press, 1984.

Yinger, Milton. *The Scientific Study of Religion.* New York: Macmillan, 1970.

Zion, Sidney. "Supreme Power-Grab: Legal Scholars Scorn the Landmark Ruling." *New York Post,* 19 December 2000.

CASES CITED

Adamson v. California, 332 U.S. 46 (1947).

Agostini v. Felton, 521 U.S. 203 (1997).

Aguilar v. Felton, 473 U.S. 405 (1985).

Allegheny County v. American Civil Liberties Union, 492 U.S. 573 (1989).

Barron v. Mayor and City Council of Baltimore, 32 U.S. 7 Pet. 243 (1833).

Board of Education v. Allen, 392 U.S. 236 (1968).

Braunfeld v. Brown, 366 U.S. 420 (1961).

Bush v. Gore, 121 S.Ct. 525 (2000).

Cantwell v. Connecticut, 310 U.S. 296 (1940).

Church of Jesus Christ of Latter-Day Saints v. United States, 136 U.S. 1 (1890).

Church of the Lukumi Babalu Aye v. City of Hialeah, 508 U.S. 520 (1993).

City of Boerne v. Flores, 521 U.S. 507 (1997).

Corporation of the Presiding Bishop of the Church of Jesus Christ of Latter Day Saints v. Amos, 483 U.S. 327 (1987).

Craig v. Boren, 429 U.S. 190 (1976).

Davis v. Beason, 133 U.S. 333 (1890).

Duncan v. Louisiana, 391 U.S. 145 (1968).

Employment Division v. Smith, 494 U.S. 872 (1990).

Estate of Thornton v. Caldor, 472 U.S. 703 (1985).
Everson v. Board of Education of Ewing Township, 330 U.S. 1 (1947).
Frazee v. Illinois Employment Security Department, 489 U.S. 829 (1989).
Goldman v. Weinberger, 475 U.S. 503 (1986).
Grand Rapids School District v. Ball, 473 U.S. 373 (1985).
Griswold v. Connecticut, 381 U.S. 479 (1965).
Grumet v.Cuomo, 900 N.Y.2d 57 1997; 681 N.E.2d 340 (1997).
Hobbie v. Unemployment Appeals Commission, 480 U.S. 136 (1987).
Jensen v. Quaring, 472 U.S. 478 (1985).
Kiryas Joel School District v. Grumet, 512 U.S. 687 (1994).
Lee v. Weisman, 505 U.S. 577 (1992).
Lemon v. Kurtzman, 403 U.S. 602 (1971).
Lynch v. Donnelly, 465 U.S. 668 (1984).
Lyng v. Northwest Indian Cemetery Protective Association, 485 U.S. 439 (1988).
McCulloch v. Maryland, 17 U.S. 4 Wheat. 316 (1819).
Meek v. Pittinger, 421 U.S. 349 (1975).
Menorah v. Illinois High School Athletic Association, 683 F.2d 1030 7th Cir. Ill. (1982).
Meyers v. Nebraska, 262 U.S. 390 (1923).
Mitchell v. Helms, 120 S.Ct. 2530, 68 U.S.L.W. 4468 (2000).
O'Lone v. Estate of Shabazz, 482 U.S. 342 (1987).
Pierce v. Society of Sisters, 268 U.S. 510 (1925).
Planned Parenthood of Southeastern Pennsylvania v. Casey, 505 U.S. 833 (1992).
Reynolds v. United States, 98 U.S. 145 (1878).
San Antonio Independent School District v. Rodriguez, 411 U.S. 1 (1973).
Sherbert v. Verner, 374 U.S. 398 (1963).
Slaughter-House Cases, 83 U.S. 16 Wall. 36 (1872).
Thomas v. Review Board, 450 U.S. 707 (1981).
United States v. Carolene Products Co., 304 U.S. 144 (1938).
United States v. Lee, 455 U.S. 252 (1982).
Wisconsin v. Yoder, 406 U.S. 205 (1972).

NEWSPAPER SOURCES

In writing about the extraordinary 2000 presidential election, contributors relied heavily on daily coverage of the presidential campaign, the Florida recount, and post-election events. Major sources are listed here.

The Catholic Advocate, 12 April 2000–28 February 2001. (This is the weekly newspaper of the Archdiocese of Newark.)
Catholic New York, 2 March 2000–26 October 2000. (This is the weekly publication of the Archdiocese of New York.)
Los Angeles Times, 13 March 2000–30 August 2000.
Miami Herald, 2 December 2000–11 May 2001.
New York Times, 15 December 1999–5 May 2001.
Star-Ledger, 16 February 2000–13 March 2001. (The *Star-Ledger,* based in Newark, is the newspaper of record and the largest-circulation daily in New Jersey.)

USA Today, 7 November 2000–22 January 2001.
Washington Post, 15 February 2000–10 August 2000.
Washington Times, 8 February 2000–8 March 2000.

In addition, two major newspapers have published special reports on the 2000 election:

Martin Merzer and Staff of the *Miami Herald. The Miami Herald Report: Democracy Held Hostage.* New York: St. Martin's, 2001.
Correspondents of the *New York Times. 36 Days: The Complete Chronicle of the 2000 Presidential Election Crisis.* New York: Times Books, Henry Holt, 2001.

Index

abortion: Bush views on, 122–23;
Catholic voters and, 89–92, 93, 96,
97; Lieberman views on, 139; *Los
Angeles Times* poll on, 108, 109, 110;
partial-birth, 109–11; Pew Research
Center polls on, 111, 112;
Republican primaries and, 60, 61,
63, 64, 69; in 2000 election, 58, 60,
64, 66, 67–68, 78, 79, 87–88, 105,
106, 107, 108–12. *See also* Christian
Right; McCain, John; *Roe v. Wade*;
RU-486
accommodation: and church–state
conflict in U.S., 206, 208, 209, 211,
212, 214, 215; in church–state issues,
5, 115–18, 151–53, 162, 183;
legislative and judicial, 184, 186–91;
Supreme Court cases concerning,
183–97
African-Americans, 22, 23, 24, 32, 118,
119, 225, 230, 231; Catholic, 89, 90,
95; in Democratic party, 116, 136,
137; and Florida election, 41; in
Republican party, 128. *See also*
Keyes, Alan
Alabama, 212–13
Amish, 158, 162, 163. *See also*
Wisconsin v. Yoder

anti-Catholicism, 62, 75–76, 79–80, 81,
87, 89, 96, 129, 157, 161. *See also*
Bob Jones University
Anti-Defamation League. *See* Lieberman,
Joseph
anti-Semitism, 4, 128, 138; history of
anti-Jewish prejudice in the U.S.,
129–32. *See also* Lieberman, Senator
Joseph
Ashcroft, John, 8, 57, 71, 97, 98, 122,
123
Associated Press, 21, 28
atheists, 138, 139, 144, 216

Baker, James, 26
Bentsen, Lloyd, 127, 136
Bill of Rights, 3, 178, 182, 188, 194, 203
Blackmun, Justice Harry. *See* Supreme
Court Justices
Bob Jones University, 8; and anti-
Catholic prejudice, 62, 64, 76–77,
79–80, 89; George W. Bush and,
76–82; controversy and George W.
Bush reaction, 62, 80, 81, 87;
controversy and Catholic reaction,
68, 79–80, 82–87, 96; controversy
and Republican reaction, 79, 80, 81,
84; interracial dating policy, 62, 76,

247

About the Contributors

Molly W. Andolina is assistant research professor of political science at Loyola University in Chicago. She earned the B.A. in history from Emory University in 1989, a Master of Public Policy degree at Georgetown in 1992, and a Ph.D. from Georgetown in 1997. She has taught courses in American politics, political behavior, public opinion, and American political culture. From 1998 through 1999, she served as survey director at the PEW Research Center for the People and the Press in Washington, D.C. She has written on public opinion and political generations. With funding from the PEW Charitable Trusts, she is currently conducting research on youth civic engagement.

Bette Novit Evans is associate professor of political science at Creighton University in Omaha, Nebraska. Her academic specializations include constitutional jurisprudence and political philosophy. Professor Evans's research has focused on constitutional rights and liberties. She has published articles on the concept of equality, on equal employment opportunity law and policy, and on the concept of race in law. Most recently her work has been directed toward the First Amendment guarantees of religious freedom. Her book, *Interpreting the Free Exercise of Religion,* was published in 1998 by the University of North Carolina Press. She continues to pursue interests at the intersection of law and religion and to relate religious pluralism to general theories of American pluralism.

George E. Garvey is professor of law at the Catholic University of America, Columbus School of Law. Among other courses, he teaches constitutional law and Catholic social teaching and law. He served as associate dean for academic affairs from 1989 to 1997. Garvey was a Senior Fulbright Lecturer at

Jagiellonian University in Krakow, Poland, in spring 1999, and a Senior Fulbright Research Scholar at the Max Planck Institute for Foreign and International Private Law in Hamburg, Germany, in 1986–87. In 1980 and 1981, he served as counsel to the Committee on the Judiciary of the U.S. House of Representatives. Garvey coauthored "Economic Law and Economic Growth: Antitrust, Rate Regulation and the Growth Cycle" (1990) and has published in numerous legal journals. His essay "A Catholic Social Teaching Critique of Law and Economics" will be published in *Christian Perspectives on Legal Thought,* forthcoming from Yale University Press. In 2000, he served as academic coordinator for a conference entitled "Jubilee Year Reflections on Catholic Social Thought: Anticipating the Kingdom" and is coediting the resulting publication.

Rachel Goldberg received her B.A. in political science and history from the University of Wisconsin in 1992, and her M.A. in political science from Georgetown University in 1998. She is currently completing her Ph.D. degree. Her specialty is American national politics. She teaches a variety of courses in that area, including courses on political parties, elections, and interest groups. Her publications have explored the role of religion in politics, as well as campaign finance. Her current research focuses on the interaction between social movements and third parties in the two-party system.

Elizabeth A. Hull is associate professor of political science at Rutgers University in Newark, where she teaches courses in American politics, constitutional law and civil liberties. She has written several books, including *Without Justice for All: The Constitutional Rights of Aliens* (Greenwood Press, 1985) and *Taking Liberties: National Barriers to the Free Flow of Ideas* (Praeger, 1990). Her publications include numerous articles in political science journals and law reviews. In 1999 she served, under the auspices of the Soros Foundation, as a guest lecturer in Kazakhstan, where she addressed law school faculties. She received the Rutgers University Award for Teaching Excellence in 1989. She is currently working on a book dealing with racial discrimination in the electoral process.

Ted G. Jelen is chair and professor of political science at the University of Nevada at Las Vegas. He has published widely in the field of religion and politics, including books on *The Political World of the Clergy, Public Attitudes toward Church and State,* and *Perspectives on the Politics of Abortion.* His most recent book is *To Serve God and Mammon: Church-State Relations in the United States* (2000). He is editor of the *Journal for the Scientific Study of Religion.*

Mark J. Rozell is professor of politics and director of the Congressional Studies Program at the Catholic University of America in Washington, D.C. His fields of expertise are religion and politics, and American politics with a focus on separation-of-power studies and the presidency. He has written widely on the role of the Christian Right in American politics. His books include: *God at the Grass Roots: The Christian Right in the 1994 Elections* (1995, with Clyde Wilcox); *Executive Privilege: The Dilemma of Secrecy and Democratic Accountability;* and *God at the Grass Roots: The Christian Right in American Elections* (1996, with Clyde Wilcox). His most recent book is *Interest Groups in American Campaigns: The New Face of Electioneering* (1999, with Clyde Wilcox).

Mary C. Segers is chair and professor of political science at Rutgers University's Newark campus, where she received the university's Distinguished Teaching Award in 1998. She has written widely about religious and ethical values underlying public policy. Her books include *A Wall of Separation Debating the Role of Religion in American Public Life* (with Ted Jelen, Rowman & Littlefield, 1998); *Abortion Politics in American States* (1995, coedited with Timothy Byrnes); *The Catholic Church and Abortion Politics: A View from the States* (1992, coedited with Timothy Byrnes); *Church Polity and American Politics* (1990); and *Elusive Equality: Liberalism, Affirmative Action, and Social Change in America* (1983, with James Foster). In 1999, she served as Fulbright Distinguished Chair in American Studies at the University of Warsaw. She held a Henry Luce fellowship in theology at Harvard Divinity School from 1987 to 1989. Professor Segers was the symposium coordinator for the religion and politics panels at the fiftieth International Conference of Americanists in Warsaw, July 2000.

Clyde Wilcox is professor of government at Georgetown University, where he teaches American politics, and religion and politics. He has written numerous books and empirical studies of the political behavior of religious believers in the United States. His books include: *Prayers in the Precincts: The Christian Right in the 1998 Elections* (1998, with John C. Green and Mark J. Rozell); *Onward Christian Soldiers: The Role of the Religious Right in American Politics* (1996); *Public Attitudes toward Church and State* (1995, with Ted G. Jelen); and *Between Two Absolutes: Public Opinion and the Politics of Abortion* (1992, with Elizabeth Adell Cook and Ted G. Jelen). He is the coeditor of the books *God at the Grass Roots: The Christian Right in the 1994 Elections* (1995, with Mark J. Rozell, Rowman & Littlefield) and *God at the Grass Roots: The Christian Right in American Elections* (1996, with Mark J. Rozell).